Companion Workbook

math expressions

Dr. Karen C. Fuson

Watch the lemur come alive in its forest as you discover and solve math challenges.

Download the *Math Worlds AR* app available on Android or iOS devices.

Grade 4

This material is based upon work supported by the
National Science Foundation
under Grant Numbers
ESI-9816320, REC-9806020, and RED-935373.

Any opinions, findings, and conclusions, or recommendations expressed in this material are those of the author and do not necessarily reflect the views of the National Science Foundation.

Cover Illustration: ©Josh Brill

Printed in the U.S.A.

ISBN 978-1-328-74493-7

3 4 5 6 7 8 9 10 0607 26 25 24 23 22 21 20 19 18

4500723986 B C D E F G

Contents

UNIT 1 - Place Value and Operations

UNIT 2 - Multiplication with Whole Numbers

Contents

UNIT 3 - Division with Whole Numbers

UNIT 4 - Equations and Word Problems

Contents

Contents

UNIT 7 - Fractions and Decimals

UNIT 8 - Geometry

Dear Family:

Your child is learning math in an innovative program called *Math Expressions*. In Unit 1, your child will use place value drawings and charts to understand that the value of each place is 10 times greater than the value of the place to its right. This understanding is essential when comparing, rounding, or adding multidigit numbers. *Math Expressions* encourages children to think about "making new groups" to help them understand place values.

We call the method below "New Groups Above Method." The numbers that represent the new groups are written above the problem.

1. Add the ones:

$5 + 7 = 12$ ones
$12 = 2$ ones $+ 10$ ones,
and 10 ones $= 1$ new ten.

$$\begin{array}{r} 1 \\ 5,175 \\ +\,3,967 \\ \hline 2 \end{array}$$

2. Add the tens:

$1 + 7 + 6 = 14$ tens
$14 = 4$ tens $+ 10$ tens,
and 10 tens $= 1$ new hundred.

$$\begin{array}{r} 11 \\ 5,175 \\ +\,3,967 \\ \hline 42 \end{array}$$

3. Add the hundreds:

$1 + 1 + 9 = 11$ hundreds
$11 = 1$ hundred $+ 10$ hundreds,
and 10 hundreds $= 1$ new thousand.

$$\begin{array}{r} 1\ 11 \\ 5,175 \\ +\,3,967 \\ \hline 142 \end{array}$$

4. Add the thousands:

$1 + 5 + 3 = 9$ thousands

$$\begin{array}{r} 1\ 11 \\ 5,175 \\ +\,3,967 \\ \hline 9,142 \end{array}$$

We call the following method "New Groups Below Method." The steps are the same, but the new groups are written below the addends.

1.
$$\begin{array}{r} 5,175 \\ +\,3,967 \\ \hline 1 \\ 2 \end{array}$$

2.
$$\begin{array}{r} 5,175 \\ +\,3,967 \\ \hline 11 \\ 42 \end{array}$$

3.
$$\begin{array}{r} 5,175 \\ +\,3,967 \\ \hline 111 \\ 142 \end{array}$$

4.
$$\begin{array}{r} 5,175 \\ +\,3,967 \\ \hline 1\ 11 \\ 9,142 \end{array}$$

It is easier to see the totals for each column (12 and 14) and adding is easier because you add the two numbers you see and then add the 1.

Activities and games to build fluency with multiplication and division are included at the end of this unit. It is important that your child maintains his or her home practice with basic multiplication and division.

Sincerely,
Your child's teacher

Estimada familia:

Su niño está aprendiendo matemáticas mediante el programa *Math Expressions*. En la Unidad 1, se usarán dibujos y tablas de valor posicional para comprender que el valor de cada lugar es 10 veces mayor que el valor del lugar a su derecha. Comprender esto es esencial para comparar, redondear o sumar números de varios dígitos. *Math Expressions* enseña a pensar en "formar grupos nuevos" para comprender los valores posicionales.

Este método se llama "Método de Grupos nuevos arriba." Los números que representan los grupos nuevos se escriben arriba del problema:

1. Suma las unidades:
5 + 7 = 12 unidades
12 = 2 unidades + 10 unidades,
y 10 unidades = 1 nueva decena.

```
     1
 5, 175
+3, 967
-------
      2
```

2. Suma las decenas:
1 + 7 + 6 = 14 decenas
14 = 4 decenas + 10 decenas,
y 10 decenas = 1 nueva centena.

```
    11
 5, 175
+3, 967
-------
     42
```

3. Suma las centenas:
1 + 1 + 9 = 11 centenas
11 = 1 centenas + 10 centenas,
y 10 centenas = 1 nuevo millar.

```
  1 11
 5, 175
+3, 967
-------
    142
```

4. Suma los millares:
1 + 5 + 3 = 9 millares

```
 1  11
 5, 175
+3, 967
-------
 9, 142
```

Este método se llama "Método de Grupos nuevos abajo". Los pasos son iguales, pero los nuevos grupos se escriben abajo de los sumandos:

```
1.   5, 175        2.   5, 175
    +3, 967            +3, 967
          1               11
    -------            -------
          2                42

3.   5, 175        4.   5, 175
    +3, 967            +3, 967
        111            1  111
    -------            -------
        142             9, 142
```

Es más fácil ver los totales de cada columna (12 y 14) y es más fácil sumar porque sumas los dos números que ves, y luego sumas 1.

Al final de esta unidad se incluyen actividades y juegos para desarrollar la fluidez con la multiplicación y división. Es importante que su niño siga practicando las multiplicaciones y divisiones básicas en casa.

Atentamente,
El maestro de su niño

addend

factor

digit

greater than (>)

expanded form

inverse operations

One of two or more numbers multiplied to find a product.

Example:

4 × 5 = 20

factor factor product

One of two or more numbers added together to find a sum.

Example:

7 + 8 = 15

addend addend sum

A symbol used to compare two numbers. The greater number is given first below.

Example:

33 > 17

33 is greater than 17.

Any of the symbols 0, 1, 2, 3, 4, 5, 6, 7, 8, or 9.

Opposite or reverse operations that undo each other. Addition and subtraction are inverse operations. Multiplication and division are inverse operations.

Examples:

4 + 6 = 10 so, 10 − 6 = 4 and 10 − 4 = 6.

3 × 9 = 27 so, 27 ÷ 9 = 3 and 27 ÷ 3 = 9.

A way of writing a number that shows the value of each of its digits.

Example:

Expanded form of 835:

800 + 30 + 5

8 hundreds + 3 tens + 5 ones

less than (<)	**product**
order	**square number**
place value	**standard form**

The answer to a multiplication problem.

Example:
9 × 7 = 63
↑
product

A symbol used to compare two numbers.
The smaller number is given first below.

Example:
54 < 78
54 is less than 78.

The product of a whole number and itself.

Example
3 × 3 = 9
↑
square number

Arrange numbers from the least number to the greatest number or from the greatest number to the least number.

Examples:
Least to greatest: 453, 526, 571, 802
Greatest to least: 3,742; 3,608; 3,295

The form of a number written using digits.

Example:
2,145

The value assigned to the place that a digit occupies in a number.

Example:
235
↑
The 2 is in the hundreds place, so its value is 200.

word form

The form of a number written using words instead of digits.

Example:

Six hundred thirty-nine

Name ____________________

Model Hundreds

You can represent numbers by making place value drawings on a dot array.

1. What number does this drawing show? ____
   Explain your thinking.

   ____

   ____

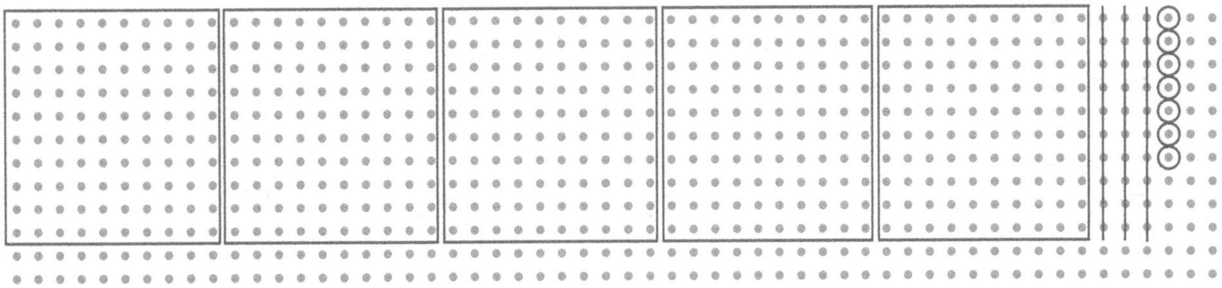

Model Thousands

Discuss this place value drawing. Write the number of each.

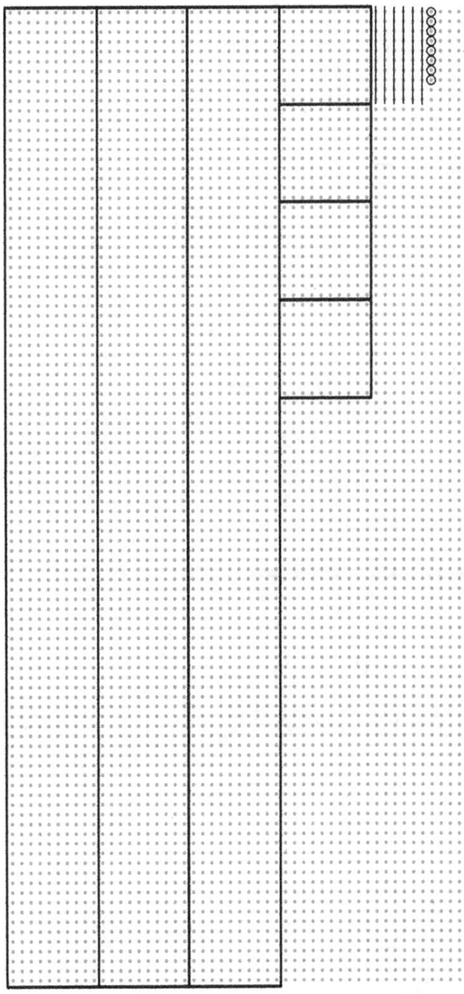

2. ones: ____
3. quick tens: ____
4. hundred boxes: ____
5. thousand bars: ____
6. How many hundred boxes could we draw inside each thousand bar? Explain.

   ____

   ____

7. What number does this drawing show?

   ____

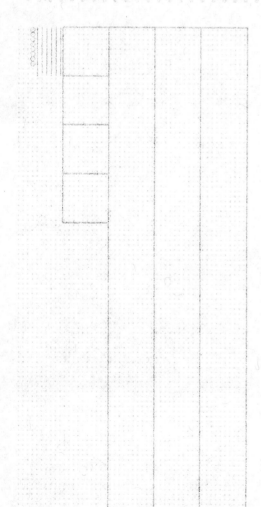

1,000 1,000	100 100
2,000 2,000	200 200
3,000 3,000	300 300
4,000 4,000	400 400
5,000 5,000	500 500
6,000 6,000	600 600
7,000 7,000	700 700
8,000 8,000	800 800
9,000 9,000	900 900

one hundred	one thousand
two hundred	two thousand
three hundred	three thousand
four hundred	four thousand
five hundred	five thousand
six hundred	six thousand
seven hundred	seven thousand
eight hundred	eight thousand
nine hundred	nine thousand

10 10	1 1
20 20	2 2
30 30	3 3
40 40	4 4
50 50	5 5
60 60	6 6
70 70	7 7
80 80	8 8
90 90	9 9

one	ten (teen) (one ten)
two	twenty (two tens)
three	thirty (three tens)
four	forty (four tens)
five	fifty (five tens)
six	sixty (six tens)
seven	seventy (seven tens)
eight	eighty (eight tens)
nine	ninety (nine tens)

 Name ______________________

Order Numbers on a Number Line

VOCABULARY
order

You can **order** numbers by arranging them from the least number to the greatest number or the greatest number to the least number.

Use the number lines.

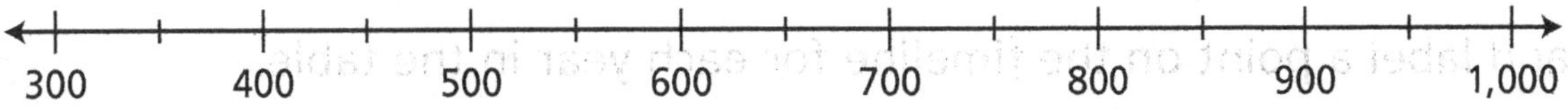
300
400
500
600
700
800
900
1,000

37 Draw and label a point on the number line for each number: 600, 350, 650.

38 Write the numbers in order from least to greatest.

350 650 600

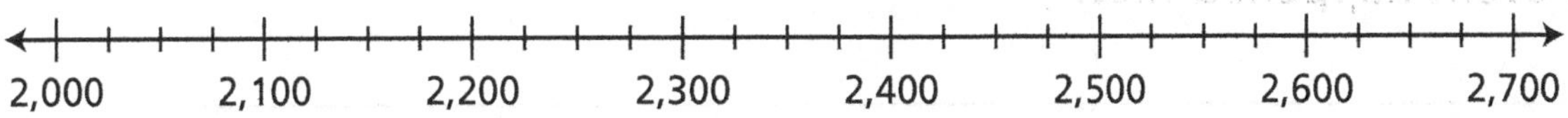
2,000
2,100
2,200
2,300
2,400
2,500
2,600
2,700

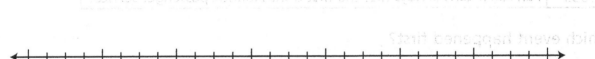

39 Draw and label a point on the number line for each number: 2,500; 2,025; 2,350; 2,575.

40 Write the numbers in order from greatest to least.

2,575 2,500 2,350 2,025

Write the numbers in order from least to greatest.

41 994, 748, 906, 876 ______________________

42 2,480; 2,078; 2,409 ______________________

Write the numbers in order from greatest to least.

43 588, 836, 498, 534 ______________________

44 2,104; 2,652; 2,008 ______________________

Name ______________________

Order Numbers on a Timeline

The timeline is divided into 10-year periods called decades.

Events in Aviation

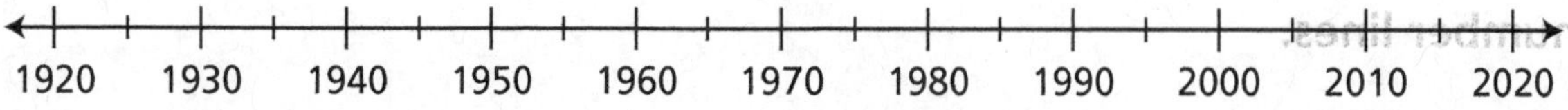
1920
1930
1940
1950
1960
1970
1980
1990
2000
2010
2020

45 Draw and label a point on the timeline for each year in the table.

Year	Event
2015	The first test of a drone tracking system occurs.
1989	*Voyager 2* first encounters Neptune.
1978	The first balloon flight over the Atlantic Ocean occurs.
1927	Lindbergh makes the first non-stop solo flight over the Atlantic Ocean.
1939	Pan American Airways flies the first trans-Atlantic passenger service.

46 Which event happened first?

____

____

47 Write the years of the events in order from the earliest year to the latest year.

____

48 Write a question that can be answered by the timeline. Include the answer.

____

____

____

Check Understanding

Explain a method you can use to round, compare, or order multidigit numbers.

Name ________________________________

Write the correct answer.

1. Rachel made this place value drawing using ones, quick tens, hundred boxes, and a thousand bar. What number did Rachel model?

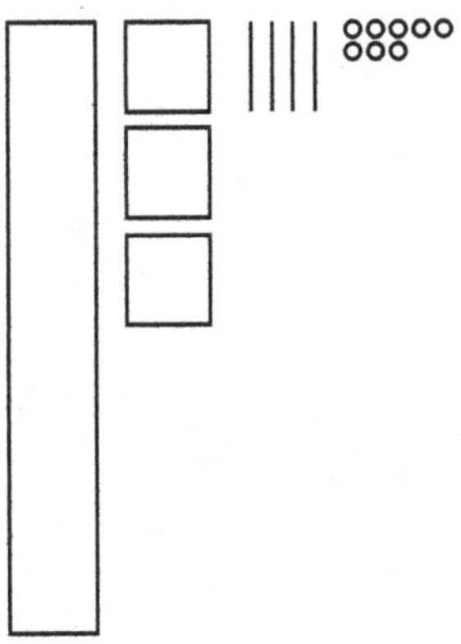

____

2. Round the number to the place value of the underlined digit.

3<u>4</u>5,209

____

3. Complete the pattern.

$5 \times 100 = 500$

$5 \times 1{,}000 = 5{,}000$

$5 \times 10{,}000 = 50{,}000$

$5 \times 100{,}000 =$ 500,000

4. Write the number in standard form.

two hundred twelve thousand, forty

____

5. Compare using >, <, or =.

72,890 (>) 72,809

Strategy Check 1

Name ____________________

❶ Make a place value drawing using ones, quick tens, hundred boxes, and thousand bars.

6,782

❷ Round 6,<u>7</u>82 to the place value of the underlined digit.

____

❸ Is the rounded number greater than or less than 6,782? Compare using >, <, or =.

____

❹ Describe the rules for rounding numbers in your own words.

____

____

____

____

____

Unit 1
Quick Quiz 2

Name ____________________

Add.

1.
$$\begin{array}{r} 45{,}616 \\ +\ 38{,}985 \\ \hline \end{array}$$

2.
$$\begin{array}{r} 645{,}732 \\ +\ 288{,}919 \\ \hline \end{array}$$

Solve.

Show your work.

3. A truck driver drove 1,438 hours last year, and another 1,767 hours this year. How many hours did he drive in all?

3,205 ____________________

4. Customers paid a total of $93,879 for an online music service one month. They paid $416,783 more the next month than the first month. How much money did customers spend on the music service during the second month?

____

5. a. What is 529,471 rounded to the nearest hundred thousand?

____

b. What is 826,513 rounded to the nearest thousand?

____

Fluency Check 1 Name ____________________

Add.

1. $$\begin{array}{r} 413 \\ +\ 227 \\ \hline \end{array}$$

2. $$\begin{array}{r} 679 \\ +\ 308 \\ \hline \end{array}$$

3. $$\begin{array}{r} 8{,}675 \\ +\ 309 \\ \hline \end{array}$$

4. $$\begin{array}{r} 4{,}721 \\ +\ 819 \\ \hline \end{array}$$

5. $$\begin{array}{r} 2{,}964 \\ +\ 6{,}120 \\ \hline \end{array}$$

6. $$\begin{array}{r} 3{,}835 \\ +\ 5{,}937 \\ \hline \end{array}$$

7. $$\begin{array}{r} 7{,}312 \\ +\ 4{,}563 \\ \hline \end{array}$$

8. $$\begin{array}{r} 8{,}783 \\ +\ 5{,}617 \\ \hline \end{array}$$

9. $$\begin{array}{r} 73{,}189 \\ +\ 8{,}413 \\ \hline \end{array}$$

10. $$\begin{array}{r} 47{,}852 \\ +\ 7{,}894 \\ \hline \end{array}$$

11. $$\begin{array}{r} 45{,}803 \\ +\ 23{,}762 \\ \hline \end{array}$$

12. $$\begin{array}{r} 19{,}328 \\ +\ 74{,}523 \\ \hline \end{array}$$

13. $$\begin{array}{r} 435{,}004 \\ +\ 144{,}067 \\ \hline \end{array}$$

14. $$\begin{array}{r} 73{,}016 \\ +\ 49{,}679 \\ \hline \end{array}$$

15. $$\begin{array}{r} 548{,}702 \\ +\ 34{,}287 \\ \hline \end{array}$$

Dear Family:

Your child is now learning about subtraction. A common subtraction mistake is subtracting in the wrong direction. Children may think that they always subtract the smaller digit from the larger digit, but this is not true. To help children avoid this mistake, the *Math Expressions* program encourages children to "fix" numbers first and then subtract.

~~1,634~~
~~− 158~~
~~1,524~~

When one or more digits in the top number are smaller than the corresponding digits in the bottom number, fix the numbers by "ungrouping." For example, 1,634 − 158 is shown below:

1. We cannot subtract 8 ones from 4 ones. We get more ones by ungrouping 1 ten to make 10 ones.

We now have 14 ones and only 2 tens.

```
    2 14
 1,6 3̸ 4̸
−   158
```

2. We cannot subtract 5 tens from 2 tens. We get more tens by ungrouping 1 hundred to make 10 tens.

We now have 12 tens and only 5 hundreds.

```
     12
    5 2̸ 14
 1,6̸ 3̸ 4̸
−   158
```

3. Now we can subtract:
1 − 0 = 1 thousand
5 − 1 = 4 hundreds
12 − 5 = 7 tens
14 − 8 = 6 ones

```
     12
    5 2̸ 14
 1,6̸ 3̸ 4̸
−   158
  1,476
```

In the method above, the numbers are ungrouped from right to left, but students can also ungroup from left to right. Children can choose whichever way works best for them.

The unit concludes with opportunities to review and practice basic multiplications and divisions by using multiplication tables, product cards, and games. Exploring patterns, such as 4s, 6s, 8s, and 10s products as doubles of 2s, 3s, 4s, and 5s products, helps build fluency.

6 × <u>2</u> = 12	6 × <u>4</u> = 24
6 × <u>3</u> = 18	6 × <u>6</u> = 36
6 × <u>4</u> = 24	6 × <u>8</u> = 48
6 × <u>5</u> = 30	6 × <u>10</u> = 60

Your child should also continue to practice multiplication and division skills at home.

If you have any questions or comments, please contact me.

Sincerely,
Your child's teacher

Estimada familia:

Ahora su niño está aprendiendo a restar. Un error muy común al restar, es hacerlo en la dirección equivocada. Los niños pueden pensar que siempre se resta el dígito más pequeño del dígito más grande, pero no es verdad. Para ayudar a los niños a no cometer este error, el programa *Math Expressions* les propone "arreglar" los números primero y luego restar.

~~1,634~~
~~− 158~~
~~1,524~~

Cuando uno o más dígitos del número de arriba son más pequeños que los dígitos correspondientes del número de abajo, se arreglan los números "desagrupándolos". Por ejemplo, 1,634 − 158 se muestra abajo:

1. No podemos restar 8 unidades de 4 unidades. Obtenemos más unidades al desagrupar 1 decena para formar 10 unidades.

   Ahora tenemos 14 unidades y solamente 2 decenas.

   2 14
   1,6~~3~~~~4~~
   − 158

2. No podemos restar 5 decenas de 2 decenas. Obtenemos más decenas al desagrupar 1 centena para formar 10 decenas.

   Ahora tenemos 12 decenas y solamente 5 centenas.

   12
   5 ~~2~~14
   1,~~6~~~~3~~~~4~~
   − 158

3. Ahora podemos restar:
   1 − 0 = 1 millar
   5 − 1 = 4 centenas
   12 − 5 = 7 decenas
   14 − 8 = 6 unidades

   12
   5 ~~2~~14
   1,~~6~~~~3~~~~4~~
   − 158
   1,476

En el método de arriba se desagrupan los números de derecha a izquierda, pero también se pueden desagrupar de izquierda a derecha. Los niños pueden escoger la manera que les resulte más fácil.

La unidad concluye con la oportunidad de revisar y practicar multiplicaciones y divisiones básicas usando tablas de multiplicación, tarjetas de productos y juegos. Explorar patrones, tales como 4, 6, 8 y 10 productos dobles de 2, 3, 4 y 5, ayuda a desarrollar la fluidez.

$6 \times \underline{2} = 12$	$6 \times \underline{4} = 24$
$6 \times \underline{3} = 18$	$6 \times \underline{6} = 36$
$6 \times \underline{4} = 24$	$6 \times \underline{8} = 48$
$6 \times \underline{5} = 30$	$6 \times \underline{10} = 60$

Su niño también debe seguir practicando las destrezas de multiplicación y de división en casa.

Si tiene alguna pregunta, por favor comuníquese conmigo.

Atentamente,
El maestro de su niño

Name ______________________________

Discuss the Steps of the Problem

Sometimes you will need to work through more than one step to solve a problem. The steps can be shown in one or more equations.

1. In the morning, 19 students were working on a science project. In the afternoon, 3 students left and 7 more students came to work on the project. How many students were working on the project at the end of the day?

____

2. Solve the problem again by finishing Anita's and Chad's methods. Then discuss what is alike and what is different about each method.

Anita's Method	Chad's Method
Write an equation for each step.	**Write an equation for the whole problem.**
Find the total number of students who worked on the project.	Let $n =$ the number of students working on the project at the end of the day.
$19 + 7 =$ ___	Students who left in the afternoon. ↘ Students who arrived in the afternoon. ↙
Subtract the number of students who left in the afternoon.	$19 -$ ___ $+$ ___ $= n$
$26 - 3 =$ ___	___ $= n$

3. Solve. Discuss the steps you used.

A team is scheduled to play 12 games. Of those games, 7 will be played at home. The other games are away games. How many fewer away games than home games will be played?

____

____

Name ______________________________

Determine Reasonable Answers

Solve each problem. Check your answers using inverse operations.

17. Mrs. Washington has $265. She wants to buy shoes for $67 and dresses for $184. Does she have enough money? Explain your answer. ______________________________

18. Terrell wants to run at least 105 miles during the month. He ran a total of 87 miles during the first 3 weeks of the month. If he runs 25 miles in the fourth week, will he make his goal? Explain. ______________________________

What's the Error?

Dear Math Students,

My friend is taking a trip to Antarctica. He gave me $112 to buy him some clothes. I tried to buy a parka and two pairs of wool socks, but the clerk said I didn't have enough money. I added the cost like this:

$98 + $12 = $110

Can you help me figure out what I did wrong?

Your friend,
Puzzled Penguin

Bill's Outdoor Wear

Pair of wool socks	$12
Hat	$15
Mittens	$10
Parka	$98

?

19. Write a response to Puzzled Penguin.

____

____

Check Understanding

If Puzzled Penguin wanted to buy a parka and a hat, what would the total be? __________ Does Puzzled Penguin have enough money? __________

Name ______________________________

Make a Bar Graph

Bridges are structures that are built to get over obstacles like water, a valley, or roads. Bridges can be made of concrete, steel, or even tree roots. Engineers and designers do a lot of math to be sure a bridge will stand up to its use and the forces of nature that affect it.

Lengths of Bridges		
Bridge	**Length Over Water (ft)**	
Manchac Swamp Bridge, U.S.A.	121,440	
Hangzhou Bay Bridge, China	117,057	
Lake Pontchartrain Causeway, U.S.A.	125,664	
Jiaozhou Bay Bridge, China	139,392	

1. Use the data in the table above to make a bar graph.

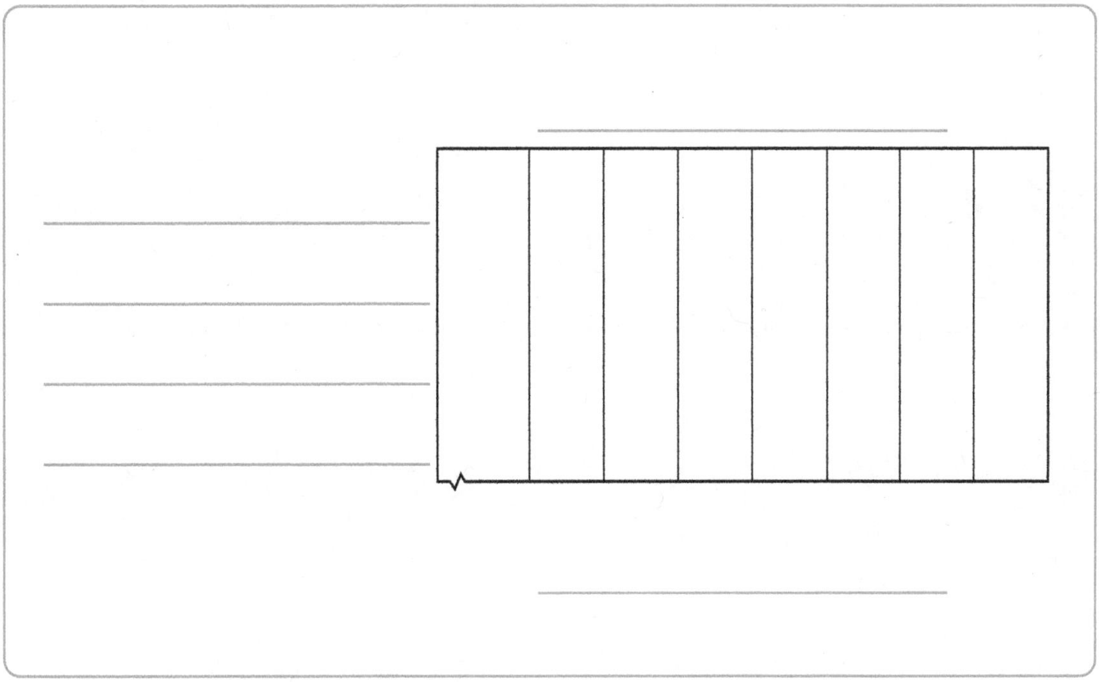

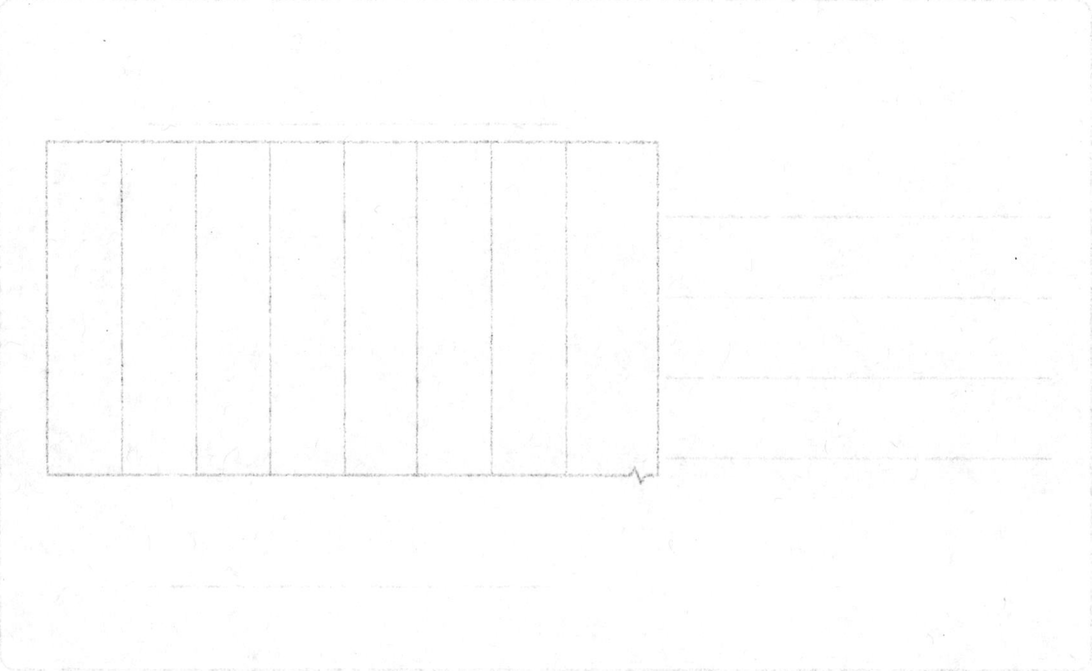

Name ______________________________

Subtract.

1. $$\begin{array}{r} 409{,}867 \\ -\ 377{,}294 \\ \hline \end{array}$$

Solve.

Show your work.

2. Most tickets were sold before Sunday. On Sunday 9,854 more tickets are sold. 92,563 tickets were sold in all. How many tickets were sold before Sunday?

____

3. Earth has an average diameter of about 7,926 miles. Mercury's approximate average diameter is 4,894 miles less than Earth's. What is Mercury's average diameter?

____

4. Lance's class read for a total of 7,842 minutes during a read-a-thon. Alex's class read for 9,310 minutes. Alex wrote this subtraction equation to show how many more minutes his class read than Lance's class.

$9{,}310 - 7{,}842 = \blacksquare$

Solve Alex's equation and write an addition equation to check the subtraction.

____

Write an equation and solve the problem.

5. Chris scored 34,809 points in one computer game. He scored 6,250 fewer points in another game. How many points did Chris score in both games?

____

____

Fluency Check 2

Name ______________________________

Add or subtract.

1. 303 + 251
2. 9,208 − 5,107
3. 32,971 + 4,643
4. 35,977 + 41,682
5. 301,429 − 78,046
6. 448,054 + 209,186
7. 437 + 259
8. 89,307 − 6,346
9. 695 + 542
10. 7,293 + 561
11. 5,259 − 1,739
12. 791 − 438
13. 2,786 + 1,433
14. 76,176 − 46,233
15. 542,711 − 358,525

Name ______________________________

VOCABULARY
factor
product

PATH to FLUENCY

Complete a Multiplication Table

1. Look at the **factors** to complete the Multiplication Table. Leave blanks for the **products** you do not know.

×	1	2	3	4	5	6	7	8	9	10
1										
2										
3										
4										
5										
6										
7										
8										
9										
10										

2. Write the multiplications you need to practice.

____

____

____

____

____

Name ________________________________

Scrambled Multiplication Tables

PATH to FLUENCY

Complete each table.

A

×	1	5	9	10	7	4	3	2	8	6
6	6	30	54	60	42	24	18	12	48	36
2	2	10	18	20	14	8	6	4	16	12
10	10	50	90	100	70	40	30	20	80	60
8	8	40	72	80	56	32	24	16	64	48
5	5	25	45	50	35	20	15	10	40	30
1	1	5	9	10	7	4	3	2	8	6
9	9	45	81	90	63	36	27	18	72	54
4	4	20	36	40	28	16	12	8	32	24
7	7	35	63	70	49	28	21	14	56	42
3	3	15	27	30	21	12	9	6	24	18

B

×	10	3	2							
10	100	30	20		70	50		90		10
5	50	15		20	35		30		40	5
1	10	3		4	7		6	9		1
		9		12	21	15		27	24	
2	20	6	4	8			12	18	16	2
		12	8	16	28	20		36	32	
4	90	27	18	36	63	45	54		72	
		18	12	24		30	36	54	48	6
		21		28	49		42		56	7
		24		32	56	40		72	64	8

C

×										
	27	6	24	21	18	15	12	9	3	
	36	8	32	28	24		16	12	4	40
	9	2	8	7	6	5	4	3	1	10
	18	4	16	14		10	8	6	2	20
		14	56	49	42		28	21	7	
	72		64	56	48	40	32	24	8	80
	45	10	40		30	25	20	15	5	
	54	12	48	42	36	30	24	18	6	60
	90		80	70	60		40	30	10	100
	81	18	72		54	45	36	27	9	

D

×										
	48		42	12	36		18	6		30
	56	28		14		70	21		63	35
			70		60			10		50
		20	35		30		15	5	45	
	32			8		40			36	
	8	4		2			3	1		5
		8	14		12		6		18	10
	64		56		48	80	24	8		40
	72	36		18			27		81	
	24		21		18	30		3	27	

Check Understanding

Complete the sentences.

The numbers in the yellow boxes are ______________________.

The numbers in the white boxes are ______________________.

2×2

$2 \bullet 3$

Hint:
What is $3 \cdot 2$?

$2 * 4$

Hint:
What is $4 * 2$?

2×5

Hint:
What is 5×2?

2×6

Hint:
What is 6×2?

$2 \bullet 7$

Hint:
What is $7 \cdot 2$?

$2 * 8$

Hint:
What is $8 * 2$?

2×9

Hint:
What is 9×2?

5×2

Hint:
What is 2×5?

$5 \bullet 3$

Hint:
What is $3 \cdot 5$?

$5 * 4$

Hint:
What is $4 * 5$?

5×5

5×6

Hint:
What is 6×5?

$5 \bullet 7$

Hint:
What is $7 \cdot 5$?

$5 * 8$

Hint:
What is $8 * 5$?

5×9

Hint:
What is 9×5?

$2\overline{)10}$

Hint: What is
☐ × 2 = 10?

$2\overline{)8}$

Hint: What is
☐ × 2 = 8?

$2\overline{)6}$

Hint: What is
☐ × 2 = 6?

$2\overline{)4}$

Hint: What is
☐ × 2 = 4?

$2\overline{)18}$

Hint: What is
☐ × 2 = 18?

$2\overline{)16}$

Hint: What is
☐ × 2 = 16?

$2\overline{)14}$

Hint: What is
☐ × 2 = 14?

$2\overline{)12}$

Hint: What is
☐ × 2 = 12?

$5\overline{)25}$

Hint: What is
☐ × 5 = 25?

$5\overline{)20}$

Hint: What is
☐ × 5 = 20?

$5\overline{)15}$

Hint: What is
☐ × 5 = 15?

$5\overline{)10}$

Hint: What is
☐ × 5 = 10?

$5\overline{)45}$

Hint: What is
☐ × 5 = 45?

$5\overline{)40}$

Hint: What is
☐ × 5 = 40?

$5\overline{)35}$

Hint: What is
☐ × 5 = 35?

$5\overline{)30}$

Hint: What is
☐ × 5 = 30?

9 × 2 Hint: What is 2 × 9? © Houghton Mifflin Harcourt Publishing Company	9 • 3 Hint: What is 3 · 9? © Houghton Mifflin Harcourt Publishing Company	9 * 4 Hint: What is 4 * 9? © Houghton Mifflin Harcourt Publishing Company	9 × 5 Hint: What is 5 × 9? © Houghton Mifflin Harcourt Publishing Company
9 × 6 Hint: What is 6 × 9? © Houghton Mifflin Harcourt Publishing Company	9 • 7 Hint: What is 7 · 9? © Houghton Mifflin Harcourt Publishing Company	9 * 8 Hint: What is 8 * 9? © Houghton Mifflin Harcourt Publishing Company	9 × 9 © Houghton Mifflin Harcourt Publishing Company
×	•	*	×
×	•	*	×

You can write any numbers on the last 8 cards. Use them to practice difficult problems or if you lose a card.

$9\overline{)45}$

Hint: What is

☐ × 9 = 45?

$9\overline{)36}$

Hint: What is

☐ × 9 = 36?

$9\overline{)27}$

Hint: What is

☐ × 9 = 27?

$9\overline{)18}$

Hint: What is

☐ × 9 = 18?

$9\overline{)81}$

Hint: What is

☐ × 9 = 81?

$9\overline{)72}$

Hint: What is

☐ × 9 = 72?

$9\overline{)63}$

Hint: What is

☐ × 9 = 63?

$9\overline{)54}$

Hint: What is

☐ × 9 = 54?

You can write any numbers on the last 8 cards. Use them to practice difficult problems or if you lose a card.

3×2

Hint:
What is 2×3?

$3 \bullet 3$

$3 * 4$

Hint:
What is $4 * 3$?

3×5

Hint:
What is 5×3?

3×6

Hint:
What is 6×3?

$3 \bullet 7$

Hint:
What is $7 \cdot 3$?

$3 * 8$

Hint:
What is $8 * 3$?

3×9

Hint:
What is 9×3?

4×2

Hint:
What is 2×4?

$4 \bullet 3$

Hint:
What is $3 \cdot 4$?

$4 * 4$

4×5

Hint:
What is 5×4?

4×6

Hint:
What is 6×4?

$4 \bullet 7$

Hint:
What is $7 \cdot 4$?

$4 * 8$

Hint:
What is $8 * 4$?

4×9

Hint:
What is 9×4?

$3\overline{)15}$

Hint: What is
☐ × 3 = 15?

$3\overline{)12}$

Hint: What is
☐ × 3 = 12?

$3\overline{)9}$

Hint: What is
☐ × 3 = 9?

$3\overline{)6}$

Hint: What is
☐ × 3 = 6?

$3\overline{)27}$

Hint: What is
☐ × 3 = 27?

$3\overline{)24}$

Hint: What is
☐ × 3 = 24?

$3\overline{)21}$

Hint: What is
☐ × 3 = 21?

$3\overline{)18}$

Hint: What is
☐ × 3 = 18?

$4\overline{)20}$

Hint: What is
☐ × 4 = 20?

$4\overline{)16}$

Hint: What is
☐ × 4 = 16?

$4\overline{)12}$

Hint: What is
☐ × 4 = 12?

$4\overline{)8}$

Hint: What is
☐ × 4 = 8?

$4\overline{)36}$

Hint: What is
☐ × 4 = 36?

$4\overline{)32}$

Hint: What is
☐ × 4 = 32?

$4\overline{)28}$

Hint: What is
☐ × 4 = 28?

$4\overline{)24}$

Hint: What is
☐ × 4 = 24?

6 × 2

Hint:
What is 2 × 6?

6 • 3

Hint:
What is 3 · 6?

6 * 4

Hint:
What is 4 * 6?

6 × 5

Hint:
What is 5 × 6?

6 × 6

6 • 7

Hint:
What is 7 · 6?

6 * 8

Hint:
What is 8 * 6?

6 × 9

Hint:
What is 9 × 6?

7 × 2

Hint:
What is 2 × 7?

7 • 3

Hint:
What is 3 · 7?

7 * 4

Hint:
What is 4 * 7?

7 × 5

Hint:
What is 5 × 7?

7 × 6

Hint:
What is 6 × 7?

7 • 7

7 * 8

Hint:
What is 8 * 7?

7 × 9

Hint:
What is 9 × 7?

$6\overline{)30}$

Hint: What is $\square \times 6 = 30$?

$6\overline{)24}$

Hint: What is $\square \times 6 = 24$?

$6\overline{)18}$

Hint: What is $\square \times 6 = 18$?

$6\overline{)12}$

Hint: What is $\square \times 6 = 12$?

$6\overline{)54}$

Hint: What is $\square \times 6 = 54$?

$6\overline{)48}$

Hint: What is $\square \times 6 = 48$?

$6\overline{)42}$

Hint: What is $\square \times 6 = 42$?

$6\overline{)36}$

Hint: What is $\square \times 6 = 36$?

$7\overline{)35}$

Hint: What is $\square \times 7 = 35$?

$7\overline{)28}$

Hint: What is $\square \times 7 = 28$?

$7\overline{)21}$

Hint: What is $\square \times 7 = 21$?

$7\overline{)14}$

Hint: What is $\square \times 7 = 14$?

$7\overline{)63}$

Hint: What is $\square \times 7 = 63$?

$7\overline{)56}$

Hint: What is $\square \times 7 = 56$?

$7\overline{)49}$

Hint: What is $\square \times 7 = 49$?

$7\overline{)42}$

Hint: What is $\square \times 7 = 42$?

8 × 2 Hint: What is 2 × 8? 	8 • 3 Hint: What is 3 • 8? 	8 * 4 Hint: What is 4 * 8? 	8 × 5 Hint: What is 5 × 8?
8 × 6 Hint: What is 6 × 8? 	8 • 7 Hint: What is 7 • 8? 	8 * 8 	8 × 9 Hint: What is 9 × 8?
×	•	*	×
×	•	*	×

You can write any numbers on the last 8 cards. Use them to practice difficult problems or if you lose a card.

$8\overline{)40}$ Hint: What is □ × 8 = 40? 	$8\overline{)32}$ Hint: What is □ × 8 = 32? 	$8\overline{)24}$ Hint: What is □ × 8 = 24? 	$8\overline{)16}$ Hint: What is □ × 8 = 16?
$8\overline{)72}$ Hint: What is □ × 8 = 72? 	$8\overline{)64}$ Hint: What is □ × 8 = 64? 	$8\overline{)56}$ Hint: What is □ × 8 = 56? 	$8\overline{)48}$ Hint: What is □ × 8 = 48?
$\overline{)\quad}$	$\overline{)\quad}$	$\overline{)\quad}$	$\overline{)\quad}$
$\overline{)\quad}$	$\overline{)\quad}$	$\overline{)\quad}$	$\overline{)\quad}$

You can write any numbers on the last 8 cards. Use them to practice difficult problems or if you lose a card.

Name Penny

Look for Patterns

VOCABULARY
square number

21 List the products in Exercises 11–20 in order. Discuss the patterns you see with your class.

____

The numbers you listed in Exercise 21 are called **square numbers** because they are the areas of squares with whole-number lengths of sides. A square number is the product of a whole number and itself. So, if n is a whole number, the product of $n \times n$ is a square number.

Patterns on the Multiplication Table

22 In the table, circle the products that are square numbers. Discuss the patterns you see with your class.

×	1	2	3	4	5	6	7	8	9	10
1	1	2	3	4	5	6	7	8	9	10
2	2	4	6	8	10	12	14	16	18	20
3	3	6	9	12	15	18	21	24	27	30
4	4	8	12	16	20	24	28	32	36	40
5	5	10	15	20	25	30	35	40	45	50
6	6	12	18	24	30	36	42	48	54	60
7	7	14	21	28	35	42	49	56	63	70
8	8	16	24	32	40	48	56	64	72	80
9	9	18	27	36	45	54	63	72	81	90
10	10	20	30	40	50	60	70	80	90	100

23 Explain why the number 16 is a square number.

____

Name

PATH to FLUENCY

Play *High Card Wins*

Read the rules for playing *High Card Wins*. Then play the game with your partner.

Rules for *High Card Wins*

Number of players: 2

What you will need: 1 set of Product Cards

1. Shuffle the cards. Deal all the cards evenly between the two players.
2. Players put their stacks in front of them, multiplication side up.
3. Each player takes the top card from his or her stack and puts it multiplication side up in the center of the table.
4. Each player says the product and then turns the card over to check. The correct product is shown in green. Then players do one of the following:
   - If one player says the wrong answer, the other player takes both cards and puts them at the bottom of his or her pile.
   - If both players say the wrong answer, both players take back their cards and put them at the bottom of their piles.
   - If both players say the correct answer, the player with the greater product takes both cards and puts them at the bottom of his or her pile. If the products are the same, the players set the cards aside and play another round. The winner of the next round takes all the cards.
5. Play continues until one player has all the cards.

4×5

Hint: What is 5×4?

$4\overline{)20}$

Hint: What is $\square \times 4 = 20$?

Name ____________________

PATH to FLUENCY Play *Solve the Stack*

Read the rules for playing *Solve the Stack*. Then play the game with your group.

Rules for *Solve the Stack*

Number of players: 2–4

What you will need: 1 set of Product Cards

1. Shuffle the cards. Place them division side up in the center of the table.
2. Players take turns. On each turn, a player says the answer to the division on the top card and then turns the card over to check the answer. The answer is shown in blue.
3. If a player's answer is correct, he or she takes the card. If it is incorrect, the card is placed at the bottom of the stack.
4. Play ends when there are no more cards in the stack. The player with the most cards wins.

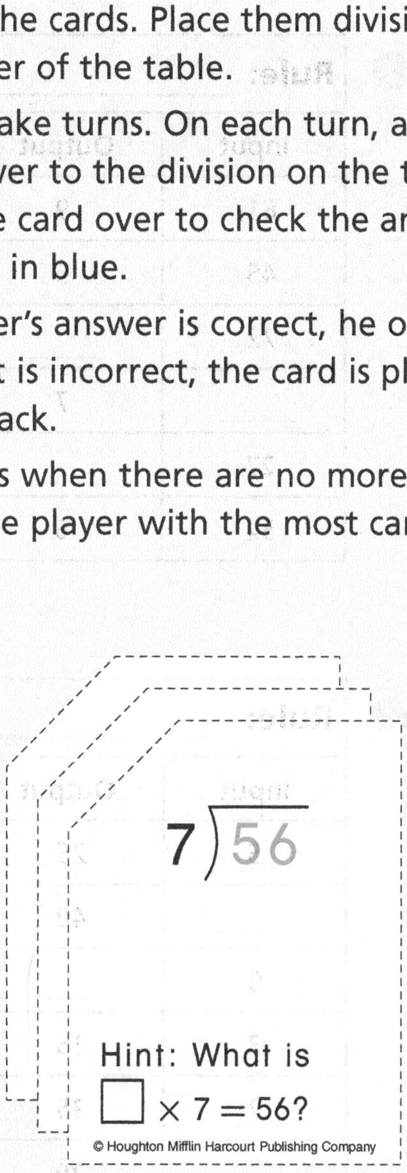
7)56
Hint: What is
□ × 7 = 56?
© Houghton Mifflin Harcourt Publishing Company

Name ______________________

PATH to FLUENCY

What's My Rule?

Look at the input/output tables below. For every input number, there is only one output number. The rule describes what to do to the input number to get the output number.

Write the rule and then complete each table.

1. **Rule:** ______

Input	Output
7	42
8	___
___	54
6	36
4	24
5	___

2. **Rule:** ______

Input	Output
81	9
45	5
72	___
___	7
27	___
54	6

3. **Rule:** ______

Input	Output
21	7
27	9
___	6
15	___
___	8
9	3

4. **Rule:** ______

Input	Output
5	25
___	40
9	___
3	15
7	35
___	20

Name

What's My Rule? (continued)

Write the rule and then complete each table.

5

Rule: ______	
Input	Output
2	4
___	18
6	12
4	___
___	14
3	___

6

Rule: ______	
Input	Output
40	5
24	3
16	___
___	4
56	___
___	1

7

Rule: ______	
Input	Output
50	5
___	8
10	___
___	4
90	___
30	3

8

Rule: ______	
Input	Output
2	___
7	28
3	12
___	36
___	20
6	___

9

Rule: ______	
Input	Output
20	4
___	2
35	7
15	___
40	___
___	5

10

Rule: ______	
Input	Output
7	___
3	21
___	28
6	42
9	___
___	35

Check Understanding

Explain how you chose the rule for the table in Exercise 9.

Name ____________________

PATH to FLUENCY

Diagnostic Checkup for Basic Multiplication

1. 7 × 5 = ___	2. 2 × 3 = ___	3. 9 × 9 = ___	4. 9 × 6 = ___
5. 6 × 2 = ___	6. 3 × 0 = ___	7. 3 × 4 = ___	8. 6 × 8 = ___
9. 5 × 9 = ___	10. 3 × 3 = ___	11. 2 × 9 = ___	12. 5 × 7 = ___
13. 6 × 10 = ___	14. 4 × 1 = ___	15. 6 × 4 = ___	16. 4 × 8 = ___
17. 5 × 2 = ___	18. 1 × 3 = ___	19. 3 × 9 = ___	20. 7 × 6 = ___
21. 7 × 2 = ___	22. 9 × 0 = ___	23. 8 × 9 = ___	24. 8 × 7 = ___
25. 8 × 10 = ___	26. 6 × 3 = ___	27. 4 × 4 = ___	28. 3 × 8 = ___
29. 5 × 5 = ___	30. 6 × 0 = ___	31. 7 × 9 = ___	32. 6 × 6 = ___
33. 9 × 2 = ___	34. 8 × 3 = ___	35. 5 × 4 = ___	36. 7 × 7 = ___
37. 5 × 10 = ___	38. 5 × 1 = ___	39. 10 × 9 = ___	40. 5 × 6 = ___
41. 6 × 5 = ___	42. 9 × 3 = ___	43. 4 × 2 = ___	44. 7 × 8 = ___
45. 8 × 2 = ___	46. 5 × 0 = ___	47. 4 × 9 = ___	48. 6 × 7 = ___
49. 9 × 5 = ___	50. 6 × 1 = ___	51. 7 × 4 = ___	52. 9 × 8 = ___
53. 4 × 10 = ___	54. 5 × 3 = ___	55. 6 × 9 = ___	56. 8 × 6 = ___
57. 8 × 5 = ___	58. 8 × 0 = ___	59. 8 × 4 = ___	60. 4 × 7 = ___
61. 3 × 5 = ___	62. 7 × 3 = ___	63. 5 × 9 = ___	64. 3 × 6 = ___
65. 7 × 10 = ___	66. 8 × 1 = ___	67. 0 × 4 = ___	68. 9 × 7 = ___

Name ______

PATH to FLUENCY

Diagnostic Checkup for Basic Division

1 12 ÷ 2 = ___	2 8 ÷ 1 = ___	3 36 ÷ 9 = ___	4 35 ÷ 7 = ___
5 20 ÷ 5 = ___	6 24 ÷ 3 = ___	7 12 ÷ 4 = ___	8 6 ÷ 6 = ___
9 6 ÷ 2 = ___	10 3 ÷ 3 = ___	11 18 ÷ 9 = ___	12 63 ÷ 7 = ___
13 20 ÷ 10 = ___	14 0 ÷ 1 = ___	15 40 ÷ 4 = ___	16 48 ÷ 8 = ___
17 18 ÷ 2 = ___	18 6 ÷ 3 = ___	19 8 ÷ 4 = ___	20 36 ÷ 6 = ___
21 8 ÷ 2 = ___	22 9 ÷ 1 = ___	23 9 ÷ 9 = ___	24 56 ÷ 7 = ___
25 40 ÷ 5 = ___	26 9 ÷ 3 = ___	27 36 ÷ 4 = ___	28 56 ÷ 8 = ___
29 80 ÷ 10 = ___	30 7 ÷ 1 = ___	31 45 ÷ 9 = ___	32 48 ÷ 6 = ___
33 5 ÷ 5 = ___	34 30 ÷ 3 = ___	35 16 ÷ 4 = ___	36 72 ÷ 8 = ___
37 10 ÷ 2 = ___	38 1 ÷ 1 = ___	39 54 ÷ 9 = ___	40 21 ÷ 7 = ___
41 25 ÷ 5 = ___	42 15 ÷ 3 = ___	43 32 ÷ 4 = ___	44 24 ÷ 8 = ___
45 90 ÷ 10 = ___	46 18 ÷ 3 = ___	47 63 ÷ 9 = ___	48 54 ÷ 6 = ___
49 45 ÷ 5 = ___	50 6 ÷ 1 = ___	51 20 ÷ 4 = ___	52 49 ÷ 7 = ___
53 15 ÷ 5 = ___	54 0 ÷ 3 = ___	55 28 ÷ 4 = ___	56 30 ÷ 6 = ___
57 16 ÷ 2 = ___	58 21 ÷ 3 = ___	59 81 ÷ 9 = ___	60 64 ÷ 8 = ___
61 30 ÷ 5 = ___	62 12 ÷ 3 = ___	63 27 ÷ 9 = ___	64 42 ÷ 7 = ___
65 40 ÷ 10 = ___	66 10 ÷ 1 = ___	67 24 ÷ 4 = ___	68 18 ÷ 6 = ___

Name

PATH to FLUENCY

Unknown Number Puzzles

Complete each Unknown Number Puzzle.

1

×	6	3	2
10	60	30	20
6	36	18	12
3	18	9	6

2

×	8	4	2
7	56	28	14
2	16	8	4
4	32	16	8

3

×	9	7	3
8	72	56	24
6	54	42	18
5	45	35	15

4

×	5	2	8
6	30	12	48
4	20	8	32
9	45	18	72

5

×		3	7
6	30	18	42
4		12	28
	40	24	56

6

×	4		8
9		81	
	12		24
	20	45	40

7

×	8		7
8		40	
	32	20	28
	24	15	

8

×	3	4	
	27	36	81
7			63
			18

9

×			10
8	48	16	
7	42	14	
	36		60

Name ____________________

What's the Error?

Dear Math Students,

Today I had to find 8 × 4. I didn't know the answer, but I figured it out by combining two multiplications I did know:

$$5 \times 2 = 10$$
$$3 \times 2 = 6$$
$$8 \times 4 = 16$$

Is my answer right? If not, please correct my work and tell me why it is wrong.

Your friend,
The Puzzled Penguin

?

10 **Write an answer to Puzzled Penguin.**

____

____

____

Unknown Number Puzzles

11 Make your own Unknown Number Puzzle. Trade with a partner and solve.

×			

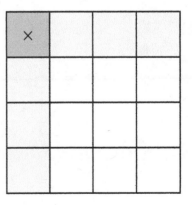

Check Understanding

I know 4 × 7 = 28.

So 8 × 7 must be ______ + ______ .

Name ____________________

What's the Error?

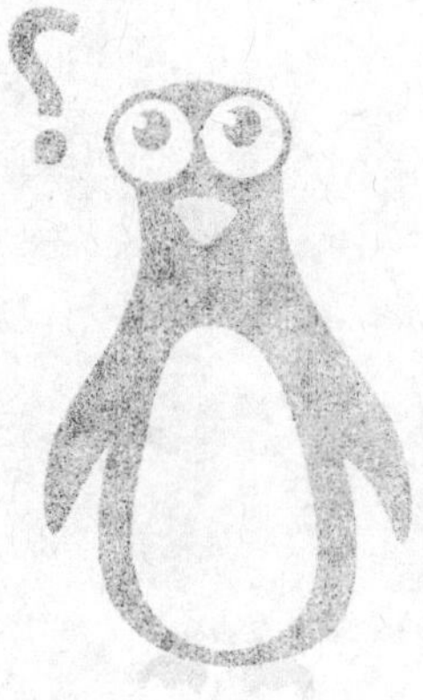

$$\overline{8 \times 4 = 16}$$

____

____

____

Unit 1
Quick Quiz 4

Name ______________________________

Write the correct answer.

1. $6 \times 9 = \square$

2. $18 \div \square = 2$

3. $8 \times \square = 56$

4. Write an equation to show the area of the large square.

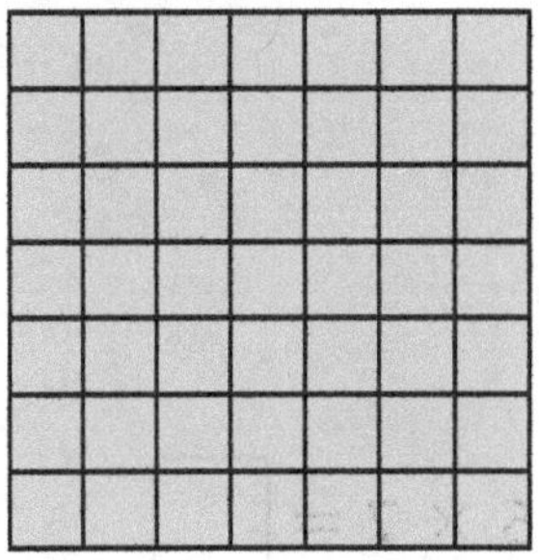

____

5. Write the rule and complete the table.

Rule:	
Input	**Output**
36	6
30	5
18	
54	
48	8

Fluency Check 3

Name ______________________

Multiply.

1. $1 \times 3 = \square$
2. $3 \times 2 = \square$
3. $4 \times 3 = \square$
4. $4 \times 1 = \square$
5. $2 \times 5 = \square$
6. $6 \times 1 = \square$
7. $6 \times 6 = \square$
8. $8 \times 4 = \square$
9. $5 \times 7 = \square$
10. $9 \times 3 = \square$
11. $8 \times 8 = \square$
12. $6 \times 9 = \square$
13. $7 \times 10 = \square$
14. $10 \times 10 = \square$
15. $8 \times 9 = \square$

Name ______________________________

1 Anthony's family drives 659 miles from Miami to Atlanta. Then they drive another 247 miles to Nashville. How far does Anthony's family drive in all? Show your work.

2 A scientist measures 3,470 milliliters of water into a beaker. She pours 2,518 milliliters of the water in a solution. If the beaker can hold 5,000 milliliters, how much water is needed to fill the beaker? Show your work. Then show a way to check your answer.

3 Fill in the blank to show the number of hundreds.

4,500 = ____________ hundreds

Explain how you know.

Name ______________________________

4 Write the rule and complete the table.

Rule:	
Input	**Output**
6	54
5	45
7	____
3	____
2	18

5 56 ÷ 8 = ☐

6 The downtown location of Mike's Bikes earned $179,456 last year. The store's riverside location earned $145,690. The store with the greater earnings gets an award. Which store gets the award? Show your work.

7 Select another form of 65,042. Mark all that apply.

Ⓐ 6 + 5 + 0 + 4 + 2

Ⓑ sixty-five thousand, forty-two

Ⓒ 60,000 + 5,000 + 40 + 2

Ⓓ six hundred fifty, forty-two

Name ____________________

8 For numbers 8a–8d, choose Yes or No to tell if the number is rounded to the nearest thousand.

8a. 234,566
235,000 ○ Yes ○ No

8b. 7,893
7,900 ○ Yes ○ No

8c. 64,498
65,000 ○ Yes ○ No

8d. 958,075
958,000 ○ Yes ○ No

9 For numbers 9a–9e, choose True or False to describe the statement.

9a. 34,639 > 34,369 ○ True ○ False

9b. 2,709 = 2,790 ○ True ○ False

9c. 480,920 > 480,902 ○ True ○ False

9d. 259 < 261 ○ True ○ False

10 3 × 4 = ☐

So, 3 × 8 = ☐ + ☐

Name ______________________________

11 Make a place value drawing for 1,534.

12 For numbers 12a–12e, write 685,203 rounded to the nearest place value.

12a. ten ____________

12b. hundred ____________

12c. thousand ____________

12d. ten thousand ____________

12e. hundred thousand ____________

13 Solve.

13a.
$$\begin{array}{r} 4{,}379 \\ +\ 3{,}284 \\ \hline \end{array}$$

13c. $6 \times 7 = \square$

13b. $63 \div 7 = \square$

13d.
$$\begin{array}{r} 648{,}939 \\ -\ 584{,}172 \\ \hline \end{array}$$

Name ______________________________

14 There were 2,683 books sold at a bookstore this year. There were 1,317 more books sold last year. How many books were sold last year? Write an equation for the problem and then solve it. Show your work.

15 Wren added the numbers 1,376 and 6,275.

Part A

Write the addends and the sum in the break-apart drawing. Then complete the two addition problems represented by the break-apart drawing.

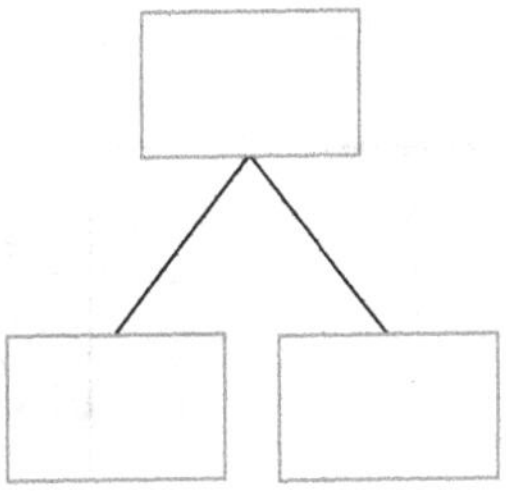

$$\begin{array}{r} 1{,}376 \\ +\ \square \\ \hline 7{,}651 \end{array} \qquad \begin{array}{r} 6{,}275 \\ +\ \square \\ \hline \square \end{array}$$

Part B

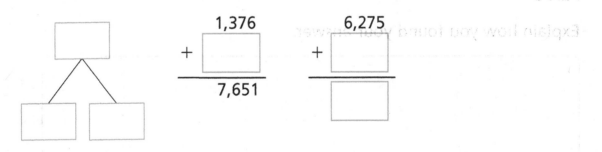

Write a word problem that requires subtracting 1,376 from 7,651.

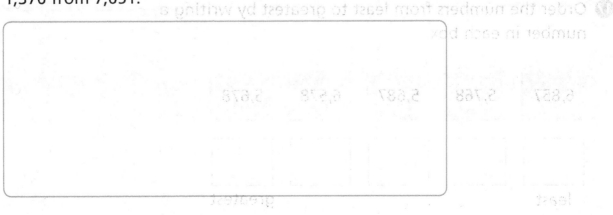

Name

16 Last week there were two soccer games. There were 3,982 people at the first soccer game. There were 1,886 fewer people at the second soccer game than at the first soccer game.

Part A

How many people attended the soccer games last week? Show your work.

Part B

Explain how you found your answer.

17 Order the numbers from least to greatest by writing a number in each box.

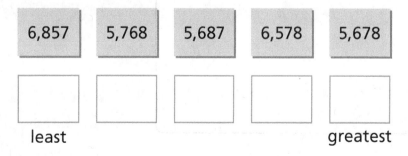

6,857	5,768	5,687	6,578	5,678
least				greatest

Name ____________________

Track Blog Traffic

James used a tool to see how much traffic his blog was getting.

Blog Traffic

Month	Unique Users	Number of Unique Users (Rounded)
January	389	400
February	3,725	4,000
March	41,692	40,000

1. James is reporting his blog's growing popularity to a journalist. She asks James how many more unique users visited the blog in February than in January. Should James find the difference using the actual number of unique users or the rounded number of unique users? Explain your answer.

2. On March 3, James's blog was featured in an online gaming journal. How many more unique users visited James's website in March than in February?

3. Look at the *Number of Unique Users (Rounded)* column in the table. Describe a pattern.

4. Is it realistic to expect this pattern to continue? Explain why or why not. Use addition or subtraction patterns to support your answer.

 Name ____________________

One of the unique users is a computer at a school library. In any given month, anywhere from 250 to 1,200 individual students use this library computer.

5 Consider what you know about the computer in the school's library. Suppose you wanted to include the number of individual students who visited James's blog from that computer. How might the data change?

Complete the table below including your new data.

Blog Traffic

Month	Unique Users + students	Number of Users (Rounded)
January		
February		
March		

6 Explain why you chose the number that you entered for January's data.

7 Explain why you chose the number that you entered for February's data.

8 Explain how you changed the data in March, after James's blog was featured in an online gaming journal.

Dear Family:

In this unit, your child will be learning about the common multiplication method that most adults know. However, they will also explore ways to draw multiplication. *Math Expressions* uses area of rectangles to show multiplication.

	30	+ 7
20	$20 \times 30 = 600$	$20 \times 7 = 140$
+ 4	$4 \times 30 = 120$	$4 \times 7 = 28$

Area Method:

$$\begin{array}{r} 20 \times 30 = 600 \\ 20 \times 7 = 140 \\ 4 \times 30 = 120 \\ 4 \times 7 = 28 \\ \hline \text{Total} = 888 \end{array}$$

Shortcut Method:

$$\begin{array}{r} {\scriptstyle 1} \\ {\scriptstyle 2} \\ 37 \\ \times\ 24 \\ \hline 148 \\ 74 \\ \hline 888 \end{array}$$

Area drawings help all students see multiplication. They also help students remember what numbers they need to multiply and what numbers make up the total.

Your child will also learn to find products involving single-digit numbers, tens, and hundreds by factoring the tens or hundreds. For example,

$$\begin{aligned} 200 \times 30 &= 2 \times 100 \times 3 \times 10 \\ &= 2 \times 3 \times 100 \times 10 \\ &= 6 \times 1{,}000 = 6{,}000 \end{aligned}$$

By observing the zeros patterns in products like these, your child will learn to do such multiplications mentally.

If your child is still not confident with single-digit multiplication and division, we urge you to set aside a few minutes every night for multiplication and division practice. In a few more weeks, the class will be doing multidigit division, so it is very important that your child be both fast and accurate with basic multiplication and division.

If you need practice materials, please contact me.

Sincerely,
Your child's teacher

Estimada familia:

En esta unidad, su niño estará aprendiendo el método de multiplicación común que la mayoría de los adultos conoce. Sin embargo, también explorará maneras de dibujar la multiplicación. Para mostrar la multiplicación, *Math Expressions* usa el método del área del rectángulo.

	30	+ 7
20	$20 \times 30 = 600$	$20 \times 7 = 140$
+ 4	$4 \times 30 = 120$	$4 \times 7 = 28$

Método del área

$$\begin{aligned} 20 \times 30 &= 600 \\ 20 \times 7 &= 140 \\ 4 \times 30 &= 120 \\ 4 \times 7 &= 28 \\ \hline \text{Total} &= 888 \end{aligned}$$

Método más corto

$$\begin{array}{r} \scriptstyle 1 \\ \scriptstyle 2 \\ 37 \\ \times\ 24 \\ \hline 148 \\ 74 \\ \hline 888 \end{array}$$

Los dibujos de área ayudan a los estudiantes a visualizar la multiplicación. También los ayuda a recordar cuáles números tienen que multiplicar y cuáles números forman el total.

Su niño también aprenderá a hallar productos relacionados con números de un solo dígito, con decenas y con centenas, factorizando las decenas o las centenas. Por ejemplo:

$$\begin{aligned} 200 \times 30 &= 2 \times 100 \times 3 \times 10 \\ &= 2 \times 3 \times 100 \times 10 \\ &= 6 \times 1{,}000 = 6{,}000 \end{aligned}$$

Al observar los patrones de ceros en productos como estos, su niño aprenderá a hacer dichas multiplicaciones mentalmente.

Si su niño todavía no domina la multiplicación y la división con números de un solo dígito, le sugerimos que dedique algunos minutos todas las noches para practicar la multiplicación y la división. Dentro de pocas semanas, la clase hará divisiones con números de varios dígitos, por eso es muy importante que su niño haga las operaciones básicas de multiplicación y de división de manera rápida y exacta.

Si necesita materiales para practicar, comuníquese conmigo.

Atentamente,
El maestro de su niño

area	**estimate**
array	**partial product**
Distributive Property	**rounding**

A number close to an exact amount or to find about how many or how much.

The number of square units that cover a figure.

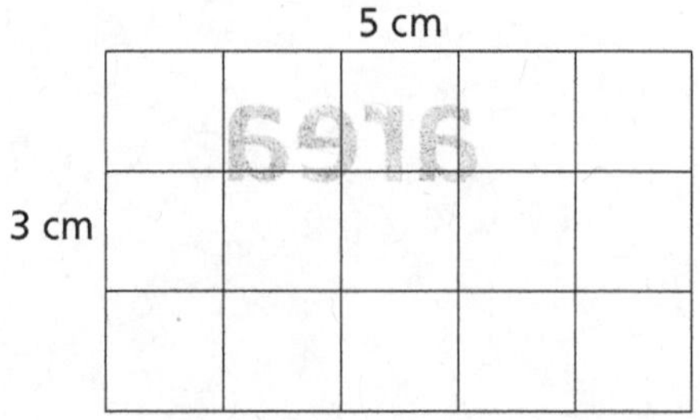
5 cm
3 cm

The product of the ones, or tens, or hundreds, and so on in multidigit multiplication.

Example:

```
   24
×   9
   36  ←  partial product (9 × 4)
  180  ←  partial product (9 × 20)
  216
```

An arrangement of objects, symbols, or numbers in rows and columns.

Finding the nearest ten, hundred, thousand, or some other place value. The usual rounding rule is to round up if the next digit to the right is 5 or more and round down if the next digit to the right is less than 5.

Example:

463 rounded to the nearest ten is 460.

463 rounded to the nearest hundred is 500.

Multiplying a sum by a number, or multiplying each addend by the number and adding the products; the result is the same.

Example:

$3 \times (2 + 4) = (3 \times 2) + (3 \times 4)$

$3 \times 6 = 6 + 12$

$18 = 18$

square unit ($unit^2$)

A unit of area equal to the area of a square with one-unit sides.

Name ______________________

VOCABULARY
square units

Factor the Tens to Multiply Ones and Tens

This 2 × 30 rectangle contains 2 groups of 30 unit squares.

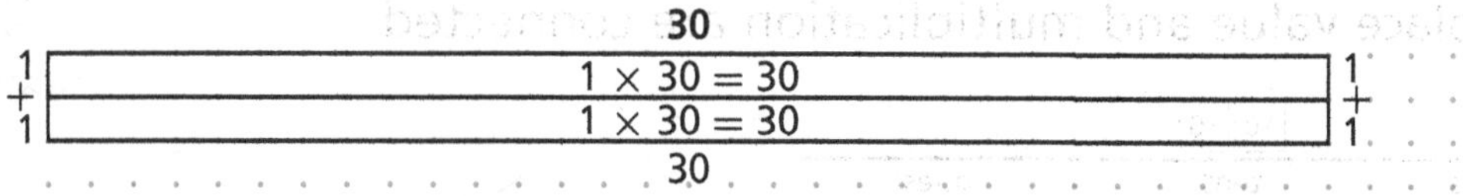
30
1 + 1
1 × 30 = 30
1 × 30 = 30
1 + 1
30

This 2 × 30 rectangle contains 3 groups of 20 unit squares.

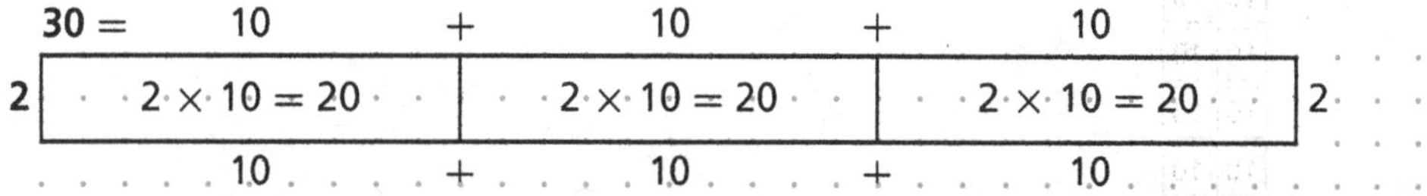
30 = 10 + 10 + 10
2
2 × 10 = 20
2 × 10 = 20
2 × 10 = 20
2
10 + 10 + 10

This 2 × 30 rectangle contains 6 groups of 10 unit squares, so its area is 60 **square units**.

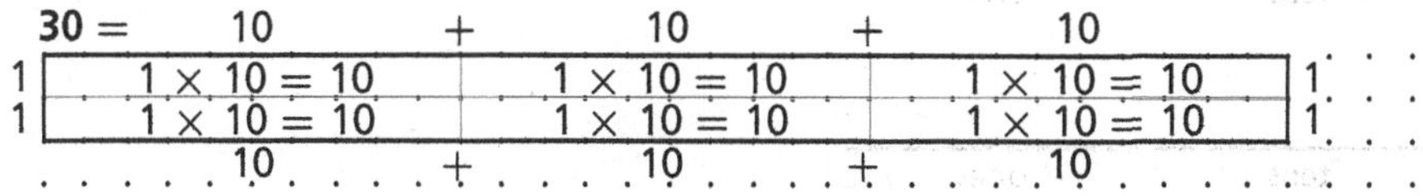
30 = 10 + 10 + 10
1
1
1 × 10 = 10
1 × 10 = 10
1 × 10 = 10
1 × 10 = 10
1 × 10 = 10
1 × 10 = 10
1
1
10 + 10 + 10

3 How can we show this numerically? Complete the steps.

$2 \times 30 = (2 \times 1) \times (\_\_\_\_ \times 10)$

$= (\_\_\_\_ \times \_\_\_\_) \times (1 \times 10)$

$= \_\_\_\_ \times 10 = 60$

4 How is a 30 × 2 rectangle similar to the 2 × 30 rectangle? How is it different?

____

____

____

____

Check Understanding

Draw a model to represent 4 × 20. Then show how to find 4 × 20 by factoring the tens.

Name ____________________

Use Place Value to Multiply

You have learned about the Base Ten Pattern in place value. This model shows how place value and multiplication are connected.

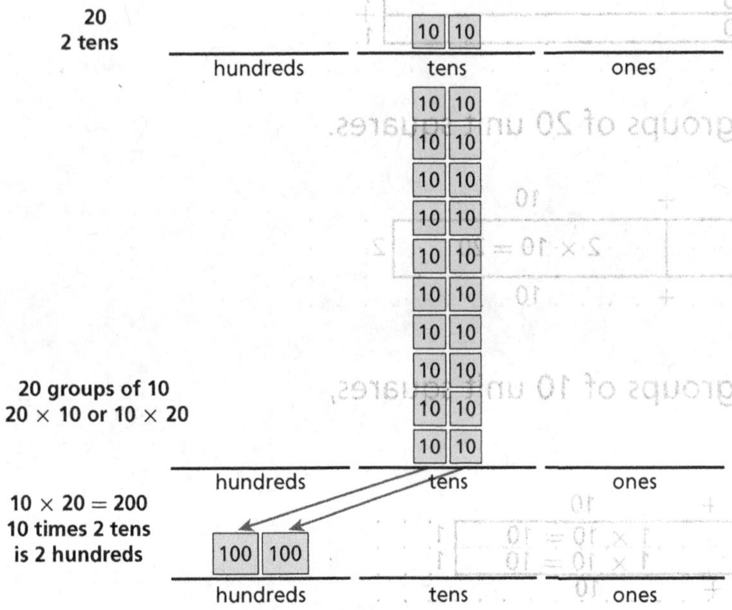
20
2 tens
10 10
hundreds
tens
ones
20 groups of 10
20 × 10 or 10 × 20
10 10
hundreds
tens
ones
10 × 20 = 200
10 times 2 tens
is 2 hundreds
100 100
hundreds
tens
ones

You can use properties to show the relationship between place value and multiplication.

Associative Property	$10 \times 20 = 10 \times (2 \times 10)$
	$= (10 \times 2) \times 10$
Commutative Property	$= (2 \times 10) \times 10$
Associative Property	$= 2 \times (10 \times 10)$
	$= 2 \times 100$
	$= 200$

1 Ten times any number of tens gives you that number of hundreds. Complete the steps to show 10 times 5 tens.

$10 \times 50 = 10 \times (\_\_\_\_\_\_ \times \_\_\_\_\_\_)$

$= (10 \times \_\_\_\_\_\_) \times \_\_\_\_\_\_$

$= (\_\_\_\_\_\_ \times 10) \times \_\_\_\_\_\_$

$= \_\_\_\_\_\_ \times (10 \times \_\_\_\_\_\_)$

$= \_\_\_\_\_\_ \times \_\_\_\_\_\_$

$= \_\_\_\_\_\_$

Name ______________________________

Model a Product of Tens

Olivia wants to tile the top of a table. The table is 20 inches by 30 inches.

2. Find the area of this 20 × 30 rectangle by dividing it into 10-by-10 squares of 100.

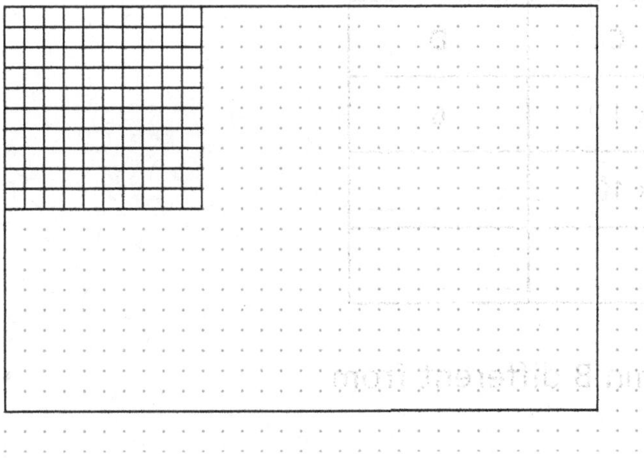

3. Each tile is a 1-inch square. How many tiles does Olivia need to cover the tabletop? __________

4. Each box of tiles contains 100 tiles. How many boxes of tiles does Olivia need to buy? __________

Factor the Tens

5. Show your work in Exercise 2 numerically.

$20 \times 30 = (\_\_\_\_\_ \times 10) \times (\_\_\_\_\_ \times 10)$

$= (\_\_\_\_\_ \times \_\_\_\_\_) \times (10 \times 10)$

$= \_\_\_\_\_ \times 100 = 600$

6. Is it true that 20 × 30 = 30 × 20? Explain how you know.

____

Check Understanding

Explain how to find 40 × 20 by factoring the tens.

Name ______________________

Look for Patterns

Multiplying greater numbers in your head is easier when you learn patterns of multiplication with tens.

Start with column A and look for the patterns used to get the expressions in each column. Complete the table.

Table 1

	A	B	C	D
	2 × 3	2 × 1 × 3 × 1	6 × 1	6
1	2 × 30	2 × 1 × 3 × 10	6 × 10	______
2	20 × 30	2 × 10 × 3 × 10	______	______

3. How are the expressions in column B different from the expressions in column A?

____

____

____

4. In column C, we see that each expression can be written as a number times a place value. Which of these factors gives more information about the size of the product?

____

5. Why is 6 the first digit of the products in column D?

____

6. Why are there different numbers of zeros in the products in column D?

____

____

____

Name ________________

Compare Tables

Complete each table.

Table 2				
	A	B	C	D
	6 × 3	6 × 1 × 3 × 1	18 × 1	18
7	6 × 30	6 × 1 × 3 × 10	18 × 10	____
8	60 × 30	6 × 10 × 3 × 10	____	____

Table 3				
	A	B	C	D
	5 × 8	5 × 1 × 8 × 1	40 × 1	40
9	5 × 80	5 × 1 × 8 × 10	40 × 10	____
10	50 × 80	____	____	____

11 Why do the products in Table 2 have more digits than the products in Table 1 on page 77?

____

____

12 Why are there more zeros in the products in Table 3 than the products in Table 2?

____

____

Check Understanding

Complete.

50 × 60 = (______ × 10) × (6 × ______) = ______ × 100 = ______

Name ______________________________

Use mental math to find the product.

1. $7 \times 8 =$ ____________

   $7 \times 80 =$ ____________

   $70 \times 80 =$ ____________

   $7 \times 800 =$ ____________

2. $3 \times 9 =$ ____________

   $3 \times 90 =$ ____________

   $30 \times 90 =$ ____________

   $3 \times 900 =$ ____________

3. $60 \times 30 =$ ____________

Solve.

Show your work.

4. Neil wants to put 1-foot square tiles in his kitchen. The floor is a rectangle. It is 40 feet long and 20 feet wide. How many square tiles does Neil need?

   ____

5. Draw an area model for 3×30. Then find the product.

   ____

   ____

Fluency Check 4

Name ____________________

PATH to FLUENCY

Add or subtract.

1. 4,002 + 8,579

2. 2,731 − 1,527

3. 271,392 + 323,689

4. 97,532 + 55,722

5. 567 + 326

6. 88,526 − 79,613

7. 85,427 + 3,496

8. 255 − 193

9. 615 − 405

10. 325 + 632

11. 370,118 − 78,684

12. 2,790 + 508

13. 786,474 − 543,586

14. 6,496 − 3,187

15. 50,278 − 8,193

Name ____________________

Explore the Area Model

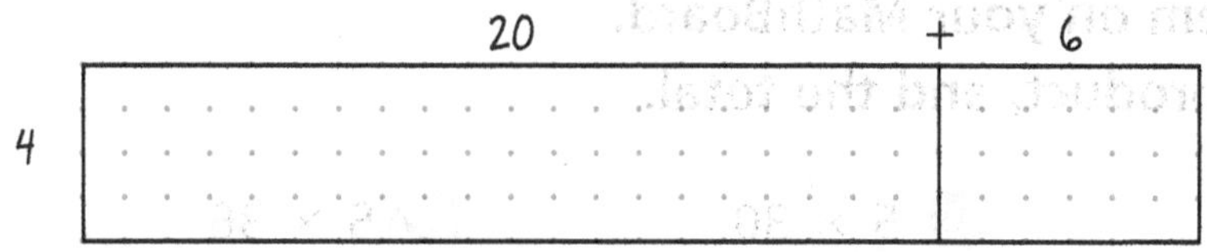
20
+ 6
4

1. How many square units of area are there in the tens part of the drawing?

   ____

2. What multiplication equation gives the area of the tens part of the drawing? Write this equation in its rectangle.

   ____

3. How many square units of area are there in the ones part?

   ____

4. What multiplication equation gives the area of the ones part? Write this equation in its rectangle.

   ____

5. What is the total of the two areas?

   ____

6. How do you know that 104 is the correct product of 4 × 26?

   ____

7. Read Problems A and B.

   A. Al's photo album has 26 pages. Each page has 4 photos. How many photos are in Al's album?

   B. Nick took 4 photos. Henri took 26 photos. How many more photos did Henri take than Nick?

   Which problem could you solve using the multiplication you just did? Explain why.

   ____

   ____

Name ______________________

Use Rectangles to Multiply

Draw a rectangle for each problem on your MathBoard. Find the tens product, the ones product, and the total.

8. 3 × 28
______
______
______

9. 3 × 29
______
______
______

10. 5 × 30
______
______
______

11. 5 × 36
______
______
______

12. 4 × 38
______
______
______

13. 8 × 38
______
______
______

14. 4 × 28
______
______
______

15. 5 × 28
______
______
______

Solve each problem. *Show your work.*

16. Maria's father planted 12 rows of tomatoes in his garden. Each row had 6 plants. How many tomato plants were in Maria's father's garden?

____

17. A library subscribes to 67 magazines. Each month the library receives 3 copies of each magazine. How many magazines does the library receive each month?

____

18. Complete this word problem. Then solve it.

__________ has _____ boxes of __________.

There are _____ __________ in each box.

How many __________ does __________

have altogether? ______________________

Name ______________________________

Use the Place Value Sections Method

You can use an area model to demonstrate the Place Value Sections Method. This strategy is used below for multiplying a one-digit number by a two-digit number.

Complete the steps.

27 = 20 + 7

	20	7
5	5 × 20 = 100	5 × 7 = 35

5 × 27: ____ + ____ = ____

Use the Place Value Sections Method to solve the problem. Complete the steps.

1. The fourth-grade class is participating in a walk-a-thon. Each student will walk 8 laps around the track. There are 92 fourth-grade students. How many laps will the fourth-grade class walk?

____

92 = 90 + 2

	90	2
8	____ × ____ = ____	____ × ____ = ____

8 × 92: ____ + ____ = ____

Draw an area model and use the Place Value Sections Method to solve the problem.

2. A football coach is ordering 3 shirts for each football player. There are 54 players in the football program. How many shirts does the coach need to order for the entire program?

____

Name ________________________________

Use the Expanded Notation Method

You can also use an area model to show how to use the Expanded Notation Method.

Use the Expanded Notation Method to solve each problem.

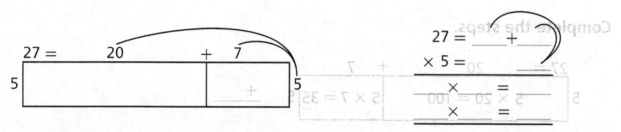

3

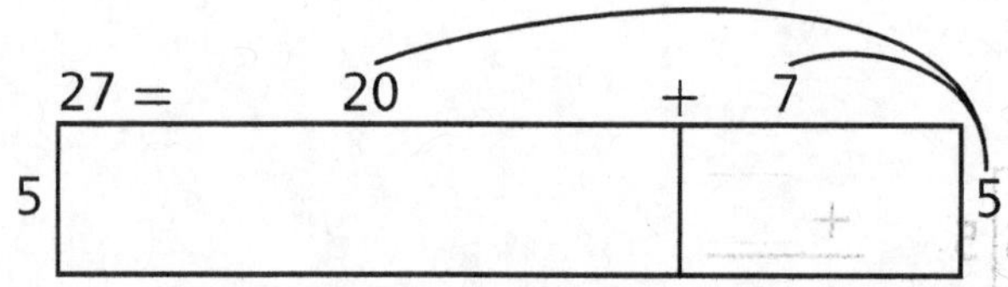
27 =
20
+ 7
5
5

27 = ____ + ____

× 5 = ____

____ × ____ = ____

____ × ____ = ____

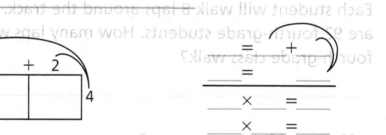

4 A farm stand sold 4 bushels of apples in one day. Each bushel of apples weighs 42 pounds. How many pounds of apples did the farm stand sell?

____

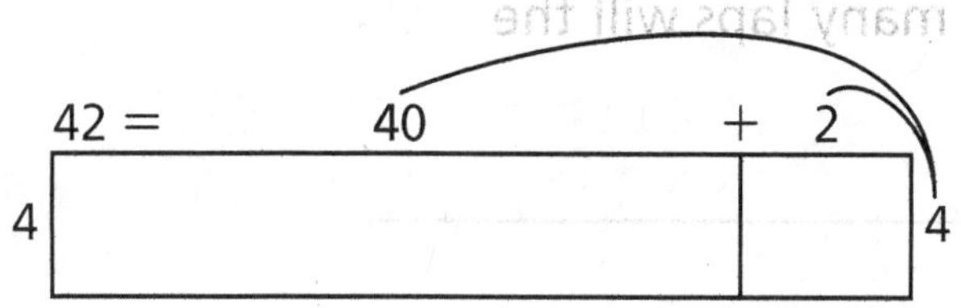
42 =
40
+ 2
4
4

____ = ____ + ____

____ = ____

____ × ____ = ____

____ × ____ = ____

5 A marina needs to replace the boards on their pier. The pier is 7 feet by 39 feet. What is the area of the pier?

____

Check Understanding

Do you prefer to use the Place Value Sections Method or the Expanded Notation Method? Explain your answer.

Name ___

Use the Algebraic Notation Method to Multiply

Another numerical multiplication method that can be represented by an area model is the Algebraic Notation Method. This method also decomposes the two-digit factor into tens and ones and then uses the Distributive Property.

Use the Algebraic Notation Method to solve each problem. Complete the steps.

4 8 · 62

62 = ___ + ___

___

8 · 62 = ___ ·(___ + ___)
= 480 + 16
= 496

5 2 · 97

97 = ___ + ___

___

2 · 97 = ___ ·(___ + ___)
= 180 + 14
= 194

Draw an area model and use the Algebraic Notation Method to solve the problem.

6 There are 9 members on the school's golf team. Each golfer hit a bucket of 68 golf balls at the driving range. How many golf balls did the entire team hit?

___

Check Understanding

Draw an area model and use it to explain how to use the Algebraic Notation Method to find 4 × 86.

Name ______________________________

Practice Different Methods

Fill in the blanks in the following solutions.

3 4 × 86

Expanded Notation

86 = _____ + 6

× 4 = _____

4 × _____ = _____

_____ × 6 = 24

Algebraic Notation

4 • 86 = _____ • (80 + 6)

= 320 + _____

= _____

4 4 × 68

Expanded Notation

_____ = 60 + 8

× 4 = _____

4 × _____ = _____

_____ × 8 = 32

_____

Algebraic Notation

4 • 68 = 4 • (_____ + _____)

= 240 + _____

= _____

Solve using a numerical method. Draw the related area model.

5 5 × 64 = _____

6 6 × 72 = _____

Check Understanding

For Exercise 6, which numerical method did you use?

____

Explain why you chose that method.

Name ____________________

Discuss Problems With Too Much Information

A word problem may sometimes include more information than you need. Read the following problem and then answer each question.

Mrs. Sanchez is putting a border around her garden. Her garden is a rectangle with dimensions 12 feet by 18 feet. The border material costs $3.00 per foot. How many feet of border material is needed?

1. Identify any extra numerical information. Why isn't this information needed?

   ____

   ____

2. Solve the problem. ____________________

Solve each problem. Cross out information that is not needed.

Show your work.

3. Judy downloaded an album for $15. The album has 13 songs. Each song is 3 minutes long. How long will it take to listen to the whole album?

   ____

4. Jerry has 64 coins in his coin collection and 22 stamps in his stamp collection. His sister has 59 stamps in her collection. How many stamps do they have altogether?

   ____

5. Adrian has been playing the piano for 3 years. He practices 20 minutes a day. He is preparing for a recital that is 9 days away. How many minutes of practice will he complete before the recital?

   ____

Name ______________________________

Mixed Problem Solving

Show your work.

16 Mr. Collins counts 54 cartons and 5 boxes of paper clips. Each carton contains 8 boxes. A box of paper clips costs $2. How many boxes of paper clips does he have?

____

17 Ms. Wu has 5 cartons of black ink and 4 cartons of color ink. Each carton contains 48 cartridges. How many ink cartridges are there in all?

____

What's the Error?

Dear Math Students,

My school is collecting cans for a food drive. There are 608 students in the school. A can of soup costs about $ 2. Each student will bring in 3 cans. I wrote this multiplication to find the number of cans the school will collect in all.

$$\begin{array}{r} {}^{2} \\ 608 \\ \times \quad 3 \\ \hline 1{,}864 \end{array}$$

?

Is my answer correct? Can you help me?

Your friend,
Puzzled Penguin

18 Write a response to Puzzled Penguin.

____

____

____

Check Understanding

Does Puzzled Penguin's problem have too much information or a hidden question?

____

Write the information that is extra or the question that is hidden.

____

Name ______________________________

Multiply using any method. Show your work.

1. 4×67

2. 5×94

Estimate the product. Solve to check your estimate.

3. 9×68

   Estimate ______________________

Solve.

Show your work.

4. A school sweatshirt costs $9. If the principal orders 195 sweatshirts, how much will the order cost?

   ____

5. Annalise bought 10 items at a computer store. She bought 2 computer games for $25 each and 3 computer games for $30 each. She paid $8 for a new mouse. How much did the computer games cost? List any extra numerical information.

   ____

Fluency Check 5

Name ______________________

PATH to FLUENCY

Add or subtract.

1. $\begin{array}{r} 819 \\ -\ 617 \\ \hline \end{array}$

2. $\begin{array}{r} 208{,}342 \\ +\ 673{,}079 \\ \hline \end{array}$

3. $\begin{array}{r} 86{,}864 \\ -\ 24{,}981 \\ \hline \end{array}$

4. $\begin{array}{r} 88{,}108 \\ -\ 4{,}342 \\ \hline \end{array}$

5. $\begin{array}{r} 55{,}551 \\ +\ 83{,}288 \\ \hline \end{array}$

6. $\begin{array}{r} 9{,}710 \\ -\ 8{,}609 \\ \hline \end{array}$

7. $\begin{array}{r} 5{,}870 \\ +\ 4{,}635 \\ \hline \end{array}$

8. $\begin{array}{r} 24{,}522 \\ +\ 6{,}397 \\ \hline \end{array}$

9. $\begin{array}{r} 162 \\ +\ 387 \\ \hline \end{array}$

10. $\begin{array}{r} 238 \\ -\ 209 \\ \hline \end{array}$

11. $\begin{array}{r} 3{,}963 \\ +\ 816 \\ \hline \end{array}$

12. $\begin{array}{r} 247 \\ +\ 531 \\ \hline \end{array}$

13. $\begin{array}{r} 937{,}771 \\ -\ 18{,}948 \\ \hline \end{array}$

14. $\begin{array}{r} 9{,}814 \\ -\ 7{,}203 \\ \hline \end{array}$

15. $\begin{array}{r} 843{,}966 \\ -\ 809{,}199 \\ \hline \end{array}$

Name ____________________

What's the Error?

Dear Math Students,

My friends and I are going to build 42 flower boxes. The building plans say each box needs 13 nails. I rounded to estimate how many nails we'll need. Since 40 × 10 = 400, I bought a box of 400 nails.

My friends say we won't have enough nails. Did I make a mistake? Can you help me estimate how many nails we need?

Your friend,
Puzzled Penguin

?

12 Write a response to Puzzle Penguin. 42 × 13

Estimate and then solve. Explain whether the estimate is problematic in each situation.

13 Sally hires a dog sitter for her 18-day trip. A dog sitter charges $14 per day. How much money will Sally need to pay the dog sitter?

14 An artist draws a plan for a mosaic pattern that has 21 rows of tiles with 47 tiles in each row. How many tiles does the artist need to buy?

Check Understanding
Describe strategies you use to estimate products.

Name

What's the Error?

13 Sally hires a dog sitter for her 18-day trip. A dog sitter charges $14 per day. How much money will Sally need to pay the dog sitter?

Name ______________________________

Multiply using any method. Show your work.

1. 48×29

2. 64×37

Estimate and then solve.

3. 68×97

4. 58×86

5. Draw an area model for 42×56.
Then find the product.

____

____

Name

PATH to FLUENCY

Add or subtract.

1. $959{,}896 - 78{,}929$
2. $361 + 728$
3. $196 - 154$
4. $7{,}718 - 3{,}683$
5. $461{,}727 + 88{,}866$
6. $821 + 107$
7. $315{,}944 - 257{,}061$
8. $71{,}656 - 1{,}966$
9. $99{,}181 + 1{,}876$
10. $1{,}951 - 1{,}311$
11. $815 - 673$
12. $22{,}688 + 98{,}205$
13. $44{,}827 - 28{,}399$
14. $1{,}236 + 9{,}535$
15. $8{,}318 + 227$

Name ______________________________

Estimate Products

Solve and then estimate to check if your answer is reasonable. Show your estimate.

20. 5 × 3,487 = ________

21. 7 × 8,894 = ________

22. 4 × 7,812 = ________

23. 3 × 4,109 = ________

What's the Error?

Dear Math Students,

My school collected 2,468 empty cartons of milk today. If the school collects about the same number of cartons each day for 5 days, I estimated that the school will collect 17,500 cartons.

$$(5 \times 3,000) + (5 \times 500) = 17,500$$

Can you help me decide if this is a reasonable estimate?

Your friend,
Puzzled Penguin

?

24. Write a response to Puzzled Penguin.

Check Understanding

Multiply 6 × 5,283 using the Shortcut Method. ________
Round and estimate to check your work.

20 $5 \times 3{,}487 =$ ______

21 $7 \times 8{,}894 =$ ______

22 $4 \times 7{,}812 =$ ______

23 $3 \times 4{,}109 =$ ______

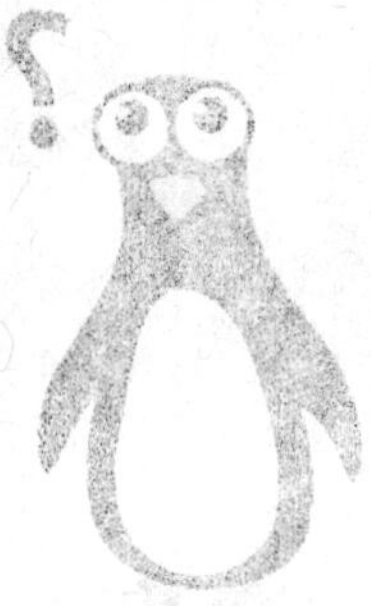

Name ____________________

Multiply using any method. Show your work.

1. 4 × 3,819

2. 6,423 × 7

Multiply and then estimate to check if your answer is reasonable.

3. 3 × 4,756

4. 6 × 5,939

Solve.

Show your work.

5. It costs $9,179 in *Big City Building* game money to build each apartment. What is the cost to build 6 apartment buildings?

____

Fluency Check 7 Name ____________________

PATH to FLUENCY

Add or subtract.

1. $\begin{array}{r} 37{,}796 \\ +\ 68{,}121 \\ \hline \end{array}$

2. $\begin{array}{r} 8{,}990 \\ +\ 8{,}501 \\ \hline \end{array}$

3. $\begin{array}{r} 638 \\ +\ 127 \\ \hline \end{array}$

4. $\begin{array}{r} 22{,}274 \\ -\ 16{,}139 \\ \hline \end{array}$

5. $\begin{array}{r} 20{,}056 \\ -\ 4{,}315 \\ \hline \end{array}$

6. $\begin{array}{r} 565 \\ +\ 234 \\ \hline \end{array}$

7. $\begin{array}{r} 920{,}443 \\ -\ 36{,}071 \\ \hline \end{array}$

8. $\begin{array}{r} 118{,}242 \\ +\ 893{,}915 \\ \hline \end{array}$

9. $\begin{array}{r} 324 \\ -\ 203 \\ \hline \end{array}$

10. $\begin{array}{r} 211{,}549 \\ -\ 144{,}096 \\ \hline \end{array}$

11. $\begin{array}{r} 4{,}759 \\ -\ 3{,}392 \\ \hline \end{array}$

12. $\begin{array}{r} 1{,}010 \\ +\ 993 \\ \hline \end{array}$

13. $\begin{array}{r} 55{,}825 \\ +\ 7{,}115 \\ \hline \end{array}$

14. $\begin{array}{r} 5{,}898 \\ +\ 3{,}251 \\ \hline \end{array}$

15. $\begin{array}{r} 842 \\ -\ 739 \\ \hline \end{array}$

Name ______________________

1. Use the numbers on the tiles to complete the steps to find 20 × 40 by factoring the tens.

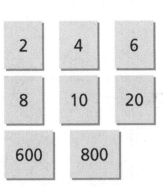

2	4	6
8	10	20
600	800	

20 × 40 = (☐ × 10) × (☐ × 10)
= (2 × 4) × (☐ × ☐)
= ☐ × 100
= ☐

2. Select the expression that is equivalent to 36 × 25. Mark all that apply.

Ⓐ 30 × 6 + 20 × 5

Ⓑ (30 × 20) + (30 × 5) + (6 × 20) + (6 × 5)

Ⓒ (5 × 6) + (5 × 3 tens) + (2 tens × 6) + (2 tens × 3 tens)

Ⓓ 30 × (20 + 5) + 6 × (20 + 5)

Ⓔ 30 + 15 + 12 + 6

3. There are 24 pencils in a box. If there are 90 boxes, how many pencils are there?

_______ pencils

4. A clown bought 18 bags of round balloons with 20 balloons in each bag. He bought 26 bags of long balloons with 35 balloons in each bag. How many more long balloons did he buy than round balloons? Show your work.

Name ______________________________

5 Draw an area model for 7×682.

Explain how you used the model to find the product.

6 For Exercises 6a–6d, choose Yes or No to tell whether the equation is true.

6a. $8 \times 4 = 32$ ○ Yes ○ No

6b. $8 \times 400 = 32{,}000$ ○ Yes ○ No

6c. $80 \times 40 = 3{,}200$ ○ Yes ○ No

6d. $8 \times 4{,}000 = 32{,}000$ ○ Yes ○ No

7 Find the product of 4×52.

Name ____________________

8 Use the numbers on the tiles to complete the area model for 29 × 48.

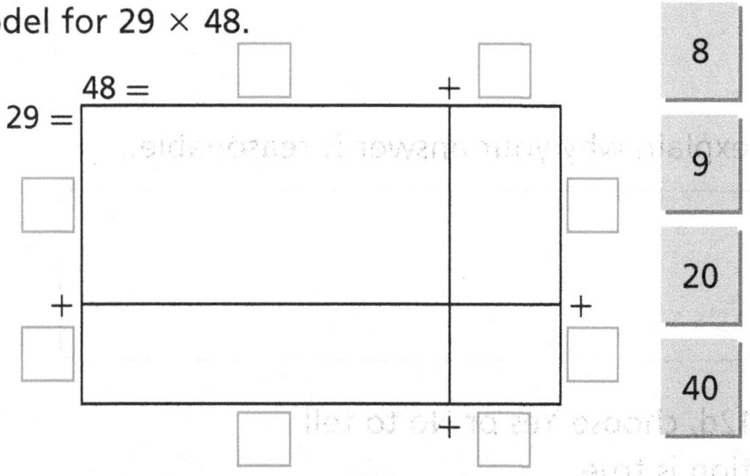
48 =
+
29 =
+
+
+
8
9
20
40

Show how to use the area model and expanded notation to find 29 × 48.

9 Estimate 15 × 34 by rounding each number to the nearest ten.

10 For Exercises 10a–10d, choose True or False to describe the statement.

10a. 8 × 93 is greater than 8 × 90. ○ True ○ False

10b. An estimate of 8 × 93 is 2,700. ○ True ○ False

10c. 8 × 93 = (8 × 9) + (8 × 3) ○ True ○ False

10d. 8 × 93 is less than 800. ○ True ○ False

Name ____________________

11 Find 4 × 7,342.

Use estimation to explain why your answer is reasonable.

12 For Exercises 12a–12d, choose Yes or No to tell whether the equation is true.

12a. 5 × 60 = 30 ○ Yes ○ No

12b. 500 × 6 = 30,000 ○ Yes ○ No

12c. 50 × 60 = 3,000 ○ Yes ○ No

12d. 5 × 6,000 = 30,000 ○ Yes ○ No

13 The best estimate for 78 × 50 is that it must be greater than __?__ but less than __?__.

Select one number from each column to make the sentence true.

Greater than	Less than
○ 3,200	○ 3,200
○ 3,500	○ 3,500
○ 4,000	○ 4,000
○ 4,200	○ 4,200

14 Choose the number from the box to complete the statement.

The product of 39 and 22 is closest to [300 | 400 | 800 | 8,000].

Name ____________________

15 A bus tour of New York City costs $48 per person. A group of 7 people go on the tour. What is the cost for the group? Explain how you found your answer.

16 There is a book sale at the library. The price for each book is $4. If 239 books are sold, how much money will be made at the sale?

Ⓐ $235

Ⓑ $243

Ⓒ $826

Ⓓ $956

17 Volunteers are needed at the animal shelter. If 245 boys and 304 girls each volunteer to work 3 hours, how many volunteer hours is this?

Part A

Identify any extra information given in the problem. Explain your reasoning.

Part B

Solve the problem. Show your work.

Name ____________________

18 Select an expression that is equivalent to 7×800. Mark all that apply.

Ⓐ $8 + (100 \times 7) + 10$

Ⓑ $(8 \times 7) \times (100 \times 1)$

Ⓒ $(7 \times 80) \times 10$

Ⓓ $(8 + 7) \times (100 + 1)$

19 Joe makes belts. He has 9 buckles. He uses 12 rivets on each of 4 belts and 15 rivets on each of 2 belts. He has 22 rivets left over. How many rivets are on the belts?

Part A

Identify any extra information given in the problem.

Part B

Solve the problem. Show your work.

20 Draw an area model for $7 \times 5{,}432$. Then write an equation to match your model.

Equation: ________ × ________ = ________

21 Use the numbers on the tiles to complete the steps to find the solution to 4×65.

4	5	9
60	64	84
240	260	

4 × 65 = ______ × (60 + ______)

= (4 × ______) + (4 × ______)

= ______ + 20

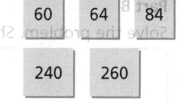

= ______

Name ______________________

Shop for a Clothing Drive

Mrs. Liston and 9 of her friends are shopping for clothes to donate to a winter clothing drive. The store has many clothing items for sale. The table shows the items Mrs. Liston and her friends can buy and the price for each item.

Clothing for Sale

Item	Price
Shirt	$15
Jeans	$25
Sweater	$45
Boots	$75
Coat	$99

1. Mrs. Liston has $259. Is it possible for her to spend the whole amount by buying only one kind of item at the store? How do you know?

2. What are 2 different ways that Mrs. Liston can spend $259 at the store?

3. If Mrs. Liston and her friends each spend $259 at the store, how much money do they spend in all? How do you know?

4. Mrs. Liston collected $1,800 for the clothing drive. She buys 24 pairs of jeans and 24 sweaters. What could she buy with the money that is left?

Name ______________________

The store puts some items on sale, as shown in the table.

Clothing for Sale

Item	Original Price	Sale Price
Shirt	$15	$12
Jeans	$25	
Sweater	$45	$42
Boots	$75	$56
Coat	$99	

5. How would these sale prices affect what Mrs. Liston could have bought with $1,800? Explain.

6. Mrs. Liston and her friends would like to buy a shirt, a pair of jeans, and a sweater for 32 people. They will hold a dinner to raise the money needed to buy these items on sale. They plan to estimate the money needed. Will this help them set an appropriate goal for their dinner? Explain your decision.

7. Explain how to write a word problem that requires multiplication and addition to solve using the information in the table. Give a problem in your explanation.

Dear Family:

Your child is familiar with multiplication from earlier units. Unit 3 of *Math Expressions* extends the concepts used in multiplication to teach your child division. The main goals of this unit are to:

- Learn methods for dividing whole numbers up to four digits by one-digit divisors and up to three digits by two-digit divisors.
- Use estimates to check the reasonableness of answers.
- Solve problems involving division and remainders.

Your child will learn and practice techniques such as the Place Value Sections, Expanded Notation, and Digit-by-Digit methods to gain speed and accuracy in division.

Examples of Division Methods:

Place Value Sections Method

$$
\begin{array}{c|c|c|}
 & 60\ + & 6 = 66 \\
\hline
5 & 330 & 30 \\
 & -\,300 & -\,30 \\
\hline
 & 30 & 0
\end{array}
$$

Expanded Notation Method

$$
\begin{array}{r}
6 \\
60 \\
5\overline{)330} \\
-300 \\
\hline
30 \\
-30 \\
\hline
0
\end{array}
\quad 6 + 60 = 66
$$

Digit-by-Digit Method

$$
\begin{array}{r}
66 \\
5\overline{)330} \\
-\,30 \\
\hline
30 \\
-\,30 \\
\hline
0
\end{array}
$$

Your child may use whatever method he or she chooses as long as he or she can explain it. Some children like to use different methods.

Your child will also learn to interpret remainders in the context of the problem being solved; for example, when the remainder alone is the answer to a word problem.

Your child will apply this knowledge to solve mixed problems with one or more steps and using all four operations.

If you have questions or problems, please contact me.

Sincerely,
Your child's teacher

Estimada familia:

En unidades anteriores su niño se ha familiarizado con la multiplicación. La Unidad 3 de *Math Expressions* amplía los conceptos usados en la multiplicación para que su niño aprenda la división. Los objetivos principales de esta unidad son:

- aprender métodos para dividir números enteros de hasta cuatro dígitos por divisores de un dígito y hasta tres dígitos por divisores de dos dígitos.
- usar la estimación para comprobar si las respuestas son razonables.
- resolver problemas que requieran división y residuos.

Su niño aprenderá y practicará técnicas tales como las de Secciones de valor posicional, Notación extendida y Dígito por dígito, para adquirir rapidez y precisión en la división.

Ejemplos de métodos de división:

Secciones de valor posicional

$$60 + 6 = 66$$

5	330	30
	− 300	− 30
	30	0

Notación extendida

$$\begin{array}{r} 6 \\ 60 \\ 5\overline{)330} \\ -300 \\ \hline 30 \\ -30 \\ \hline 0 \end{array} \quad \Big] 66$$

Dígito por dígito

$$\begin{array}{r} 66 \\ 5\overline{)330} \\ -30 \\ \hline 30 \\ -30 \\ \hline 0 \end{array}$$

Su niño puede usar el método que elija siempre y cuando pueda explicarlo. A algunos niños les gusta usar métodos diferentes.

Su niño también aprenderá a interpretar los residuos en el contexto del problema que se esté resolviendo; por ejemplo, cuando solamente el residuo es la respuesta a un problema.

Su niño aplicará este conocimiento para resolver problemas mixtos de uno o más pasos, usando las cuatro operaciones.

Si tiene alguna pregunta o comentario, por favor comuníquese conmigo.

Atentamente,
El maestro de su niño

compatible numbers

overestimate

dividend

quotient

divisor

remainder

Make an estimate that is too big.

Numbers that are easy to compute mentally.

Example:

$9\overline{)5,841}$

Some compatible numbers for the divisor and dividend are 9 and 5,400, and 9 and 6,300.

The answer to a division problem.

Example:

$\begin{array}{r} 7 \\ 9\overline{)63} \end{array}$

7 is the quotient.

The number that is divided in division.

Example:

$\begin{array}{r} 7 \\ 9\overline{)63} \end{array}$

63 is the dividend.

The number left over after dividing two numbers that are not evenly divisible.

Example:

$\begin{array}{r} 8\text{ R3} \\ 5\overline{)43} \end{array}$

The remainder is 3.

The number you divide by in division.

Example:

$\begin{array}{r} 7 \\ 9\overline{)63} \end{array}$

9 is the divisor.

underestimate

Make an estimate that is too small.

Name ____________________

Multiplying and Dividing

Complete the steps.

1 Sam divides 738 by 6. He uses the Place Value Sections Method and the Expanded Notation Method.

a. Sam thinks: I'll draw the Place Value Sections that I know from multiplication. To divide, I need to find how many hundreds, tens, and ones to find the unknown factor.

Place Value Sections Method

__ hundreds + __ tens + __ ones

	__00	__0	__
6	738		

Expanded Notation Method

$6\overline{)738}$

b. 6 × 100 = 600 will fit. 6 × 200 = 1,200 is too big.

	__00 +	__0 +	__
6	738		

$6\overline{)738}$

c. I have 138 left for the other sections.
6 × 20 = 120 will fit. 6 × 30 = 180 is too big.

	100 +	__0 +	__
6	738 −600	138	
	138		

$$\begin{array}{r} 100 \\ 6\overline{)738} \\ -600 \\ \hline 138 \end{array}$$

d. 6 × 3 = 18

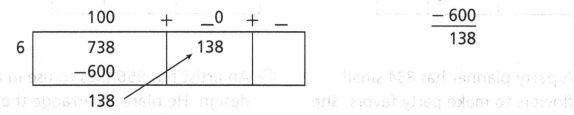

	100 +	20 +	__ = ______
6	738 −600	138 −120	18
	138	18	0

$$\begin{array}{r} 20 \\ 100 \\ 6\overline{)738} \\ -600 \\ \hline 138 \\ -120 \\ \hline 18 \end{array}$$

Name ___

Practice the Place Value Sections Method

Solve. Use Place Value Sections Method for division.

1. The area of the new rectangular sidewalk at the mall will be 3,915 square feet. It will be 9 feet wide. How long will it be? 435 ft

400 + 30 + 5 = 435

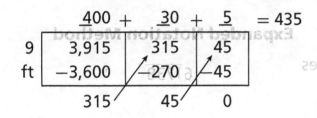

	400	30	5
9 ft	3,915	315	45
	−3,600	−270	−45
	315	45	0

2. The rectangular sidewalk at the theater will have an area of 2,748 square feet. It will be 6 feet wide. How long will it be? ___

_00 + _0 + _ = ___

3. Pens are packaged in boxes of 8. The store received a shipment of 4,576 pens. How many boxes of pens did they receive? ___

_00 + _0 + _ = ___

4. A factory has 2,160 erasers. They package them in groups of 5. How many packages of erasers does the factory have? ___

___ + ___ + ___ = ___

5. A party planner has 834 small flowers to make party favors. She will put 3 flowers in each party favor. How many party favors can she make? ___

___ + ___ + ___ = ___

6. An artist has 956 tiles to use in a design. He plans to arrange the tiles in groups of 4 tiles. How many groups of 4 tiles can he make? ___

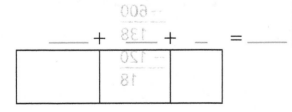

___ + ___ + ___ = ___

Name ______________________________

Two-Digit and Four-Digit Quotients

Solve. Use the Place Value Sections and the Expanded Notation Methods for division.

1

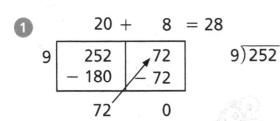

	20 +	8 = 28
9	252 − 180	72 − 72
	72	0

$9\overline{)252}$

2

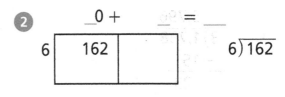

	_0 +	_ = __
6	162	

$6\overline{)162}$

3

	_,000 +	_00 +	_0 +	_ = ____
8	8,984			

$8\overline{)8,984}$

4

	_,000 +	_00 +	_0 +	_ =
3	7,722			

$3\overline{)7,722}$

Name ________________________________

What's the Error?

Dear Math Students,

Here is a division problem I tried to solve.

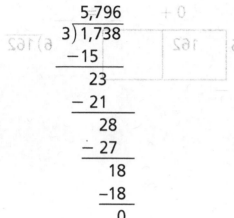

```
   5,796
3)1,738
  -15
    23
  - 21
     28
   - 27
      18
     -18
       0
```

?

Is my answer correct? If not, please help me understand why it is wrong.

Thank you,
Puzzled Penguin

2 Write a response to Puzzled Penguin.

____

____

____

Solve. Use the Digit-by-Digit Method.

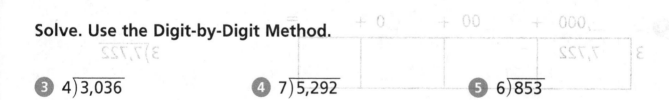

3 $4\overline{)3{,}036}$

4 $7\overline{)5{,}292}$

5 $6\overline{)853}$

Name ______________________________

Division Practice

Use any method to solve.

7. $6\overline{)2{,}238}$

8. $5\overline{)2{,}431}$

9. $7\overline{)2{,}198}$

10. $8\overline{)2{,}512}$

11. $4\overline{)5{,}027}$

12. $5\overline{)5{,}624}$

13. $9\overline{)3{,}631}$

14. $6\overline{)6{,}305}$

What's the Error?

Dear Math Students,

This is a problem from my math homework. My teacher says my answer is not correct, but I can't figure out what I did wrong. Can you help me find and fix my mistake?

Your friend,
Puzzled Penguin

```
   7,069 R2
5)3,847
 - 35
    34
  - 30
     47
   - 45
      2
```

?

15. Write a response to Puzzled Penguin.

____

____

____

____

Check Understanding

Describe the advantages and disadvantages of the three division methods used in this lesson.

Name ______________________________

Use any method to solve.

1. $3\overline{)684}$

2. $7\overline{)926}$

3. $6\overline{)7,281}$

Solve.

Show your work.

4. Khalil filled an album with 104 postcards. If there are 4 postcards on each page, how many pages are in the album?

____

5. Whistles are in packages of 8 at a sporting goods store. How many packages can be made from 336 whistles?

____

Name

PATH to FLUENCY

Add or subtract.

1. $909 - 747$

2. $488{,}927 - 99{,}274$

3. $33{,}876 + 15{,}788$

4. $631 - 400$

5. $90{,}639 - 87{,}392$

6. $400{,}672 - 272{,}115$

7. $134{,}919 + 92{,}683$

8. $7{,}891 + 1{,}423$

9. $9{,}152 - 6{,}001$

10. $79{,}153 - 6{,}881$

11. $5{,}634 + 625$

12. $493 + 406$

13. $64{,}822 + 6{,}342$

14. $2{,}716 - 1{,}391$

15. $338 + 491$

Name ______________________________

What's the Error?

Dear Math Students,

I started to solve this division problem and realized there was a problem. Some friends suggested different ways to fix it.

Your friend,
Puzzled Penguin

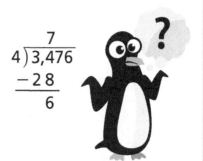

$$\begin{array}{r} 7 \\ 4\overline{)3{,}476} \\ -2\,8 \\ \hline 6 \end{array}$$

?

Jacob suggested that Puzzled Penguin erase the 7 and write 8 in its place. Puzzled Penguin would also need to erase the calculations and do them over.

$$\begin{array}{r} 8 \\ 4\overline{)3{,}476} \\ -3\,2 \\ \hline 2 \end{array}$$

Fred told Puzzled Penguin to cross out the 7 and write 8 above it. The next step would be to subtract one more 4.

$$\begin{array}{r} 8 \\ \not{7} \\ 4\overline{)3{,}476} \\ -2\,8 \\ \hline 6 \\ -\ 4 \\ \hline \end{array}$$

Amad showed Puzzled Penguin how to use the Expanded Notation Method and just keep going.

$$\begin{array}{r} 100 \\ 700 \\ 4\overline{)3{,}476} \\ -2{,}800 \\ \hline 676 \\ -\ 400 \\ \hline 276 \end{array}$$

Kris showed Puzzled Penguin how, with the Place Value Sections Method, another section can be added.

	700 +	100
4	3,476	676
	−2,800	−400
	676	276

1 What was Puzzled Penguin's problem?

____

2 Discuss the solutions above. Which friend was right?

____

$$\begin{array}{r} 8 \\ \not{7} \\ 4\overline{)3{,}476} \\ -2\,8 \\ \hline 6 \\ -\,4 \\ \hline \end{array}$$

Unit 3
Quick Quiz 2

Name ________________________________

Use rounding and estimation to decide whether the quotient makes sense.

① $7\overline{)368}$ = 52 R4

____

____

Use any method to divide.

② $4\overline{)8,392}$

③ $5\overline{)6,037}$

Solve.

Show your work.

④ It takes 9 tickets to ride a Ferris wheel. Luis has 158 tickets. How many times can Luis ride the Ferris wheel?

____

⑤ Puzzles are packaged in groups of 3. If the store has 183 nature puzzles and 165 animal puzzles, how many packages of puzzles are there?

____

____

Fluency Check 9

Name ______________________________

PATH to FLUENCY

Add or subtract.

1. 333 + 270

2. 87,827 − 79,363

3. 568 − 197

4. 19,785 + 9,512

5. 4,329 − 3,110

6. 987 − 162

7. 48,096 − 2,168

8. 799,780 + 993,903

9. 941,259 − 398,739

10. 39,740 + 96,510

11. 8,624 + 7,813

12. 1,460 + 4,541

13. 342,824 − 96,590

14. 8,461 + 197

15. 212 + 614

Name ______________________

Use any method to divide.

1. $34\overline{)958}$

2. $18\overline{)864}$

Solve. Then use compatible numbers to check the solution.

3. $\begin{array}{r} 459 \\ \times \quad 6 \\ \hline \end{array}$

4. $6\overline{)2{,}280}$

5. There are 864 seats. There are 24 seats in each row. How many rows of seats are there?

____

Fluency Check 10

Name ______

PATH to FLUENCY

Divide.

1. $3 \div 3 = \square$
2. $8 \div 2 = \square$
3. $9 \div 3 = \square$
4. $16 \div 2 = \square$
5. $25 \div 5 = \square$
6. $28 \div 4 = \square$
7. $32 \div 8 = \square$
8. $40 \div 4 = \square$
9. $48 \div 6 = \square$
10. $56 \div 7 = \square$
11. $63 \div 9 = \square$
12. $54 \div 6 = \square$
13. $64 \div 8 = \square$
14. $72 \div 8 = \square$
15. $90 \div 9 = \square$

Name ______________________________

1. For 1a–1d, choose True or False to indicate if the statement is correct.

1a. $245 \div 6 = 40$ R5	○ True	○ False
1b. $803 \div 2 = 400$	○ True	○ False
1c. $492 \div 7 = 69$ R7	○ True	○ False
1d. $355 \div 5 = 71$	○ True	○ False

2. A train has a total of 216 seats in 3 cars. Each train car has the same number of seats. How many seats are in each train car?

__________ seats

3. Kayla puts together gift boxes of fruit to sell at her fruit stand. She places exactly 6 pieces of fruit in each box. She only sells full boxes of fruit.

Part A

Kayla has 256 apples. How many boxes of fruit can she fill? Explain how you found your answer.

Part B

Kayla has enough peaches to fill 31 gift boxes. How many apples and peaches did Kayla put in gift boxes to sell at her fruit stand? Show your work.

Name

4 Margaret is dividing 829 by 4.

Part A

Explain why Margaret needs to write a zero in the tens place of the quotient.

Part B

How would the digit in the tens place of the quotient change if Margaret were dividing 829 by 2?

5 A storage shelf where Carmen works can hold about 165 pounds. The storage shelf can hold 8 boxes of car parts. About how many pounds does each box weigh? Does this problem require an exact answer or an estimate? Then find the answer.

6 What is $945 \div 45$?

- (A) 20
- (B) 21
- (C) 22
- (D) 31

Name ______________________________

7 Divide 4,124 by 2.

8 Joshua carried 52 loads of sand to make a play area. Each load weighed 21 pounds. How many pounds of sand does Joshua use to make the play area? Use the numbers and symbols on the keypad to write the expression needed to solve this problem. Then solve the problem.

7	8	9
4	5	6
1	2	3
0	÷	×

expression: ____________

____________ pounds

9 There are 118 boys and 121 girls signed up for a volleyball league. The coaches first make teams of 9 players and then assign any remaining players to make some of the teams have 10 players.

Part A

How many teams of 10 players will there be? Explain.

Part B

How many teams of 9 players will there be? Explain.

Name ______________________________

10. A florist has 2,388 flowers to make into small bouquets. She wants 6 flowers in each bouquet. How many bouquets can she make? Complete the Place Value Sections to solve.

___00 + ___0 + ___ = ___ bouquets

11. Divide 840 by 46. Show your work.

12. For Exercises 12a–12d, choose Yes or No to tell if the quotient is reasonable.

12a. $6\overline{)297}$ = 39 R3 ○ Yes ○ No

12b. $4\overline{)3,256}$ = 814 ○ Yes ○ No

12c. $8\overline{)4,229}$ = 228 R5 ○ Yes ○ No

12d. $8\overline{)5,136}$ = 1,007 R1 ○ Yes ○ No

Name ______________________________

13. Hailey finds 24 seashells on Friday and another 38 seashells on Saturday. She shares as many of the seashells as she can equally among herself and 3 friends. She keeps the leftover seashells for herself. How many seashells does Hailey get? Show your work.

14. Ethan has 203 geodes to put into display cases. Each case holds 8 geodes. How many cases does Ethan need to hold all the geodes? Explain how you know.

15. Select one number from each column to make the equation true.

$5{,}155 \div 3 = \blacksquare \text{ R } \blacksquare$

Quotient	Remainder
○ 1,715	○ 1
○ 1,717	○ 2
○ 1,718	○ 3
○ 1,720	○ 4

Name ______________________________

16. Julie divided 2,526 by 6 and found a quotient of 421. For 16a–16c, choose True or False to tell if the statement is correct.

16a. $2{,}400 \div 6 = 400$, so 421 is reasonable. ○ True ○ False

16b. $2{,}526 \div 6 = 421$ R5 ○ True ○ False

16c. $421 \times 6 = 2{,}526$, so 421 makes sense. ○ True ○ False

17. Which expression has a quotient of 400? Circle all that apply.

1,600 ÷ 4	2,000 ÷ 5	400 ÷ 4	3,600 ÷ 9

18. Kyle wrote his first step in dividing 3,325 ÷ 5 using the Expanded Notation Method.

$$\begin{array}{r} 500 \\ 5\overline{)3{,}325} \\ -2{,}500 \\ \hline 825 \end{array}$$

Part A

Write an equation to calculate a reasonable estimate for the quotient of 3,325 ÷ 5.

Part B

Explain how Kyle's division work would be different if he had used your estimate instead of 500 as his first step. Then find the exact quotient of 3,325 ÷ 5.

Name

Make a Reading Plan

Matthew has 63 pages to read in 2–5 days. He wants to read the same number of pages each day and the greatest number of pages in the fewest days possible.

1. What is the best number of days for Matthew's reading plan?

2. How did you decide?

Sophia has 131 pages to read in 2–5 days.

3. Would it be possible for her to read the same number of pages each day? Explain.

4. Sophia decides to read the same number of pages on as many days as possible. What reading plan could Sophia follow? Show work to support your answer.

Name ______________________________

5 Suppose Sophia read 23 pages on the first day. She plans to read the remaining pages in 3–5 days. She wants to read the same number of pages on each of these days and the greatest number of pages in the fewest days possible. What is the best choice for the number of days for Sophia's reading plan? Explain how you decided.

6 Explain how to write your own division problem with any given quotient and remainder. Give an example that includes the relationship between multiplication and division in your explanation.

Dear Family:

In Unit 4 of *Math Expressions,* your child will apply the skills he or she has learned about operations with whole numbers while solving real world problems involving addition, subtraction, multiplication, and division.

Your child will simplify and evaluate expressions. Parentheses will be introduced to show which operation should be done first. The symbols "=" and "≠" will be used to show whether numbers and expressions are equal.

Other topics of study in this unit include situation and solution equations for addition and subtraction, as well as multiplication and division. Your child will use situation equations to represent real world problems and solution equations to solve the problems. This method of representing a problem is particularly helpful when the problems contain greater numbers and students cannot solve mentally.

Your child will also solve multiplication and addition comparison problems and compare these types of problems identifying what is the same or different.

Addition Comparison	**Multiplication Comparison**
Angela is 14 years old. She is 4 years older than Damarcus. How old is Damarcus?	Shawn colored 5 pages in a coloring book. Anja colored 4 times as many pages as Shawn colored. How many pages did Anja color?

Students learn that in the addition problem they are adding 4, while in the multiplication problem, they are multiplying by 4.

Your child will apply this knowledge to solve word problems using all four operations and involving one or more steps.

Finally, your child will find factor pairs for whole numbers and generate and analyze numerical and geometric patterns.

If you have any questions or comments, please contact me.

Sincerely,
Your child's teacher

Estimada familia:

En la Unidad 4 de Math Expressions, su hijo aplicará las destrezas relacionadas con operaciones de números enteros que ha adquirido, resolviendo problemas cotidianos que involucran suma, resta, multiplicación y división.

Su hijo simplificará y evaluará expresiones. Se introducirán los paréntesis como una forma de mostrar cuál operación deberá completarse primero. Los signos "=" y "≠" se usarán para mostrar si los números o las expresiones son iguales o no.

Otros temas de estudio en esta unidad incluyen ecuaciones de situación y de solución para la suma y resta, así como para la multiplicación y división. Su hijo usará ecuaciones de situación para representar problemas de la vida cotidiana y ecuaciones de solución para resolver esos problemas. Este método para representar problemas es particularmente útil cuando los problemas involucran números grandes y los estudiantes no pueden resolverlos mentalmente.

Su hijo también resolverá problemas de comparación de multiplicación y suma, y comparará este tipo de problemas para identificar las semejanzas y diferencias.

Comparación de suma	Comparación de multiplicación
Ángela tiene 14 años. Ella es 4 años mayor que Damarcus. ¿Cuántos años tiene Damarcus?	Shawn coloreó 5 páginas de un libro. Ana coloreó 4 veces ese número de páginas. ¿Cuántas páginas coloreó Ana?

Los estudiantes aprenderán que en el problema de suma están sumando 4, mientras que en el problema de multiplicación, están multiplicando por 4.

Su hijo aplicará estos conocimientos para resolver problemas de uno o más pasos usando las cuatro operaciones.

Finalmente, su hijo hallará pares de factores para números enteros y generará y analizará patrones numéricos y geométricos.

Si tiene alguna pregunta por favor comuníquese conmigo.

Atentamente,
El maestro de su niño

compare	**equation**
composite number	**evaluate an expression**
difference	**expression**

A statement that two expressions are equal. It has an equal sign.

Example:

32 + 35 = 67

67 = 32 + 34 + 1

(7 × 8) + 1 = 57

Describe quantities as greater than, less than, or equal to each other.

Substitute a value for a letter (or symbol) and then simplify the expression.

A number greater than 1 that has more than one factor pair. Examples of composite numbers are 10 and 18. The factor pairs of 10 are 1 and 10, 2 and 5. The factor pairs of 18 are 1 and 18, 2 and 9, 3 and 6.

A number, variable, or a combination of numbers and variables with one or more operations.

Example:

4

$6x$

$6x - 5$

7 + 4

The result of a subtraction.

Example:

54 − 37 = 17 ⟵ difference

factor pair	**pattern**
function	**pictograph**
multiple	**prime number**

A sequence that can be described by a rule.

A factor pair for a number is a pair of whole numbers whose product is that number.

Example:

$5 \times 7 = 35$

factor pair (5 and 7) → product (35)

A graph that uses pictures or symbols to represent data.

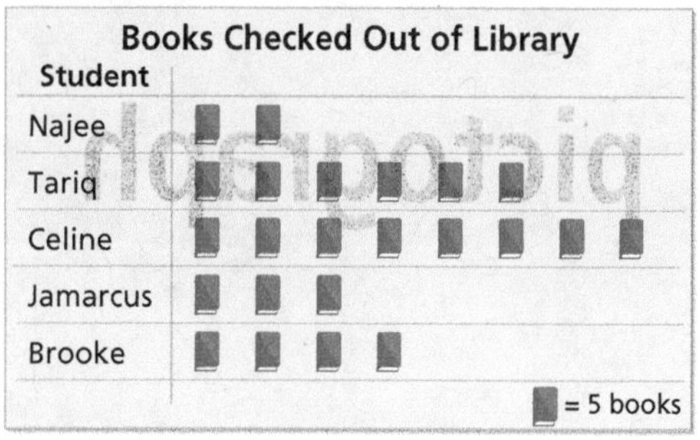

Books Checked Out of Library
Student
Najee
Tariq
Celine
Jamarcus
Brooke
= 5 books

A mathematical relationship between two sets of numbers. Each number in one of the sets is paired with exactly one number in the other set. A function may be displayed in a table.

Example:

The rule for this function is *Add 2*.

Input	1	4	5	8	12
Output	3	6	7	10	14

A number greater than 1 that has 1 and itself as the only factor pair. Examples of prime numbers are 2, 7, and 13. The only factor pair of 7 is 1 and 7.

A number that is the product of a given number and any whole number.

Examples:

$4 \times 1 = 4$, so 4 is a multiple of 4.

$4 \times 2 = 8$, so 8 is a multiple of 4.

simplify an expression

sum

term

Combining like terms and performing operations until all possible terms have been combined.

The answer when adding two or more addends.

Example:

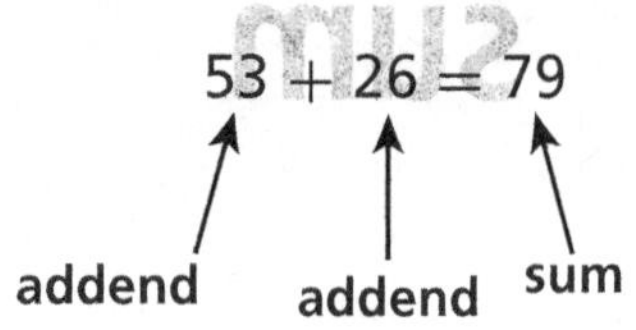
53 + 26 = 79
addend
addend
sum

A number, variable, product, or quotient in an expression or equation. Each term is separated by an operation sign (+, −).

Example:

$3n + 5$ has two terms, $3n$ and 5.

Name ______________________________

Practice Solving Problems (continued)

Show your work.

19 Terrence is planning a 760-mile trip. He travels 323 miles the first two days. How many miles does Terrence have left to travel on this trip?

____

20 There were some people at the football stadium early last Sunday, and then 5,427 more people arrived. Then there were 79,852 people at the stadium. How many people arrived early?

____

What's the Error?

Dear Math Students,

The problem below was part of my homework assignment.

Mrs. Nason had a collection of 1,845 stamps. She bought some more stamps. Now she has 2,270 stamps. How many stamps did Mrs. Nason buy?

To solve the problem, I wrote this equation:
$s - 1,845 = 2,270$. I solved the equation and wrote $s = 4,115$.

My teacher says that my answer is not correct. Can you help me understand what I did wrong and explain how to find the correct answer?

Your friend,
Puzzled Penguin

?

21 Write a response to Puzzled Penguin.

____

____

____

Check Understanding

Explain the difference between a situation equation and a solution equation. Use Puzzled Penguin's homework problem to give examples of each type of equation.

Unit 4
Quick Quiz 1

Name ______________________________

Solve for ■ or *n*.

1. $84 \div n = 6$

   $n =$ ________

2. $(14 + 7) \cdot 8 = ■ \cdot 8$

   ■ = ________

Write an equation to show the problem. Then solve. *Show your work.*

3. Miguel drove 197 miles on Monday. He drove some more miles on Tuesday. He drove 542 miles in all. How many miles did Miguel drive on Tuesday?

   ____

   ____

4. A theater has a seating capacity of 748 seats. If 3 performances are sold out, how many tickets are sold?

   ____

   ____

5. Britney is saving $996 to pay for summer camp. She wants to save the same amount of money each month for 6 months. How much money does Britney need to save each month?

   ____

   ____

   ____

Fluency Check 11

Name ______________________________

PATH to FLUENCY

Add or subtract.

1. $\begin{array}{r} 242 \\ +\ 316 \\ \hline \end{array}$

2. $\begin{array}{r} 681 \\ -\ 375 \\ \hline \end{array}$

3. $\begin{array}{r} 2{,}945 \\ +\ 713 \\ \hline \end{array}$

4. $\begin{array}{r} 5{,}839 \\ -\ 3{,}427 \\ \hline \end{array}$

5. $\begin{array}{r} 17{,}649 \\ +\ 2{,}431 \\ \hline \end{array}$

6. $\begin{array}{r} 48{,}600 \\ -\ 29{,}728 \\ \hline \end{array}$

7. $\begin{array}{r} 6{,}739 \\ +\ 3{,}847 \\ \hline \end{array}$

8. $\begin{array}{r} 5{,}069 \\ -\ 4{,}853 \\ \hline \end{array}$

9. $\begin{array}{r} 371 \\ +\ 542 \\ \hline \end{array}$

10. $\begin{array}{r} 574 \\ -\ 350 \\ \hline \end{array}$

11. $\begin{array}{r} 26{,}366 \\ -\ 7{,}382 \\ \hline \end{array}$

12. $\begin{array}{r} 34{,}278 \\ +\ 57{,}341 \\ \hline \end{array}$

13. $\begin{array}{r} 693{,}317 \\ -\ 47{,}592 \\ \hline \end{array}$

14. $\begin{array}{r} 242{,}730 \\ +\ 79{,}527 \\ \hline \end{array}$

15. $\begin{array}{r} 809{,}411 \\ -\ 472{,}389 \\ \hline \end{array}$

Name

Practice

Write and solve an equation to solve each problem. Draw comparison bars when needed.

Show your work.

11 On the last day of school, 100 more students wore shorts than wore jeans. If 130 students wore jeans, how many students wore shorts?

12 Matthew completed a puzzle with 90 pieces. Wendy completed a puzzle with 5 times as many pieces. How many pieces are in Wendy's puzzle?

13 There were 19,748 adults at a baseball game. There were 5,136 fewer children at the baseball game than adults. How many children were at the baseball game?

What's the Error?

Dear Math Students,

I was asked to find the number of stamps that Amanda has if her friend Jesse has 81 stamps and that is 9 times as many stamps as Amanda has.

I wrote $81 \times 9 = s$. So, $s = 729$. My teacher says that my answer is not correct. Can you explain what I did wrong?

Your friend,
Puzzled Penguin

?

14 Write a response to Puzzled Penguin.

Check Understanding

Explain how addition comparison problems differ from multiplication comparison problems.

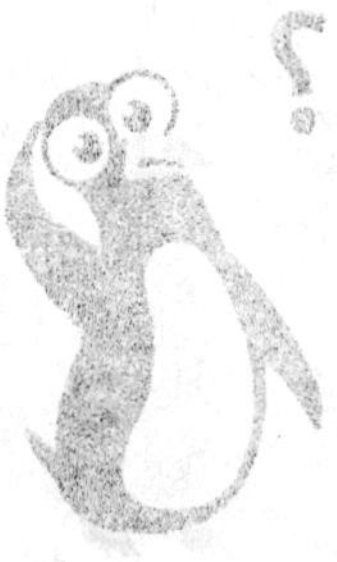

Name ____________________

Write an equation.

1. Nicole swims 6 times as many laps as Evan. What multiplication equation compares the laps Nicole and Evan swim?

____

Write an equation to show the problem. Then solve.

Show your work.

2. There are 34 hats at a shop. There are 2 times as many scarves as hats at the shop. How many scarves are at the shop?

____

3. Liam has 51 stickers. He has 3 times as many stickers as Jade. How many stickers does Jade have?

____

4. There are 16,492 people at a car race. There are 3,271 fewer people at the race this year than last year. How many people were at the car race last year?

____

Use the bar graph. Write an equation to solve the problem.

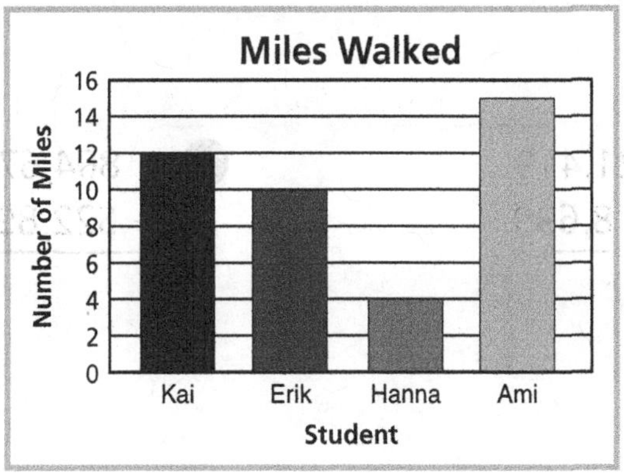
Miles Walked
Number of Miles
0
2
4
6
8
10
12
14
16
Kai
Erik
Hanna
Ami
Student

5. Kai walked how many times as many miles as Hanna?

____

Name ______________________

PATH to FLUENCY

Add or subtract.

1. 214 + 180

2. 427 − 345

3. 4,592 + 3,667

4. 6,953 − 3,812

5. 8,931 + 658

6. 50,730 − 42,694

7. 83,314 + 20,894

8. 9,063 − 1,842

9. 397 + 411

10. 694 − 642

11. 76,836 − 8,565

12. 367,530 + 246,597

13. 477,713 − 80,722

14. 21,419 + 8,639

15. 804,672 − 522,891

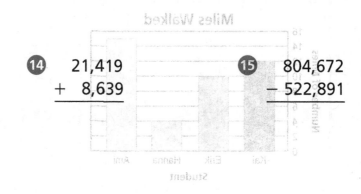

 Name ______________________

Discuss the Steps

1. Mr. Stills makes bags of school supplies for the 9 students in his class. He has 108 pencils and 72 erasers. He puts the same number of pencils and the same number of erasers into each bag. How many more pencils than erasers are in each bag of school supplies?

Solve the problem by finishing Nicole's and David's methods. Discuss what is alike and what is different about the methods.

Nicole's Method

Write an equation for each step.

Divide to find the number of pencils that Mr. Stills puts in each bag of school supplies. $108 \div 9 = \_\_\_\_$

Divide to find the number of erasers that Mr. Stills puts in each bag of school supplies. $72 \div 9 = \_\_\_\_$

Subtract the number of erasers in each bag from the number of pencils in each bag. $12 - 8 = \_\_\_\_$

There are ____ more pencils than erasers in each bag of school supplies.

David's Method

Write an equation for the whole problem.

Let p = how many more pencils than erasers are in each bag of school supplies.

The number of pencils in each bag of school supplies — The number of erasers in each bag of school supplies

$\_\_\_\_ \div 9 - \_\_\_\_ \div 9 = p$

$12 - 8 = p$

$\_\_\_\_ = p$

There are ____ more pencils than erasers in each bag of school supplies.

Name ____________________

Discuss the Steps (continued)

2 John is selling bags of popcorn for a school fundraiser. So far, John has sold 45 bags of popcorn for $5 each. His goal is to earn $300 for the school fundraiser. How many more bags of popcorn must John sell to reach his goal?

Solve the problem by writing an equation for each step. Then solve the problem by writing one equation for the whole problem.

Write an equation for each step.

Multiply to find how much money John has earned so far selling popcorn.

_____ × $5 = $_____

Subtract to find how much money John has left to earn to reach his goal.

$300 − $_____ = $_____

Divide to find the number of bags of popcorn John must sell to reach his goal.

$75 ÷ $5 = _____

John must sell _____ more bags of popcorn to reach his goal.

Write an equation for the whole problem.

Let b = the number of bags of popcorn John must sell to reach his goal.

John's fundraiser goal amount — Amount of money John has raised so far

(_____ − _____ × $5) ÷ $5 = b

($300 − $_____) ÷ $5 = b

$_____ ÷ $5 = b

_____ = b

John must sell _____ more bags of popcorn to reach his goal.

Name ___

What's the Error?

Dear Math Students,

My friend and I are planning a hike. We will hike from Point A to Point B, which is a distance of 28 miles. Then we will hike from Point B to Point C, which is a distance of 34 miles. We will walk 7 miles each day for 8 days. We are trying to figure out how many miles we need to walk on the ninth day to reach Point C.

I wrote and solved this equation.

$28 + 34 - 7 \times 8 = t$

$62 - 7 \times 8 = t$

$55 \times 8 = t$

$440 = t$

?

This answer doesn't make sense. Did I do something wrong? What do you think?

Your friend,
Puzzled Penguin

8 Write a response to Puzzled Penguin.

___

___

___

___

___

___

___

Check Understanding

Describe how to solve a multistep problem.

Name ______________________________

Write an equation to show the problem. Then solve.

Show your work.

1. Anika spent $128 on 3 sweaters and 1 skirt. The sweaters cost $38 each. What was the cost of the skirt?

____

____

2. Lily has 144 ceramic beads and 108 wooden beads. She plans to store the beads equally in 6 boxes. How many beads will be in each box?

____

____

Write one or more equations to show the problem. Then solve.

3. Emma has 14 rocks in her collection. Tyler has 6 times as many rocks as Emma. How many rocks do Emma and Tyler have altogether?

____

____

4. Joaquin is saving $250 to buy a surfboard. He saved $8 each week for 12 weeks. He wants to buy the surfboard in 7 more weeks. How much does Joaquin need to save each week?

____

____

Fluency Check 13

Name ____________________

PATH to FLUENCY

Add or subtract.

1. $\begin{array}{r} 60{,}047 \\ -\ 35{,}689 \\ \hline \end{array}$

2. $\begin{array}{r} 472 \\ -\ 364 \\ \hline \end{array}$

3. $\begin{array}{r} 5{,}682 \\ +\ 2{,}497 \\ \hline \end{array}$

4. $\begin{array}{r} 5{,}897 \\ -\ 4{,}352 \\ \hline \end{array}$

5. $\begin{array}{r} 89{,}431 \\ -\ 8{,}650 \\ \hline \end{array}$

6. $\begin{array}{r} 298 \\ +\ 311 \\ \hline \end{array}$

7. $\begin{array}{r} 67{,}538 \\ +\ 22{,}685 \\ \hline \end{array}$

8. $\begin{array}{r} 429 \\ -\ 117 \\ \hline \end{array}$

9. $\begin{array}{r} 409{,}274 \\ -\ 38{,}528 \\ \hline \end{array}$

10. $\begin{array}{r} 342 \\ +\ 342 \\ \hline \end{array}$

11. $\begin{array}{r} 5{,}630 \\ -\ 3{,}428 \\ \hline \end{array}$

12. $\begin{array}{r} 587{,}390 \\ +\ 136{,}428 \\ \hline \end{array}$

13. $\begin{array}{r} 984{,}208 \\ -\ 796{,}159 \\ \hline \end{array}$

14. $\begin{array}{r} 79{,}472 \\ +\ 8{,}927 \\ \hline \end{array}$

15. $\begin{array}{r} 3{,}219 \\ +\ 628 \\ \hline \end{array}$

Name ______________________

Find Factor Pairs

A factor pair for a number is two whole numbers whose product is that number. For example, 2 and 5 is a factor pair for 10.

1. Draw arrays to show all the factor pairs for 12 on the grid below. The array for 1 and 12 is shown.

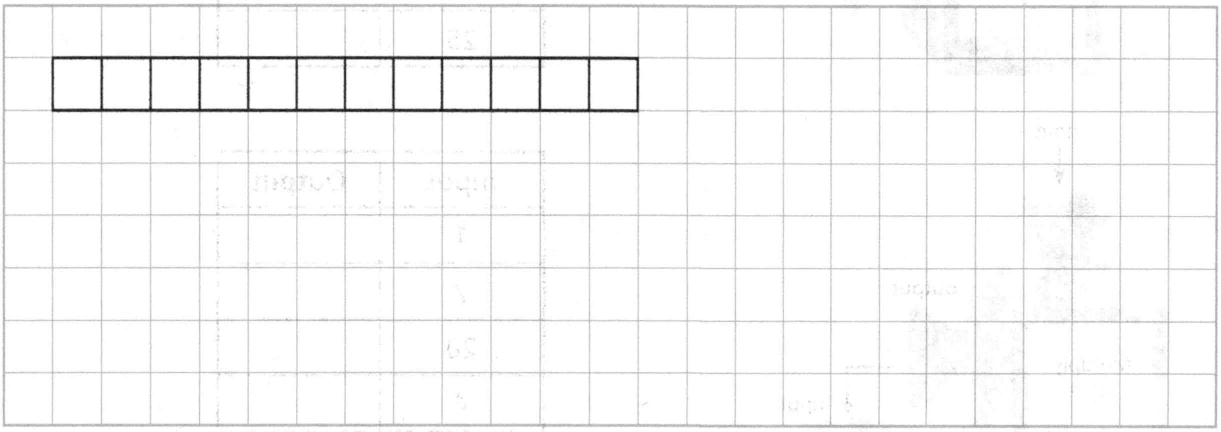

2. List all the factor pairs for 12. ______________________

Use the table to list all the factors pairs for each number.

3. 32

1	32
2	

4. 44

1	44

5. 100

1	100

List all the factor pairs for each number.

6. 29 ______________________

7. 63 ______________________

Name ____________________

Input/Output Machines

Use the input/output machines to complete the tables.

16

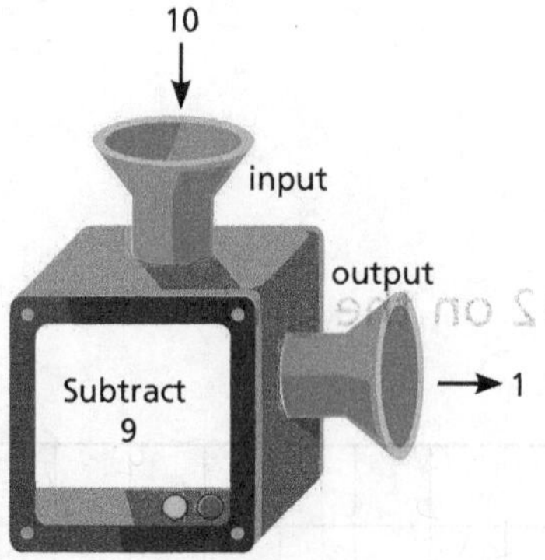
10
input
output
Subtract
9
1

Input	Output
10	1
13	
16	
22	
25	

17

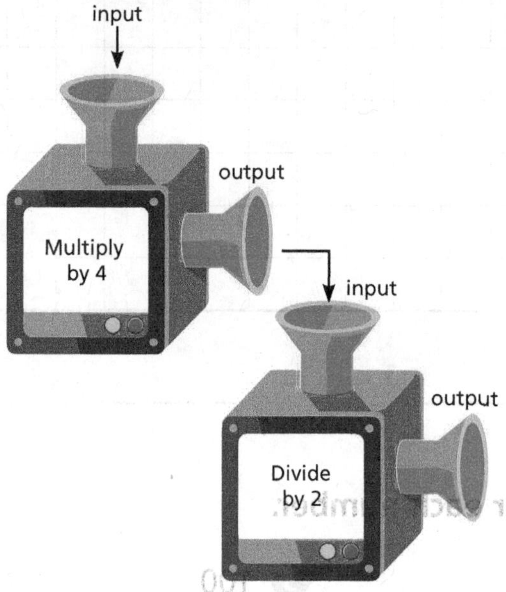
input
output
Multiply
by 4
input
output
Divide
by 2

Input	Output
1	
7	
20	
4	
11	

Use Inverse Operations

Use the given operation, or its inverse operation, to find the missing values in each table.

18

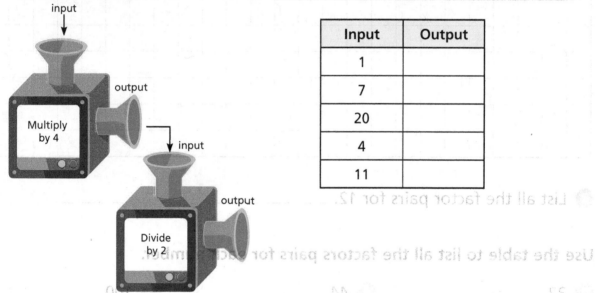

Add 3					
Input	1	4			9
Output			8	15	

19

Divide by 10					
Input	20		10	50	
Output		6			10

Name

One-Operation Functions

VOCABULARY
function

A **function** is a mathematical relationship that is shared by two sets of numbers. A rule describes the relationship. A table is a way to display a function.

For each function below, one operation is given. Use the operation, or the inverse operation, to complete the table.

20

Subtract 1					
Input	4	2		5	
Output			8		0

21

Add 5					
Input	2		3		7
Output		10		6	

22

Multiply by 11					
Input		12		9	
Output	77		110		121

Two-Operation Functions

For each function below, two operations are given. Complete the table.

23

Multiply by 3, then subtract 1					
Input	1	2	6	4	7
Output					

24

Divide by 2, then add 3					
Input	4	2	10	8	6
Output					

Name ______________________________

Write a Rule

This table shows that the number of legs is a function of the number of dogs. Use the table to complete Exercise 25.

Number of Dogs	1	2	3	4	5	6	7	8
Number of Legs	4	8	12	16	20	24	28	32

25 Using words, write the rule of the function.

____

____

Make a Table

26 Write a function rule in words that includes two operations.

____

____

27 Write your rule from Exercise 26 in the table below. Then write five inputs. Then use the rule and write the missing outputs.

Rule: ______					
Input					
Output					

28 At a bakery, bran muffins are baked by the dozen. In the table below, write a rule to describe the relationship. Then complete the table to show the number of muffins baked for any number of dozen.

Rule: ______								
Number of Dozen								
Number of Muffins								

Name

Functions and Equations

The function below describes the number of legs (*l*) for any number of spiders (*s*).

Number of Spiders (*s*)	1	2	3	4	5	6	7	8
Number of Legs (*l*)	8	16	24	32	40	48	56	64

29 Using the variables *s* and *l*, write an equation which shows that the number of legs (*l*) is a function of the number of spiders (*s*). ________

30 Write an equation that uses the variables *x* and *y* and shows *y* as a function of *x*.

x	0	1	2	3	4
y	1	2	3	4	5

____

Solve.

31 Each ticket to a school musical costs $6. Write an equation to represent the cost in dollars (*d*) for any number of tickets (*t*). ________

Jon spent $30 buying tickets. Explain how to find the number of tickets he bought. Name the number of tickets.

____

32 The rule for the table is $y = 3x + 2$. Use the rule to complete the table.

x	1	2	4	7	8
y					

Check Understanding

Use the rule to write the first five terms in the pattern.
First term: 8; Rule: multiply by 4

____

Unit 4
Quick Quiz 4

Name ____________________

Write whether the number is *prime* or *composite*.

1. 91 ____________

2. 41 ____________

3. List all factor pairs for the number.

64

____

4. The rule for the table is $y = 2x + 1$. Use the rule to complete the table.

x	0	1	2	3	4
y					

5. Describe the next term in the pattern.

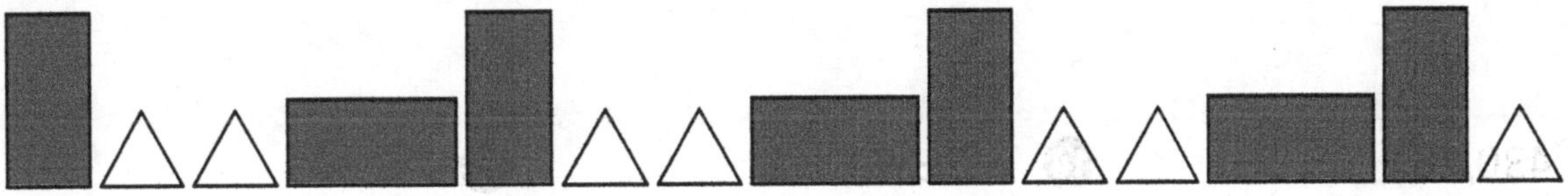

____

____

Fluency Check 14

Name ____________________

PATH to FLUENCY

Add or subtract.

1. 24,389 + 18,710

2. 506 − 382

3. 5,537 + 4,548

4. 637 + 462

5. 43,000 − 6,782

6. 52,896 − 36,952

7. 11,934 + 4,572

8. 692,375 + 227,964

9. 353,785 − 177,841

10. 409 + 570

11. 4,507 − 3,384

12. 755 − 314

13. 430,761 − 78,914

14. 5,396 − 3,352

15. 8,342 + 177

Name ______________________________

1 The number of ash trees on a tree farm is 5 times the number of pine trees. Choose one expression from each column to create an equation that compares the number of ash trees (a) and pine trees (p).

○ $a - 5$		○ p
○ $5a$	=	○ $5p$
○ a		○ $p + 5$
○ $a \div 5$		○ $p - 5$

2 Use the rule to find the value of y.

Rule: $y = 4x + 3$

value of x: 2

value of y: ______________________

3 Eliot sends 217 text messages each week. Write equations to find how many text messages he sends in 4 weeks and in 7 weeks.

Equations: ______________________

____

Use the equations to complete the table.

Weeks	Total Text Messages
1	217
4	
7	

4 Solve for n.

$(16 + 12) \div (11 - 7) = n$ $n =$ ☐

Name ______________________________

5 There are 1,342 players in the baseball league. That is 2 times the number of players in the football league. How many players are in the football league? Write an equation. Then solve.

6 A school ordered 688 T-shirts in 3 sizes: small, medium, and large. There are 296 small and 268 medium T-shirts. How many large T-shirts were ordered? Select numbers from the list to complete the equation. Then solve.

3	268	296	688

$l = \square - (\square + \square)$

$l =$ ______ large T-shirts

7 Select the factor pair for 45. Mark all that apply.

- (A) 4, 11
- (B) 3, 15
- (C) 6, 7
- (D) 4, 12
- (E) 1, 45
- (F) 5, 9

8 Is a multiple of the prime number 3 also a prime number? Circle your answer.

Yes No

Explain your reasoning.

Name ______________________

9 A baker's dozen is a group or set of 13. Select the equation that shows the number of cookies (c) in any number of baker's dozens (b). Select all that apply.

Ⓐ $c = 13b$

Ⓑ $c = 12b + 1$

Ⓒ $c = 13 + b$

Ⓓ $c = b(12 + 1)$

Complete the table to show the number of cookies.

Baker's Dozens	1	3	5	7	9
Cookies					

10 Classify each number from the list as being a multiple of 2, 3, or 5. Write each number in the correct box. A number can be written in more than one box.

18 30 20 24 55 39

Multiple of 2	**Multiple of 3**	**Multiple of 5**

11 Use the rule to find the next 3 terms in the pattern.

Rule: multiply by 2

4, 8, 16, 32, ☐, ☐, ☐, ...

12 Draw the next term in the pattern.

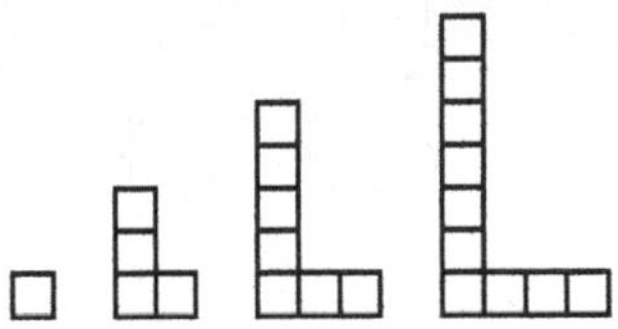

Name ______________________________

13 A team of workers is building a 942-foot trail. They plan to complete 6 feet per hour. How many hours will it take to build the trail?

Choose the equation that can be used to solve this problem. Mark all that apply.

Ⓐ $942 \times 6 = h$

Ⓑ $942 \div 6 = h$

Ⓒ $942 \div h = 6$

Ⓓ $6 \times h = 942$

Ⓔ $6 = 942 \times h$

Ⓕ $942 = 6 \div h$

14 Roger ships a large number of packages on Monday. Then he ships 3,820 more packages on Tuesday. Roger ships 22,540 packages in all. How many packages did he ship on Monday? Identify the type of comparison as addition or multiplication. Then write and solve an equation to solve the problem.

Type of comparison: ______________________

Equation: __________________________

Answer: __________ packages

15 For Exercises 15a–15d, select True or False for the calculation.

15a. $72 \div (6 + 2) = 9$ ○ True ○ False

15b. $(2 + 7) + (6 - 2) = 36$ ○ True ○ False

15c. $(12 + 8) \div 4 = 10 \div (5 - 3)$ ○ True ○ False

15d. $(35 - 8) \div (2 + 1) = 32$ ○ True ○ False

Name ______________________________

16 Charlotte made this pictograph to show the number of dogs attending a dog training class this week.

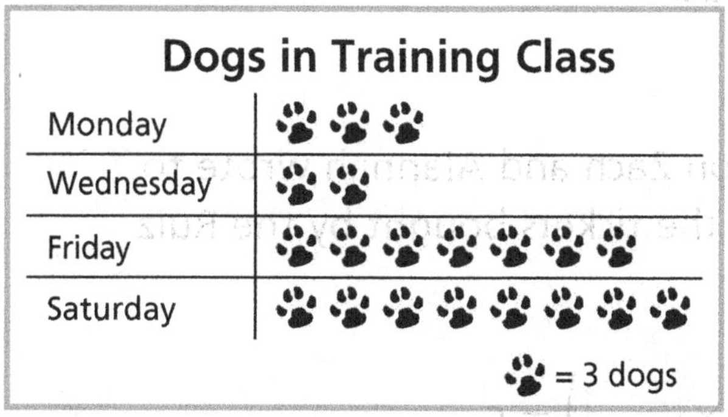
Dogs in Training Class
Monday
Wednesday
Friday
Saturday
= 3 dogs

Part A

How many fewer dogs were in training class on Monday than on Friday? Write and solve an equation.

Equation: ______________________

Answer: ____________ fewer dogs

Part B

Choose the number that makes the sentence true.

Charlotte forgot to include Thursday on her graph. There were two times as many dogs at Thursday's class than at Monday's class.

There were [2 | 6 | 15 | 18] dogs in the training class on Thursday.

Part C

Explain how you determined the number of dogs at Thursday's class.

Name

17 The Ruiz family bought 2 adult tickets and 4 child tickets to the fair. The adult tickets cost $8 each. The child tickets cost $3 each.

Part A

Complete the equation Zach and Alannah wrote to find the total cost of the tickets bought by the Ruiz family.

$(\square \times \square) + (4 \times \square) = c$

Part B

Zach's answer is $72, and Alannah's answer is $28. Who has the wrong answer? Explain what error he or she made.

18 A store has 4 bins of planet posters with 23 posters in each bin. It has 3 bins of planet calendars with 26 calendars in each bin. Yesterday, 72 calendars were sold. How many planet posters and calendars are left in all? Explain how you found your answer and how you know if your answer is reasonable.

Name ______________________________

Find Their Ages

Tricia, Molly, and Becky are cousins. At a family reunion, their Aunt Sasha makes it a game for the other relatives to find the age of each cousin. Aunt Sasha tells the relatives that Becky is 2 years older than Molly. She says that Tricia's age is 3 times Molly's age right now.

1. Write an equation relating Becky's age to Molly's age.

2. Write an equation relating Tricia's age to Molly's age.

3. If Molly is 3, how old is Becky? Show your work.

4. How old is Tricia? Show your work.

5. Write an equation that relates Tricia's age to Becky's age. Show that your equation is true.

Name ____________________

James, Ben, and David are cousins who are also at the family reunion. James is 12 years old, Ben is 16 years old, and David is 18 years old. The cousins decide to play a game for the other relatives to find the ages of their uncles.

6 The cousins said that Uncle Reggie is twice as many years old as James' and Ben's ages together. Use one or more equations to find out how old Uncle Reggie is. Show your work.

7 Then the cousins said that Uncle Tony is 4 years younger than 3 times David's age. Use one or more equations to find out how old Uncle Tony is. Show your work.

8 The cousins also said that Uncle Ed is half as old as all of their ages combined. Use one or more equations to find out how old Uncle Ed is. Show your work.

9 Write and solve an equation relating your age to the age of someone in your family. Use at least one variable. Explain how you wrote the equation.

Dear Family:

This unit includes the customary and metric measurement systems. During this unit, students will become familiar with metric units of length, liquid volume, and mass, as well as the size of each when compared to each other.

One **meter** is about the distance an adult man can reach, or a little longer than a yard.

One **liter** is about two large glasses of liquid, or a little more than a quart.

One **gram** is about the mass of a paper clip or a single peanut.
One **kilogram** is a little more than 2 pounds.

Students will also discover that the metric system is based on multiples of 10. Prefixes in the names of metric measurements tell the size of a measure compared to the size of the base unit.

Units of Length

kilometer	hectometer	decameter	meter	decimeter	centimeter	millimeter
km	hm	dam	m	dm	cm	mm
10 × 1 hm	10 × 1 dam	10 × 1 m	10 × 1 dm	10 × 1 cm	10 × 1 mm	
1 km = 1,000 m	1 hm = 100 m	1 dam = 10 m		10 dm = 1 m	100 cm = 1 m	1,000 mm = 1 m

The most commonly used length units are **kilometer, meter, centimeter**, and **millimeter**.

The most commonly used units of liquid volume are **liter** and **milliliter**.

The most commonly used units of mass are **gram, kilogram,** and **milligram**.

Students solve real world problems involving metric and customary measures including finding perimeter and area of rectangles.

If you have any questions or comments, please contact me.

Sincerely,
Your child's teacher

Estimada familia:

Esta unidad incluye el sistema métrico y usual de medidas. Durante esta unidad, los estudiantes se familiarizarán con unidades métricas de longitud, volumen del líquido y masa, así como con el tamaño de cada una comparada con las otras.

Un **metro** es aproximadamente la distancia que un hombre adulto puede alcanzar extendiendo el brazo, o un poco más de una yarda.

Un **litro** es aproximadamente dos vasos grandes de líquido, o un poco más de un cuarto de galón.

Un **gramo** es aproximadamente la masa de un clip o un cacahuate.
Un **kilogramo** es un poco más de 2 libras.

Los estudiantes también descubrirán que el sistema métrico está basado en múltiplos de 10. Los prefijos de los nombres de las medidas métricas indican el tamaño de la medida comparado con el tamaño de la unidad base.

Unidades de longitud

kilómetro	hectómetro	decámetro	metro	decímetro	centímetro	milímetro
km	hm	dam	m	dm	cm	mm
10 × 1 hm	10 × 1 dam	10 × 1 m	10 × 1 dm	10 × 1 cm	10 × 1 mm	
1 km = 1,000 m	1 hm = 100 m	1 dam = 10 m		10 dm = 1 m	100 cm = 1 m	1,000 mm = 1 m

Las unidades de longitud más comunes son **kilómetro, metro, centímetro** y **milímetro**.

Las unidades de volumen del líquido más comunes son **litro** y **mililitro**.

Las unidades de masa más comunes son **gramo, kilogramo** y **miligramo**.

Los estudiantes resuelven problemas del mundo real que incluyen medidas usuales y métricas para hallar el perímetro y el área de rectángulos.

Si tiene alguna pregunta o algún comentario, por favor comuníquese conmigo.

Atentamente,
El maestro de su niño

centimeter (cm)	**fluid ounce (fl oz)**
cup (c)	**foot (ft)**
decimeter (dm)	**formula**

A unit of liquid volume in the U.S. customary system.
8 fluid ounces = 1 cup

A unit of measure in the metric system that equals one hundredth of a meter.
100 cm = 1 m

A U.S. customary unit of length equal to 12 inches.

A unit of liquid volume in the U.S. customary system that equals 8 fluid ounces.

An equation with letters or symbols that describes a rule.

The formula for the area of a rectangle is:

$A = l \times w$

where A is the area, l is the length, and w is the width.

A unit of measure in the metric system that equals one tenth of a meter.
10 dm = 1 m

gallon (gal)

kilogram (kg)

gram (g)

kiloliter (kL)

inch (in.)

kilometer (km)

A unit of mass in the metric system that equals one thousand grams.
1 kg = 1,000 g

A unit of liquid volume in the U.S. customary system that equals 4 quarts.

A unit of liquid volume in the metric system that equals one thousand liters.
1 kL = 1,000 L

The basic unit of mass in the metric system.

A unit of length in the metric system that equals 1,000 meters.
1 km = 1,000 m

A U.S. customary unit of length.

Example:

1 inch

length	**liter (L)**
line plot	**mass**
liquid volume	**meter (m)**

The basic unit of liquid volume in the metric system.
1 liter = 1,000 milliliters

The measure of a line segment or the distance across the longer side of a rectangle.

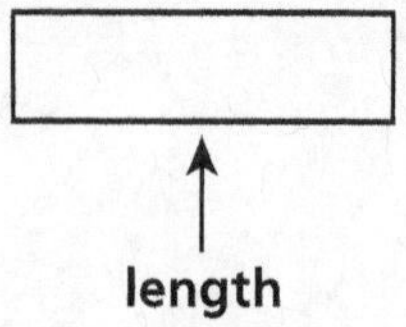
length

The measure of the amount of matter in an object.

A diagram that shows the frequency of data on a number line. Also called a dot plot.

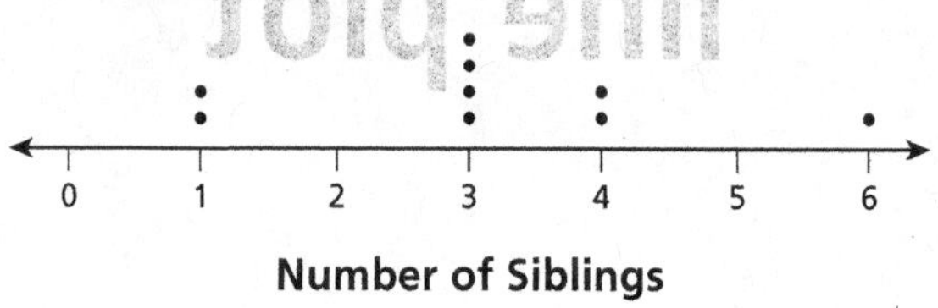
0
1
2
3
4
5
6
Number of Siblings

The basic unit of length in the metric system.

A measure of the space a liquid occupies.

metric system	**milliliter (mL)**
mile (mi)	**millimeter (mm)**
milligram (mg)	**ounce (oz)**

A unit of liquid volume in the metric system. 1,000 mL = 1 L

A base ten system of measurement.

A unit of length in the metric system. 1,000 mm = 1 m

A U.S. customary unit of length equal to 5,280 feet.

A U.S. customary unit of weight.
16 ounces = 1 pound

A U.S. customary unit of liquid volume (also called a fluid ounce). 8 ounces = 1 cup

A unit of mass in the metric system. 1,000 mg = 1g

perimeter

quart (qt)

pint (pt)

ton

pound (lb)

width

A U.S. customary unit of liquid volume that equals 32 fluid ounces or 4 cups.

The distance around a figure.

A U.S. customary unit of weight that equals 2,000 pounds.

A U.S. customary unit of liquid volume that equals 16 fluid ounces.

The distance across the shorter side of a rectangle.

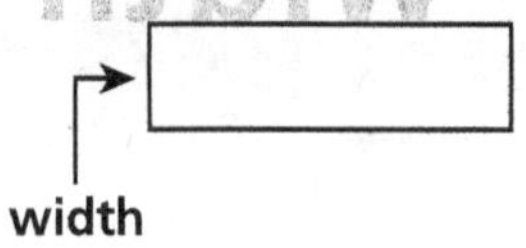
width

A unit of weight in the U.S. customary system.

yard (yd)

A U.S. customary unit of length equal to 3 feet.

Name ______________________________

Convert Metric Units of Measure

You can use a table to convert measurements.

Meters	Decimeters
2	2 × 10 = 20
4	___ × 10 = ___
6	6 × ___ = ___
8	___ = ___

20 How many decimeters are in one meter? ________

21 Complete the equation.

1 meter = ________ decimeters

22 Complete the table. Explain how you found the number of decimeters in 8 meters.

____

____

You can also use a number line to convert measurements.

23 Complete the equation. 1 kilometer = ________ meters

24 Label the double number line to show how kilometers (km) and meters (m) are related.

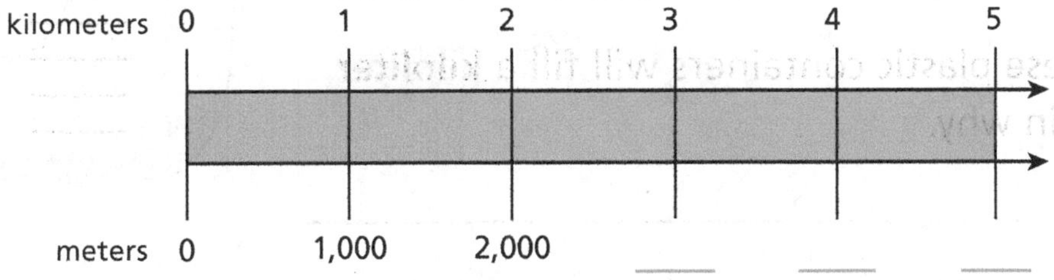
kilometers
0
1
2
3
4
5
meters
0
1,000
2,000
___
___
___

Solve each problem. Label your answers with the correct units.

25 Marsha drove her car 6,835 kilometers last year. How many meters did Marsha drive last year?

____

26 John's television is 160 centimeters wide. How many millimeters wide is the television?

____

Solve.

27 5 m = ________ cm **28** 3 hm = ________ m **29** 7 km = ________ m

Check Understanding

Describe the relationship between meters and kilometers, decimeters, centimeters, and millimeters.

Name ______________________________

Measure Liquid Volume

VOCABULARY
liquid volume
liter
milliliter
kiloliter

The base metric unit of **liquid volume** is a **liter.**

Units of Liquid Volume

kiloliter	hectoliter	decaliter	liter	deciliter	centiliter	milliliter
kL	hL	daL	L	dL	cL	mL
10 × 1 hL	10 × 1 daL	10 × 1 L	10 × 1 dL	10 × 1 cL	10 × 1 mL	
1 kL = 1,000 L	1 hL = 100 L	1 daL = 10 L		10 dL = 1 L	100 cL = 1 L	1,000 mL = 1 L

Ms. Lee cut a two-liter plastic bottle in half to make a one-liter container. She marked the outside to show equal parts.

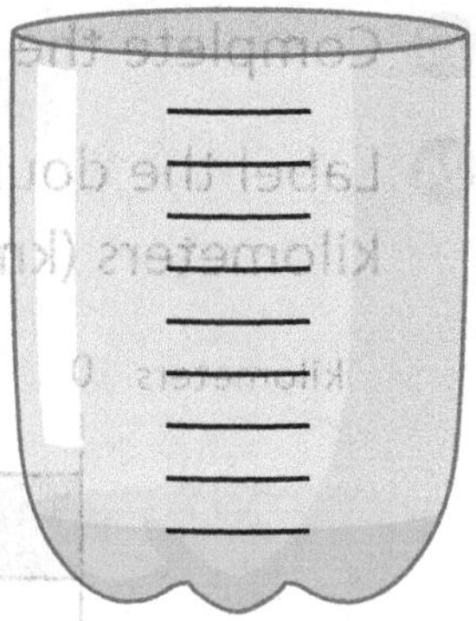

1. How many **milliliters** of water will fit in the container?

   ____

2. How many of these plastic containers will fill a **kiloliter** container? Explain why.

   ____

You can use a table or a double number line to convert units of liquid measure.

3. Complete the table.

Liters	Deciliters
3	3 × 10 = 30
5	___ × 10 = ___
7	7 × ___ = ___
12	________ = ___

4. Label the double number line to show how liters (L) and milliliters (mL) are related.

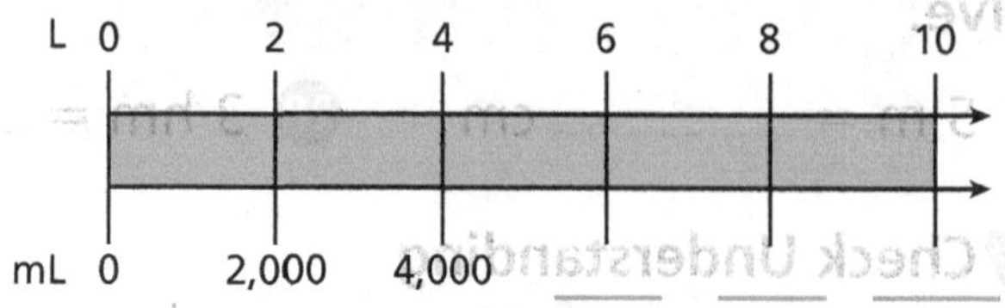
L 0 2 4 6 8 10
mL 0 2,000 4,000

Name ____________________

What's the Error?

Dear Math Students,

Today I had to solve this problem.

Meredith wanted to make some punch for a party. The recipe to make the punch called for 3 liters of fruit juice, 2 liters of apple juice, and 1 liter of grape juice. How many milliliters of juice is needed for the recipe? I said that the recipe calls for 600 milliliters of juice.
Here is how I solved the problem.

3 L + 2 L + 1 L = 6 L x 100 = 600 mL

Is my answer correct? If not, please help me understand why it is wrong.

Your friend,
Puzzled Penguin

?

5 Is Puzzled Penguin correct? Explain your thinking.

6 Use the table to show the conversion from liters to milliliters for each type of juice needed for the recipe.

Liters	Milliliters

7 Describe another way that you could show the conversion from liters to milliliters for each type of juice.

Name ______________________________

VOCABULARY
mass
gram
kilogram
milligram

Measure Mass

The basic unit of **mass** is a **gram**.

Units of Mass

kilogram	hectogram	decagram	gram	decigram	centigram	milligram
kg	hg	dag	g	dg	cg	mg
10 × 1 hg	10 × 1 dag	10 × 1 g	10 × 1 dg	10 × 1 cg	10 × 1 mg	
1 kg = 1,000 g	1 hg = 100 g	1 dag = 10 g		10 dg = 1 g	100 cg = 1 g	1,000 mg = 1 g

8 How many **milligrams** are equal to 1 gram? ______________

9 How many grams are equal to 1 **kilogram**? ______________

If you weighed 1 mL of water, you would find that its mass would be one gram (1 g).

10 Is the gram a small or large unit of measurement? Explain your thinking.

____

Convert Mass

You can use a table or a double number line to convert units of mass.

11 Complete the table.

Grams	Milligrams
4	4 × 1,000 = 4,000
8	___ × 1,000 = ______
12	12 × ______ = ______
15	__________ = ______

12 Label the double number line to show how kilograms (kg) and grams (g) are related.

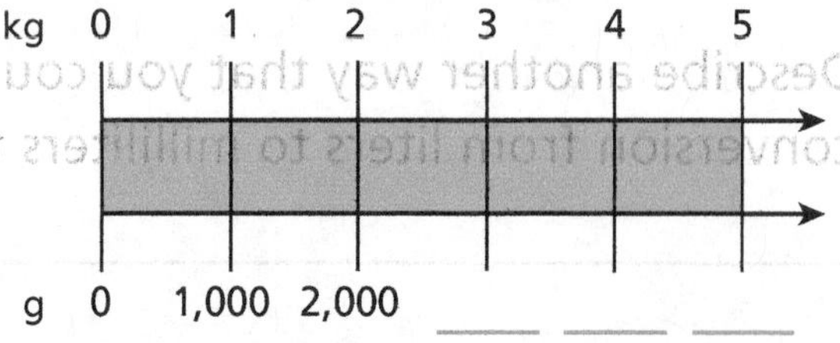
kg 0 1 2 3 4 5
g 0 1,000 2,000 ____ ____ ____

Name ______________________

Practice Converting Metric Units

Solve.

13 Martin measured the mass in grams of four different objects and recorded the information in the table below. Complete the table to find the mass of each object in milligrams.

Grams	Milligrams
4	4,000
7	
11	
15	

14 Olivia bought four different-sized containers and filled them each with water. She recorded the liquid volume of each container in liters below. Complete the table to find the liquid volume of each container in centiliters.

Liters	Centiliters
1	
3	
4	400
6	

15 Hayden has a crayon with a mass of 8 grams. Complete the double number line to find the mass of the crayon in centigrams.

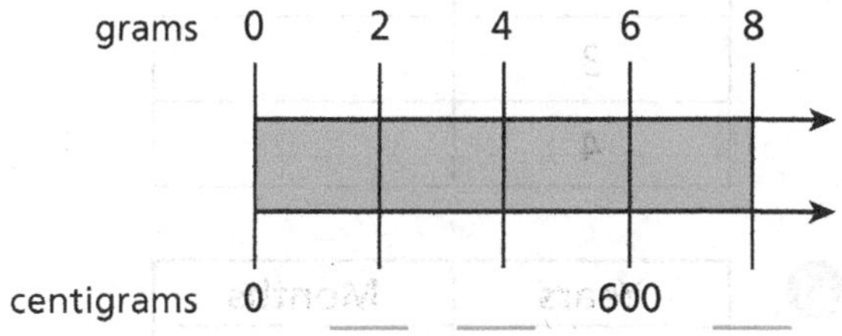
grams
0
2
4
6
8
centigrams
0
600

16 Jennifer buys a 2-liter bottle of apple juice and a 3-liter bottle of orange juice at the market. How many deciliters of juice does Jennifer buy in all?

____

17 Elena has a cat with a mass of 4 kilograms. Ginger's dog has a mass that is 2 times as much as Elena's cat. What is the mass of Ginger's dog in grams?

____

Check Understanding

Draw and label a double number line to show the relationship between liters and kiloliters. Include whole numbers from 0 to 10 to represent kiloliters.

Name ______________________________

Basic Units of Time

Complete the table.

Units of Time	
1 1 minute = _____ seconds	5 1 year = _____ days
2 1 hour = _____ minutes	6 1 year = _____ weeks
3 1 day = _____ hours	7 1 year = _____ months
4 1 week = _____ days	8 1 leap year = _____ days

Convert Units of Time

Complete the table.

9

Days	Hours
1	24
2	
3	
4	

10

Hours	Minutes
1	60
3	
5	
7	

11

Years	Months
3	36
6	
9	
12	

12

Hours	Seconds
1	3,600
2	
3	
4	

Solve.

13 36 minutes = _________ seconds

14 41 days = _________ hours

15 72 hours = _________ minutes

16 16 weeks = _________ days

17 6 years = _______ days

18 2 weeks = _________ hours

Name ______________________________

VOCABULARY
line plot

Make a Line Plot

A **line plot** displays data above a number line. Jamal asked his classmates about the time they spend reading. He organized the data in a table.

19 Use the table to complete the line plot.

Time Spent Reading	Number of Students
0 hours	0
$\frac{1}{4}$ hour	2
$\frac{1}{2}$ hour	5
$\frac{3}{4}$ hour	4
1 hour	4

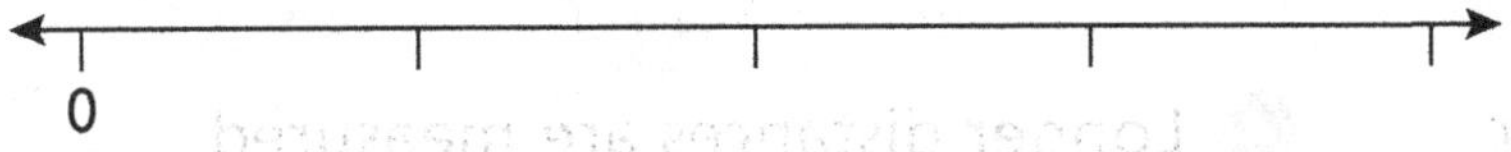
0

Time Spent Reading Each Night (in hours)

20 How many classmates did Jamal ask about time spent reading? ______

21 What amount of time had the most responses? ______

Practice

Solve.

22 Fiona asked her friends how much time they spend using a computer at home each night. Use the information in the table at right to make a line plot.

Time Spent on Computer	Number of Students
0 hours	4
$\frac{1}{4}$ hour	4
$\frac{1}{2}$ hour	7
$\frac{3}{4}$ hour	3
1 hour	9

23 Marissa wants to know how many minutes she has practiced the piano. Label the double number line to show how hours and minutes are related. How many minutes has she practiced if she practiced for 4 hours?

____

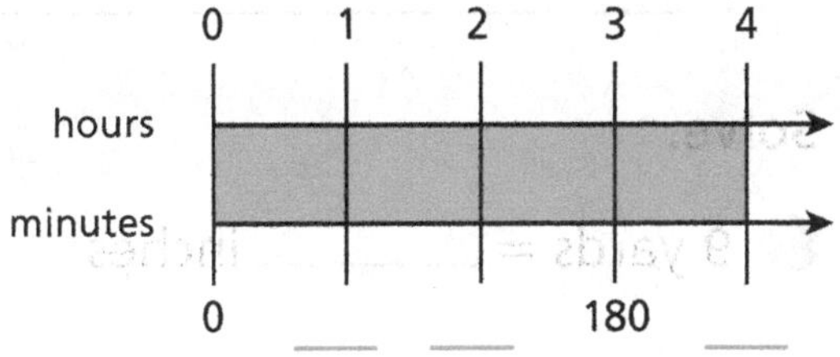
0
1
2
3
4
hours
minutes
0
180

Name ______________________________

VOCABULARY
inch yard
foot mile

Units of Length

1. This line segment is 1 **inch** long. Name an object that is about 1 inch long.

____

2. One **foot** is equal to 12 inches. Name an object that is about 1 foot long.

____

3. One **yard** is equal to 3 feet or 36 inches. Name an object that is about 1 yard long.

____

4. Longer distances are measured in miles. One **mile** is equal to 5,280 feet or 1,760 yards. Name a distance that is about 1 mile long.

____

Convert Customary Units of Length

5. Complete the table.

Feet	Inches
1	12
2	
3	
4	
5	

6. Complete the table.

Yards	Feet
2	6
4	
6	
8	
10	

Solve.

7. 9 yards = ________ inches

8. 26 feet = ________ inches

9. 4 miles = ________ feet

10. 2 miles = ________ yards

Name ______________________

Measure Length

Write the measurement of each line segment to the nearest $\frac{1}{8}$ inch.

11
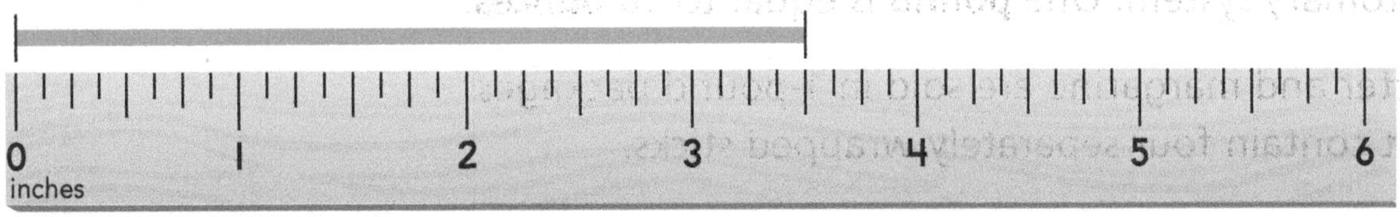
0
1
2
3
4
5
6
inches

12
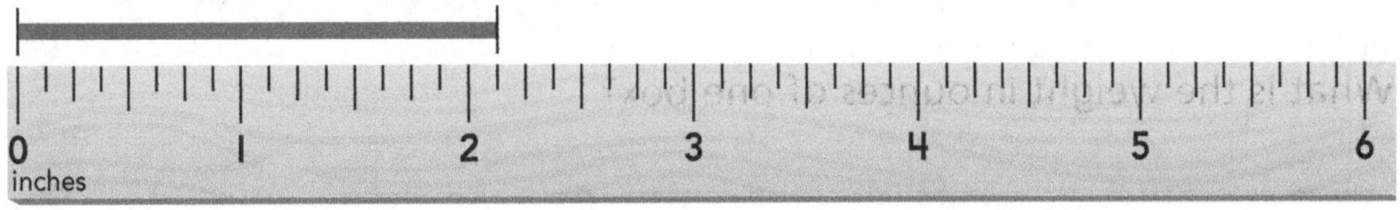
0
1
2
3
4
5
6
inches

13
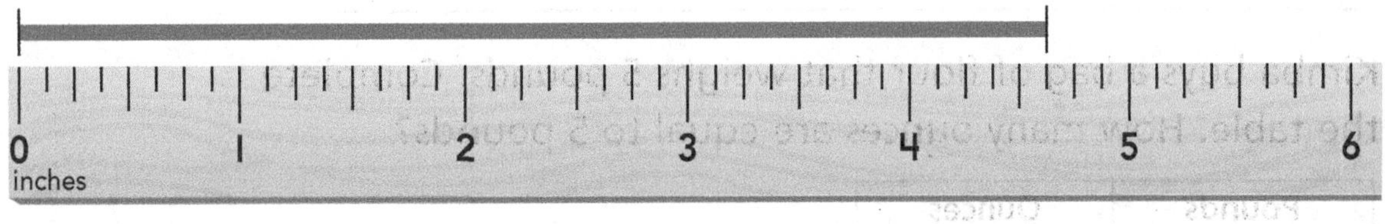
0
1
2
3
4
5
6
inches

14
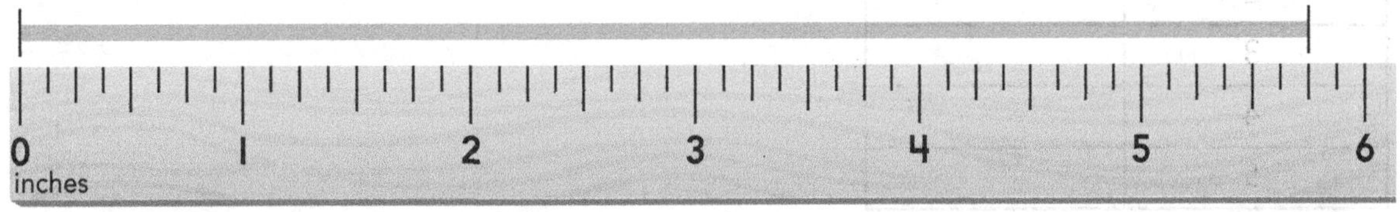
0
1
2
3
4
5
6
inches

15
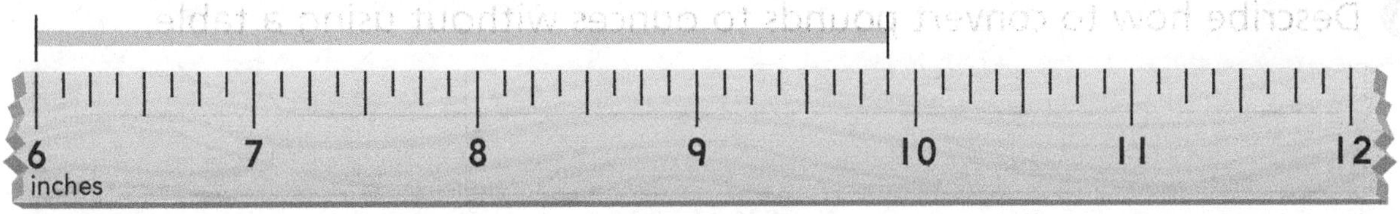
6
7
8
9
10
11
12
inches

Check Understanding

Explain how to convert a larger unit of length to a smaller unit of length using customary units. Give an example.

Name ______________________________

Pounds and Ounces

VOCABULARY
pound
ounce

The pound is the primary unit of weight in our customary system. One **pound** is equal to 16 **ounces**.

Butter and margarine are sold in 1-pound packages that contain four separately wrapped sticks.

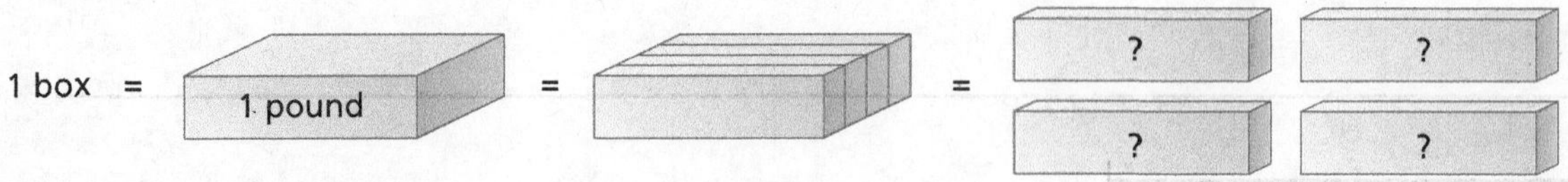
1 box =
1 pound
=
=
?
?
?
?

1 What is the weight in ounces of one box?

____

2 What is the weight in ounces of one stick?

____

3 Kimba buys a bag of flour that weighs 5 pounds. Complete the table. How many ounces are equal to 5 pounds?

Pounds	Ounces
1	16
2	
3	
4	
5	

____

4 Describe how to convert pounds to ounces without using a table.

____

____

5 When Martin weighed his dog in April, the dog weighed 384 ounces. When he weighed the dog in August, the dog weighed 432 ounces. How many ounces did Martin's dog gain between April and August?

____

Name ______________________

Liquid Volume

VOCABULARY
cup
pint
fluid ounce
gallon
quart

In the customary system, the primary unit of liquid volume is a **cup**.

1 cup 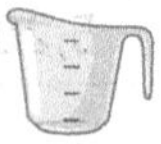 = 8 **fluid ounces**

2 cups 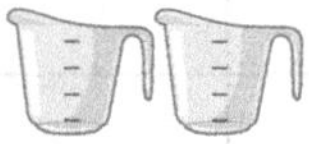 = 1 **pint**

4 cups 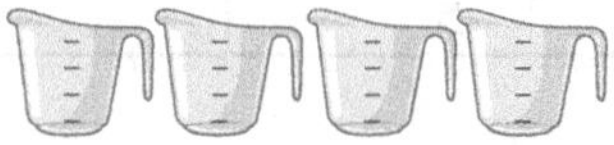 = 1 **quart**

4 quarts = 1 **gallon**

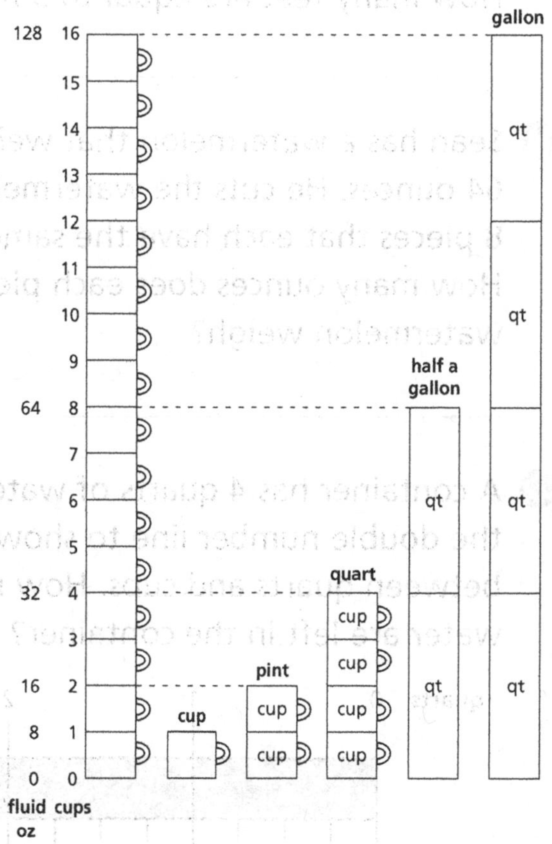
gallon
128
16
15
14
13
12
11
10
9
64
8
7
6
5
32
4
3
16
2
8
1
0
0
fluid oz
cups
half a gallon
quart
pint
cup
qt
qt
qt
qt
qt
qt
cup
cup
cup
cup
cup
cup
cup

15 Complete the table.

Quarts	Fluid Ounces
1	32
2	
3	
4	
5	
6	

16 Label the double number line to show how gallons (gal) and cups (c) are related.

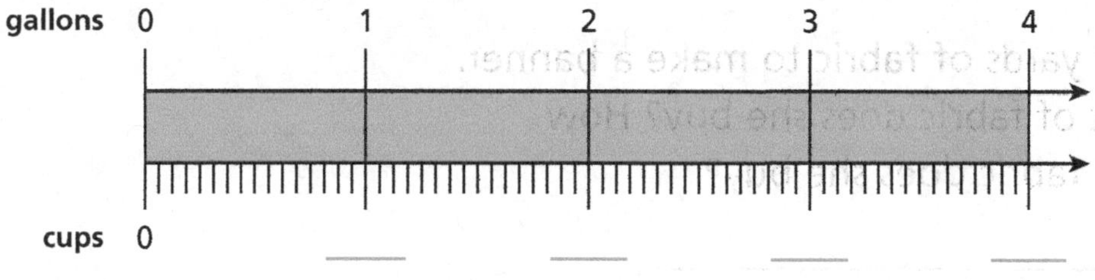
gallons
0
1
2
3
4
cups
0

Solve.

17 3 qt = ______ c

18 10 c = ______ fl oz

19 2 gal = ______ pt

Name ____________________

Solve Real World Problems

Solve.

20 A race is 5 miles long. Complete the table. How many feet are equal to 5 miles?

Miles	Feet
1	5,280
2	
3	
4	
5	

____

21 Sean has a watermelon that weighs 64 ounces. He cuts the watermelon into 8 pieces that each have the same weight. How many ounces does each piece of watermelon weigh?

Show your work.

____

22 A container has 4 quarts of water left in it. Complete the double number line to show the relationship between quarts and cups. How many cups of water are left in the container?

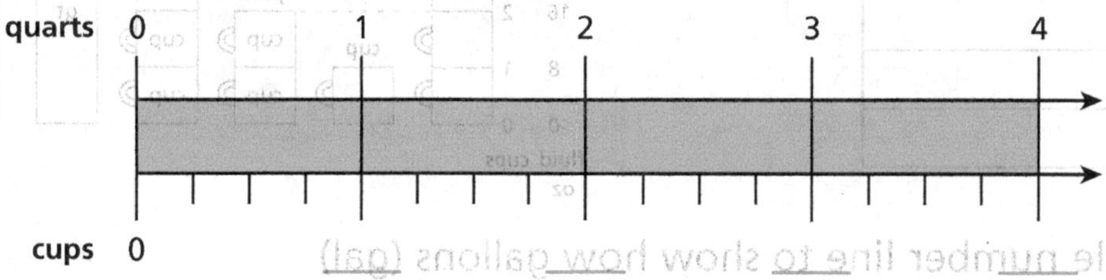
quarts
0
1
2
3
4
cups
0

____

23 Melinda buys 2 yards of fabric to make a banner. How many feet of fabric does she buy? How many inches of fabric does she buy?

____

Check Understanding

When converting from a larger unit of measure to a smaller unit, which operation do you use?

____

Unit 5
Quick Quiz 1

Name ______________________________

Convert.

1. 9 m = ________ cm

2. 5 L = ________ mL

Solve.

Show your work.

3. Brianna started mowing the lawn at 1:40 P.M. She mowed for 55 minutes. At what time did Brianna stop mowing the lawn?

____

4. Sam cut a 28-foot rope into 4 equal pieces. How long is each piece of rope in inches?

____

5. Sadie drew a double number line to find the number of fluid ounces in 4 cups. What numbers for fluid ounces will complete the labels?

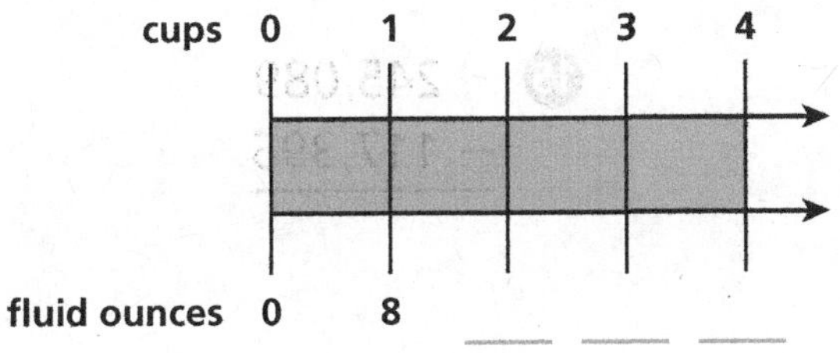

cups 0 1 2 3 4
fluid ounces 0 8 ___ ___ ___

Fluency Check 15

Name ____________________

PATH to FLUENCY

Add or subtract.

1. $\begin{array}{r} 146 \\ +\ 313 \\ \hline \end{array}$

2. $\begin{array}{r} 65{,}783 \\ +\ 37{,}149 \\ \hline \end{array}$

3. $\begin{array}{r} 3{,}908 \\ +\ 281 \\ \hline \end{array}$

4. $\begin{array}{r} 751 \\ -\ 340 \\ \hline \end{array}$

5. $\begin{array}{r} 18{,}934 \\ +\ 7{,}225 \\ \hline \end{array}$

6. $\begin{array}{r} 589{,}831 \\ +\ 46{,}230 \\ \hline \end{array}$

7. $\begin{array}{r} 3{,}792 \\ +\ 1{,}436 \\ \hline \end{array}$

8. $\begin{array}{r} 70{,}409 \\ -\ 7{,}382 \\ \hline \end{array}$

9. $\begin{array}{r} 463 \\ +\ 572 \\ \hline \end{array}$

10. $\begin{array}{r} 7{,}833 \\ -\ 6{,}312 \\ \hline \end{array}$

11. $\begin{array}{r} 67{,}492 \\ -\ 28{,}561 \\ \hline \end{array}$

12. $\begin{array}{r} 417 \\ -\ 332 \\ \hline \end{array}$

13. $\begin{array}{r} 954{,}612 \\ -\ 47{,}831 \\ \hline \end{array}$

14. $\begin{array}{r} 5{,}067 \\ -\ 3{,}543 \\ \hline \end{array}$

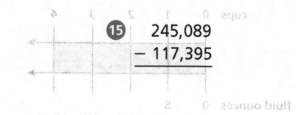

15. $\begin{array}{r} 245{,}089 \\ -\ 117{,}395 \\ \hline \end{array}$

Name ______________________________

Perimeter and Area of Complex Figures (continued)

Find the perimeter of each figure. Then divide each figure into rectangles and find the area. In these drawings, the side of each square unit represents 1 yard.

30
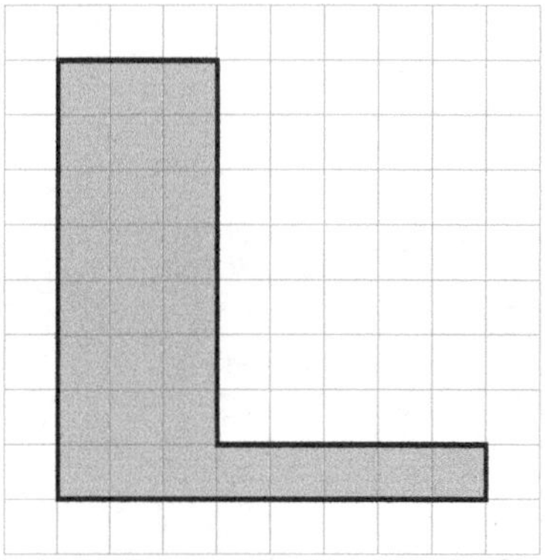

Perimeter: ______________________

Area: ______________________

31
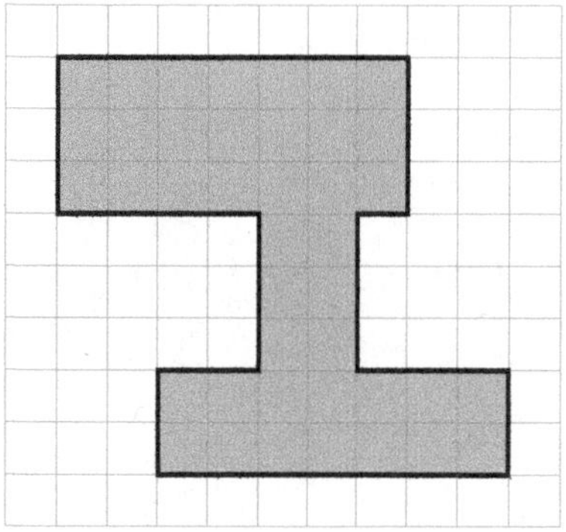

Perimeter: ______________________

Area: ______________________

32
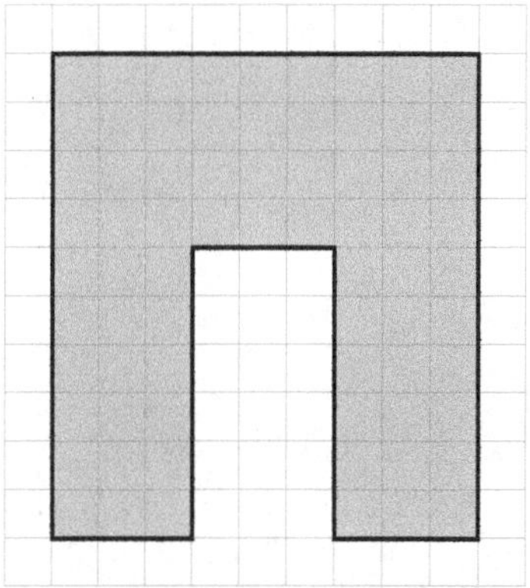

Perimeter: ______________________

Area: ______________________

33
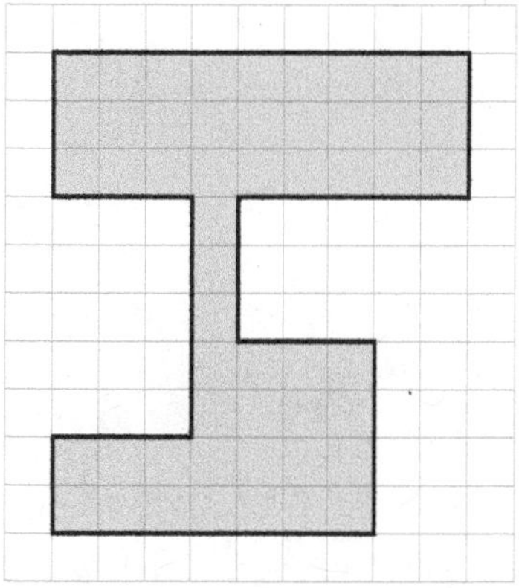

Perimeter: ______________________

Area: ______________________

34 Explain why you divided the figure in Exercise 30 the way you did.

____

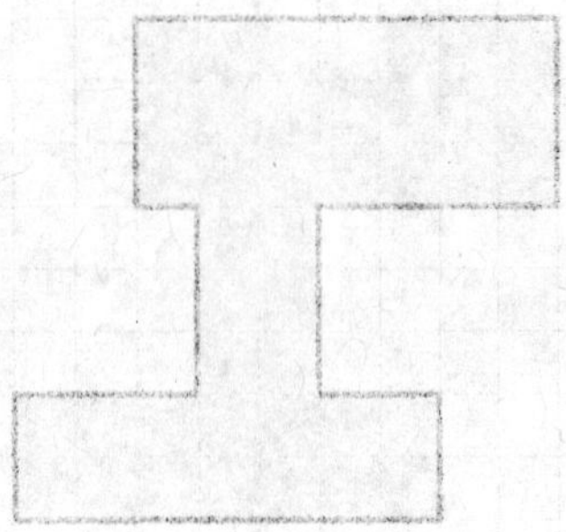

Unit 5
Quick Quiz 2

Name ______________________

Solve.

Show your work.

1. The drawing shows the plan for a path. What is the area of the path?

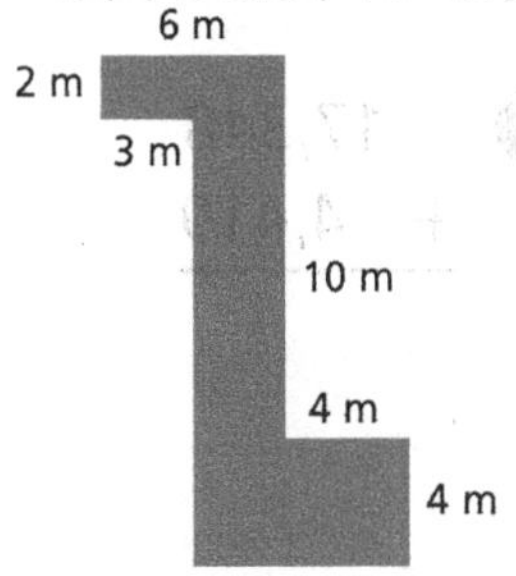
6 m
2 m
3 m
10 m
4 m
4 m

____

2. Hayden put 2 cups of lemon juice and 5 times as much water into a jar to make a jar of lemonade. How many fluid ounces of lemonade were in the jar?

____

3. Jasmine bought a 4-kilogram block of modeling clay. She wants to divide it into 8 equal blocks. What will be the mass of each block in grams?

____

4. The perimeter of the rectangle is 40 meters. What is the length of one of the long sides?

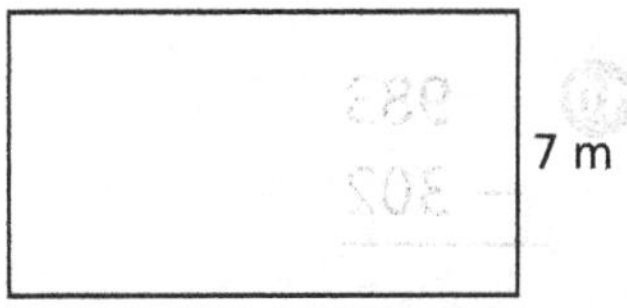
7 m

____

____

5. A crew is paving the parking lot shown in the diagram. They will pave it in two stages.

The total area of the parking lot is 207 square yards. What is the length of one of the long sides of the parking lot?

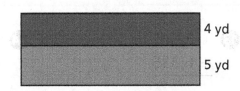
4 yd
5 yd

____

Fluency Check 16

Name ____________________

PATH to FLUENCY

Add or subtract.

1. 17,348 + 4,419

2. 817 − 736

3. 29,713 − 1,882

4. 4,385 − 2,241

5. 9,405 + 793

6. 40,219 − 34,477

7. 384 + 614

8. 4,970 − 3,548

9. 612,498 − 61,579

10. 983 − 302

11. 990,054 − 247,175

12. 32,184 + 68,472

13. 7,569 + 6,335

14. 519,045 + 453,788

15. 578 + 333

Name ____________________

1. A photograph is 8 centimeters wide. After Kari enlarges the photograph, it is 3 times as wide as the original. How wide is the new photograph in millimeters?

_______ millimeters

2. Describe the relationship between these units of time: hours, minutes, and seconds.

3. Complete the table that relates meters and centimeters.

Meters	Centimeters
1	______
2	______
3	300
4	______

4. What is the area of the rectangle?

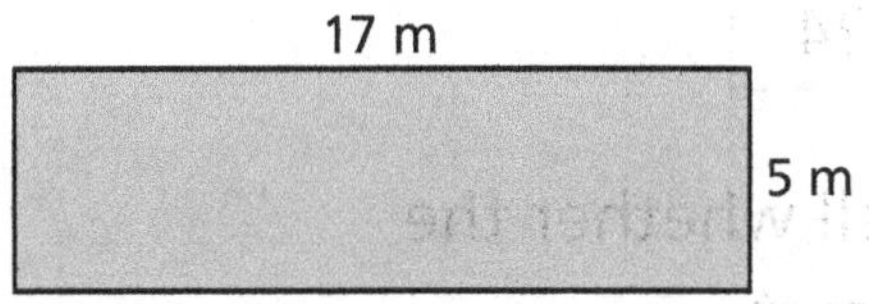
17 m
5 m

_______ square meters

5. Classify the conversion below as using $\times$ 10, $\times$ 100, or $\times$ 1,000. Write the letter of the conversion in the correct box.

A kilograms to grams
B meters to centimeters
C deciliters to centiliters
D hectograms to decagrams
E liters to milliliters
F decameters to decimeters

$\times$ 10	$\times$ 100	$\times$ 1,000

Name ______________________

6 The drawing shows plans for a sandbox. Find the perimeter and area of the sandbox if the side of each square unit represents 1 foot.

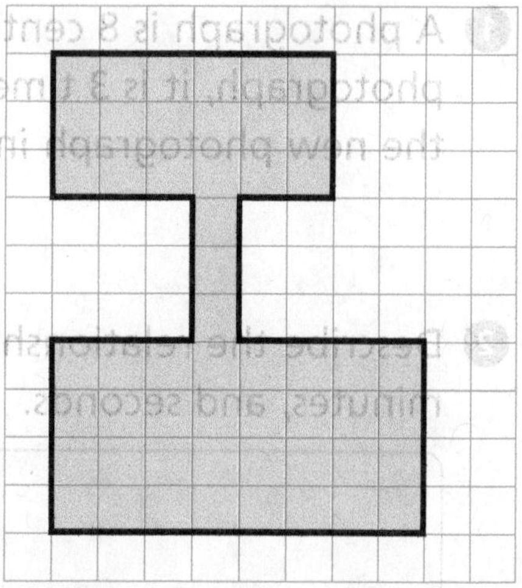

Perimeter: ______________

Area: ______________

7 For Exercises 7a and 7b, complete the conversion. Then choose the operation and complete the equation to show how you found your answer.

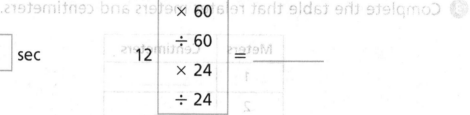

7a. 12 min = ☐ sec

12 [× 60 / ÷ 60 / × 24 / ÷ 24] = ______

7b. 96 hours = ☐ days

96 [× 60 / ÷ 60 / × 24 / ÷ 24] = ______

8 For Exercises 8a–8d, choose Yes or No to tell whether the conversion between the metric units is correct.

8a. Divide by 100 to convert kiloliters to decaliters. ○ Yes ○ No

8b. Multiply by 10 to convert milligrams to centigrams. ○ Yes ○ No

8c. Divide by 1,000 to convert grams to kilograms. ○ Yes ○ No

8d. Divide by 10 to convert kilometers to hectometers. ○ Yes ○ No

Name ______________________________

9 Find the perimeter and area of the rectangle.

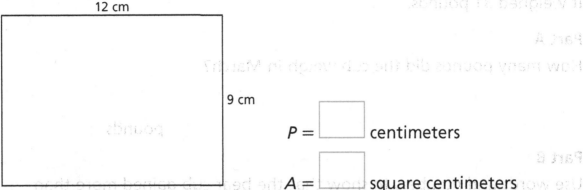

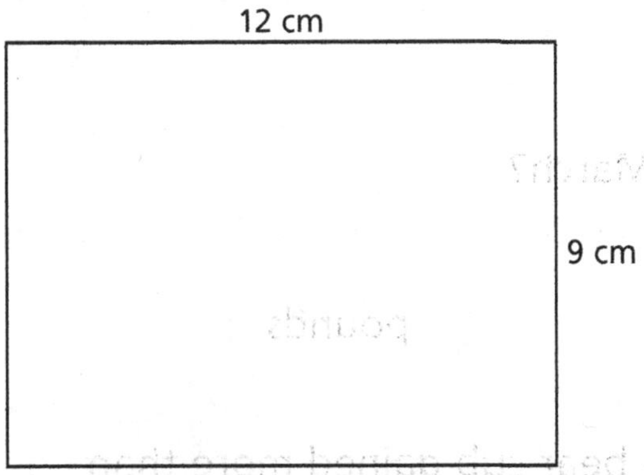
12 cm
9 cm

$P =$ ☐ centimeters

$A =$ ☐ square centimeters

10 Draw a line to match equivalent measurements.

48 inches	9 tons	24 cups	18 pounds
18,000 pounds	288 ounces	4 feet	192 fluid ounces

11 During a speech, a motivational speaker says, "There are 1,440 seconds in each day. How will you spend yours?" Do you agree or disagree with the speaker? Explain your reasoning using words and numbers.

Name ______________________________

12 A bear cub weighed 64 ounces in March. After three months, it weighed 31 pounds.

Part A

How many pounds did the cub weigh in March?

_____ pounds

Part B

Use words and numbers to show that the bear cub gained more than 25 pounds after three months.

13 Jill asked her classmates how many hours of sleep they got last night. She displayed the data in the line plot shown. How many classmates did Jill ask about the time spent sleeping?

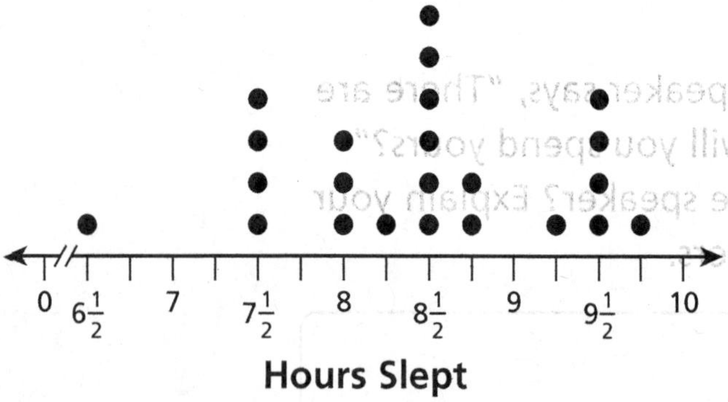
0
$6\frac{1}{2}$
7
$7\frac{1}{2}$
8
$8\frac{1}{2}$
9
$9\frac{1}{2}$
10
Hours Slept

Jill asked ☐ classmates.

14 Which mass is equivalent to 55 decagrams? Mark all that apply.

Ⓐ 55 kilograms

Ⓑ 550 grams

Ⓒ 5,500 centigrams

Ⓓ 5 hectograms

Ⓔ 550,000 milligrams

Ⓕ 55,000 decigrams

Name ______________________________

15 A rectangular scarf has an area of 192 square inches. The short sides of the scarf are each 6 inches long.

Part A

Use the labels from the list to complete the model. Labels can be used more than once.

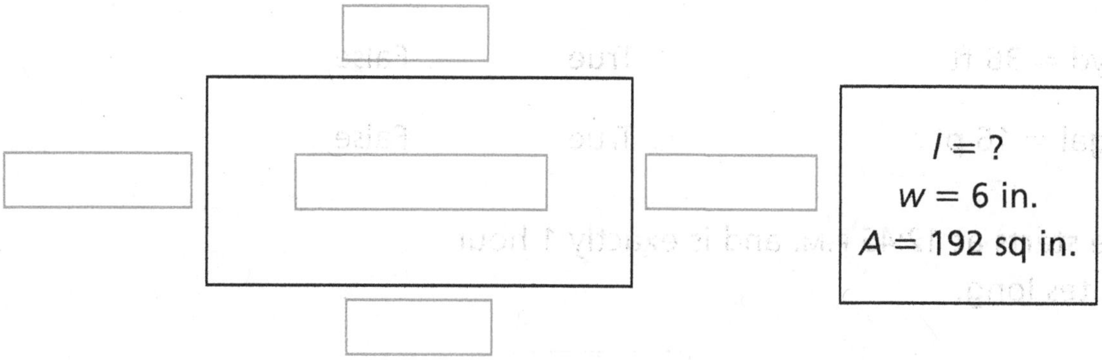
$l = ?$
$w = 6$ in.
$A = 192$ sq in.

Part B

What is the perimeter of the scarf? Show your work.

16 A rectangular cafeteria tray measures 18 inches on the long sides. It measures 12 inches on the short sides. What is the perimeter of the tray?

______ inches

17 A bag of rice has a mass of 3 kilograms. Jackie buys 17 bags of rice for the school cafeteria. How many grams of rice did Jackie buy? Explain how you solved this problem.

Name ______________________________

18 For Exercises 18a–18e, choose True or False for the conversion.

18a. 8 ft = 96 in. ○ True ○ False

18b. 9 lb = 72 oz ○ True ○ False

18c. 8 pt = 4 qt ○ True ○ False

18d. 3 yd = 36 ft ○ True ○ False

18e. 4 gal = 16 pt ○ True ○ False

19 A movie starts at 12:45 P.M. and is exactly 1 hour 35 minutes long.

Part A
What time does the movie end? ☐

Part B
It takes Lynn 25 minutes to get to the movie theater. She wants to meet her friends at the theater at least 15 minutes before the movie starts. What is the latest time Lynn can leave her house? Explain how you found your answer.

20 Choose a number from the first column and a unit from the second column to make a measurement that is equivalent to 2 meters.

Number	Unit
○ 100	○ decimeters
○ 20,000	○ centimeters
○ 200	○ millimeters

Name

Patio Design Plans

Gio wants to build a fenced rectangular patio. He has a box of 36 one-foot by one-foot slate tiles.

1. List all the possible rectangular floor designs (length × width) using only whole tiles. Which floor designs do not make sense for this problem? Explain.

2. Find the perimeter for each floor plan. Why do some floor plans have the same perimeter?

3. Gio wants to include a fence around the patio. He needs to keep the cost under $200. He is interested in two kinds of fence. One kind costs $7 per foot and the other costs $9 per foot. Which floor plans could he choose? Identify the least expensive choice.

Name ____________________

4 Gio decides to use the floor plan that is 9 feet by 4 feet. He wants to put a rectangular table that is 48 inches long and 36 inches wide on the patio. Also, on one end of the patio, he wants to put a flower box that is 24 inches long and 12 inches wide. How much floor area will the table and the flower box cover? How much open area will remain for use on the patio? Explain how you solved the problem.

5 Suppose Gio changes his mind and decides the patio can be a combination of rectangular areas, such as an L-shape, instead of a single rectangular shape. Draw and label a diagram of the new design. Be sure to use all of the tiles. What is the perimeter of the patio you drew?

6 Gio estimates it will take about 15 minutes per tile to lay the 36 tiles. How many hours will it take him to build the patio? If he starts at 9:00 A.M. and takes a one-hour break at 12:00 noon, what time will he finish the patio? Show your work.

Dear Family:

Your child has experience with fractions through measurements and in previous grades. Unit 6 of *Math Expressions* builds on this experience. The main goals of this unit are to:

- understand the meaning of fractions.
- compare unit fractions.
- add and subtract fractions and mixed numbers with like denominators.
- multiply a fraction by a whole number.

Your child will use fraction bars and fraction strips to gain a visual and conceptual understanding of fractions as parts of a whole. Later, your child will use these models to add and subtract fractions and to convert between fractions equal to or greater than 1 and mixed numbers.

Examples of Fraction Bar Modeling:

Fraction Comparisons

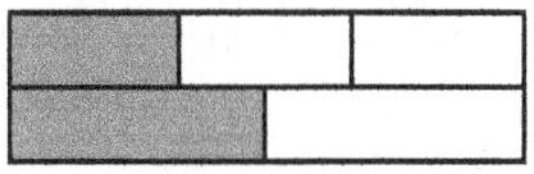

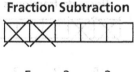

$\frac{1}{3} < \frac{1}{2}$

Fraction Subtraction

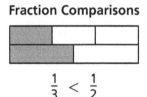

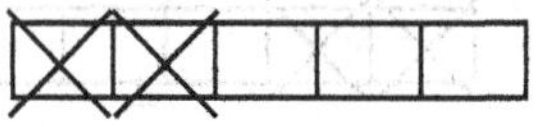

$\frac{5}{5} - \frac{2}{5} = \frac{3}{5}$

Your child will apply this knowledge about fractions and fraction operations to solve real world problems.

If you have questions or problems, please contact me.

Sincerely,
Your child's teacher

Estimada familia:

Su niño ha usado fracciones al hacer mediciones y en los grados previos. La Unidad 6 de *Math Expressions* amplía esta experiencia. Los objetivos principales de la unidad son:

- comprender el significado de las fracciones.
- comparar fracciones unitarias.
- sumar y restar fracciones y números mixtos con denominadores iguales.
- multiplicar una fracción por un número entero.

Su niño usará barras y tiras de fracciones para comprender y visualizar el concepto de las fracciones como partes de un entero. Luego, usará estos modelos para sumar y restar fracciones y para convertir fracciones igual a o mayor que 1 y números mixtos.

Ejemplos de modelos con barras de fracciones:

Comparaciones de fracciones

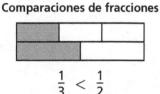

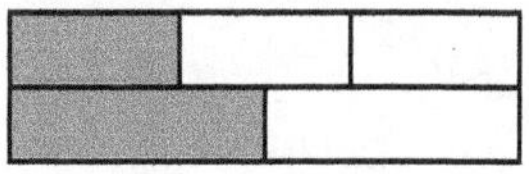

$\frac{1}{3} < \frac{1}{2}$

Resta de fracciones

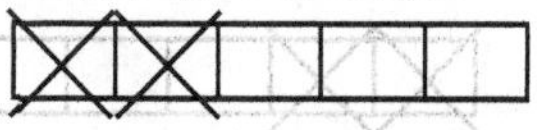

$\frac{5}{5} - \frac{2}{5} = \frac{3}{5}$

Su niño aplicará este conocimiento de las fracciones y operaciones con fracciones para resolver problemas cotidianos.

Si tiene alguna duda o algún comentario, por favor comuníquese conmigo.

Atentamente,
El maestro de su niño

denominator

numerator

fraction

unit fraction

mixed number

The number above the bar in a fraction. It shows the number of equal parts.

Example:

$\frac{3}{4}$ ← numerator $\quad \frac{3}{4} = \frac{1}{4} + \frac{1}{4} + \frac{1}{4}$

The number below the bar in a fraction. It shows the total number of equal parts in the whole.

Example:

$\frac{3}{4}$ ← denominator

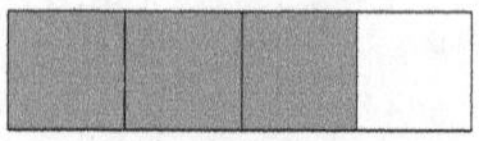

A fraction whose numerator is 1. It shows one equal part of a whole.

Example:

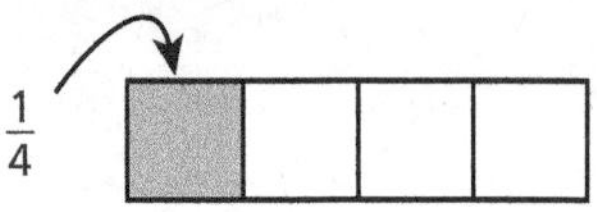
1/4

A number that is the sum of unit fractions, each an equal part of a set or part of a whole.

Example:

$\frac{3}{4} = \frac{1}{4} + \frac{1}{4} + \frac{1}{4}$

$\frac{5}{4} = \frac{1}{4} + \frac{1}{4} + \frac{1}{4} + \frac{1}{4} + \frac{1}{4}$

A number that can be represented by a whole number and a fraction.

Example:

$4\frac{1}{2} = 4 + \frac{1}{2}$

Name ________________________________

Sums of Unit Fractions

Shade the fraction bar to show each fraction. Then write the fraction as a sum of unit fractions and as a product of a whole number and a unit fraction. The first one is done for you.

9 $\frac{3}{4} = \frac{1}{4} + \frac{1}{4} + \frac{1}{4} = 3 \times \frac{1}{4}$

$\frac{1}{4}$	$\frac{1}{4}$	$\frac{1}{4}$	$\frac{1}{4}$

10 $\frac{3}{8}$ = __________ = ________

$\frac{1}{8}$	$\frac{1}{8}$	$\frac{1}{8}$	$\frac{1}{8}$	$\frac{1}{8}$	$\frac{1}{8}$	$\frac{1}{8}$	$\frac{1}{8}$

11 $\frac{5}{5}$ = ____________________ = ________

$\frac{1}{5}$	$\frac{1}{5}$	$\frac{1}{5}$	$\frac{1}{5}$	$\frac{1}{5}$

12 $\frac{2}{12}$ = ________ = ________

$\frac{1}{12}$	$\frac{1}{12}$	$\frac{1}{12}$	$\frac{1}{12}$	$\frac{1}{12}$	$\frac{1}{12}$	$\frac{1}{12}$	$\frac{1}{12}$	$\frac{1}{12}$	$\frac{1}{12}$	$\frac{1}{12}$	$\frac{1}{12}$

13 $\frac{4}{7}$ = ______________ = ________

$\frac{1}{7}$	$\frac{1}{7}$	$\frac{1}{7}$	$\frac{1}{7}$	$\frac{1}{7}$	$\frac{1}{7}$	$\frac{1}{7}$

14 $\frac{7}{9}$ = ________________________________ = ________

$\frac{1}{9}$	$\frac{1}{9}$	$\frac{1}{9}$	$\frac{1}{9}$	$\frac{1}{9}$	$\frac{1}{9}$	$\frac{1}{9}$	$\frac{1}{9}$	$\frac{1}{9}$

Name ______________________________

Fifths that Add to One

Every afternoon, student volunteers help the school librarian put returned books back on the shelves. The librarian puts the books in equal piles on a cart.

One day, Jean and Maria found 5 equal piles on the return cart. They knew there were different ways they could share the job of reshelving the books. They drew fraction bars to help them find all the possibilities.

1 On each fifths bar, circle two groups of fifths to show one way Jean and Maria could share the work. (Each bar should show a different possibility.) Then complete the equation next to each bar to show their shares.

1 whole = all of the books

1 whole = Jean's share + Maria's share

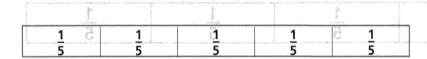

$\frac{1}{5}$	$\frac{1}{5}$	$\frac{1}{5}$	$\frac{1}{5}$	$\frac{1}{5}$

$\frac{5}{5} = \frac{\square}{5} + \frac{\square}{5}$

$\frac{1}{5}$	$\frac{1}{5}$	$\frac{1}{5}$	$\frac{1}{5}$	$\frac{1}{5}$

$\frac{5}{5} = \frac{\square}{5} + \frac{\square}{5}$

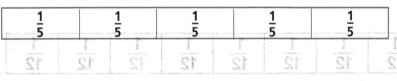

$\frac{1}{5}$	$\frac{1}{5}$	$\frac{1}{5}$	$\frac{1}{5}$	$\frac{1}{5}$

$\frac{5}{5} = \frac{\square}{5} + \frac{\square}{5}$

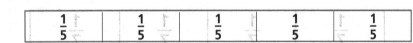

$\frac{1}{5}$	$\frac{1}{5}$	$\frac{1}{5}$	$\frac{1}{5}$	$\frac{1}{5}$

$\frac{5}{5} = \frac{\square}{5} + \frac{\square}{5}$

Name ______________________________

Sixths that Add to One

The librarian put 6 equal piles of returned books on the cart for Liu and Henry to reshelve. They also drew fraction bars.

2 On each sixths bar, circle two groups of sixths to show one way that Liu and Henry could share the work. (Each bar should show a different possibility.) Then complete the equation next to each bar to show their shares.

1 whole = all of the books						1 whole		Liu's share		Henry's share
$\frac{1}{6}$	$\frac{1}{6}$	$\frac{1}{6}$	$\frac{1}{6}$	$\frac{1}{6}$	$\frac{1}{6}$	$\frac{6}{6}$	=	$\frac{\underline{\quad}}{6}$	+	$\frac{\underline{\quad}}{6}$
$\frac{1}{6}$	$\frac{1}{6}$	$\frac{1}{6}$	$\frac{1}{6}$	$\frac{1}{6}$	$\frac{1}{6}$	$\frac{6}{6}$	=	$\frac{\underline{\quad}}{6}$	+	$\frac{\underline{\quad}}{6}$
$\frac{1}{6}$	$\frac{1}{6}$	$\frac{1}{6}$	$\frac{1}{6}$	$\frac{1}{6}$	$\frac{1}{6}$	$\frac{6}{6}$	=	$\frac{\underline{\quad}}{6}$	+	$\frac{\underline{\quad}}{6}$
$\frac{1}{6}$	$\frac{1}{6}$	$\frac{1}{6}$	$\frac{1}{6}$	$\frac{1}{6}$	$\frac{1}{6}$	$\frac{6}{6}$	=	$\frac{\underline{\quad}}{6}$	+	$\frac{\underline{\quad}}{6}$
$\frac{1}{6}$	$\frac{1}{6}$	$\frac{1}{6}$	$\frac{1}{6}$	$\frac{1}{6}$	$\frac{1}{6}$	$\frac{6}{6}$	=	$\frac{\underline{\quad}}{6}$	+	$\frac{\underline{\quad}}{6}$

Find the Unknown Addend

Write the fraction that will complete each equation.

3 $1 = \frac{7}{7} = \frac{1}{7} +$ ________

4 $1 = \frac{4}{4} = \frac{3}{4} +$ ________

5 $1 = \frac{8}{8} = \frac{3}{8} +$ ________

6 $1 = \frac{5}{5} = \frac{2}{5} +$ ________

7 $1 = \frac{3}{3} = \frac{2}{3} +$ ________

8 $1 = \frac{10}{10} = \frac{6}{10} +$ ________

9 $1 = \frac{6}{6} = \frac{2}{6} +$ ________

10 $1 = \frac{8}{8} = \frac{5}{8} +$ ________

Name ______________________

Compare and Order Unit Fractions

Write the unit fractions in order from least to greatest.

18 $\frac{1}{6}, \frac{1}{8}, \frac{1}{5}$

19 $\frac{1}{11}, \frac{1}{4}, \frac{1}{8}$

20 $\frac{1}{3}, \frac{1}{10}, \frac{1}{7}$

Solve.

21 Andi and Paolo both ordered small pizzas. Andi ate $\frac{1}{4}$ of her pizza. Paolo ate $\frac{1}{6}$ of his pizza. Who ate more pizza?

22 Elena ordered a small pizza. Max ordered a large pizza. Elena ate $\frac{1}{3}$ of her pizza. Max ate $\frac{1}{4}$ of his pizza. Elena said she ate more pizza because $\frac{1}{3} > \frac{1}{4}$. Do you agree? Explain.

What's the Error?

Dear Math Students,

I had to compare $\frac{1}{4}$ and $\frac{1}{2}$ on my math homework. I reasoned that $\frac{1}{4}$ is greater than $\frac{1}{2}$ because 4 is greater than 2. My friend told me this isn't right. Can you help me understand why my reasoning is wrong?

Your friend,
Puzzled Penguin

?

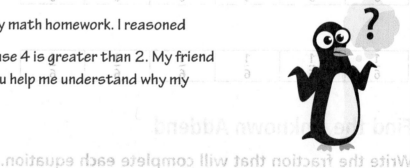

23 Write a response to Puzzled Penguin.

Check Understanding

Explain how to find pairs of fractions that have a sum of $\frac{5}{5}$.

Name ______________________________

Add Fractions

The circled parts of this fraction bar show an addition problem.

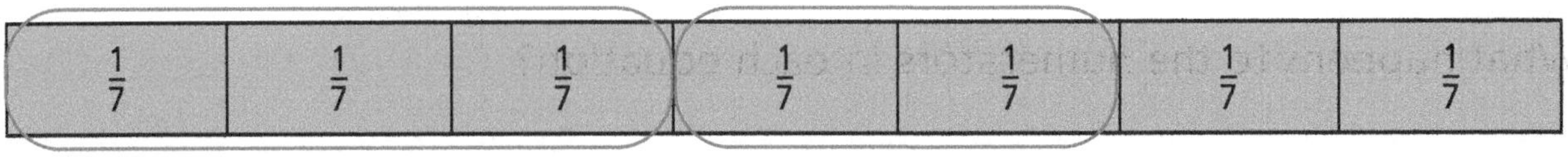
1/7
1/7
1/7
1/7
1/7
1/7
1/7

1 Complete this addition equation to match the problem above.

$\frac{}{7} + \frac{}{7} = \frac{ + }{7} = \frac{}{7}$

Write the numerators to complete each addition equation.

2 $\frac{3}{9} + \frac{4}{9} = \frac{ + }{9} = \frac{}{9}$ **3** $\frac{1}{5} + \frac{3}{5} = \frac{ + }{5} = \frac{}{5}$ **4** $\frac{2}{8} + \frac{5}{8} = \frac{ + }{8} = \frac{}{8}$

5 What happens to the numerators in each equation?

____

6 What happens to the denominators in each equation?

____

Subtract Fractions

The circled and crossed-out parts of this fraction bar show a subtraction problem.

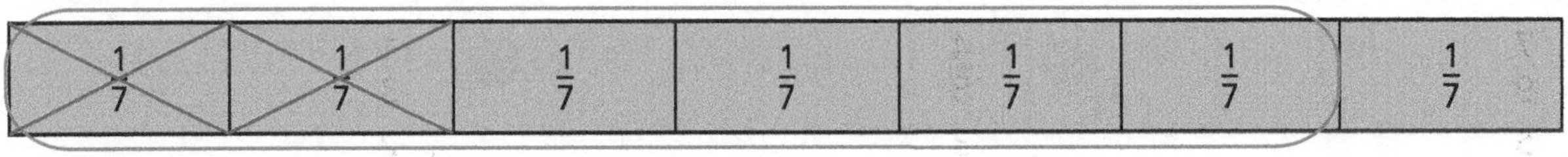
1/7
1/7
1/7
1/7
1/7
1/7
1/7

7 Write the numerators to complete the subtraction equation.

$\frac{}{7} - \frac{}{7} = \frac{ - }{7} = \frac{}{7}$

Name ____________________

Subtract Fractions (continued)

Write the numerators to complete each subtraction equation.

8 $\frac{5}{6} - \frac{4}{6} = \frac{\_ - \_}{6} = \frac{\_}{6}$

9 $\frac{9}{10} - \frac{5}{10} = \frac{\_ - \_}{10} = \_$

10 $\frac{14}{16} - \frac{9}{16} = \frac{\_ - \_}{16} = \_$

11 What happens to the numerators in each equation?

____

12 How is subtracting fractions with like denominators similar to adding fractions with like denominators?

____

____

Mixed Practice with Addition and Subtraction

Solve each problem. Include the "circled" step in Exercises 16–21.

13 $\frac{1}{4} + \frac{2}{4} = \frac{\_ + \_}{4} =$

14 $\frac{3}{9} + \frac{5}{9} = \frac{\_ + \_}{9} =$

15 $\frac{6}{6} - \frac{2}{6} = \frac{\_ - \_}{6} =$

16 $\frac{4}{10} + \frac{5}{10} =$

17 $\frac{2}{5} + \frac{4}{5} =$

18 $\frac{8}{12} - \frac{3}{12} =$

19 $\frac{5}{7} + \frac{2}{7} =$

20 $\frac{7}{11} - \frac{4}{11} =$

21 $\frac{8}{8} - \frac{5}{8} =$

Solve.

22 $\frac{7}{9} - \frac{5}{9}$

23 $\frac{4}{5} - \frac{3}{5}$

24 $\frac{1}{3} + \frac{2}{3}$

25 $\frac{2}{11} + \frac{7}{11}$

26 $\frac{5}{6} - \frac{1}{6}$

27 $\frac{1}{8} + \frac{1}{8}$

Name ____________________

Fraction Bars

one whole												$\frac{1}{1}$
$\frac{1}{2}$	$\frac{1}{2}$											$\frac{2}{2}$
$\frac{1}{3}$	$\frac{1}{3}$	$\frac{1}{3}$										$\frac{3}{3}$
$\frac{1}{4}$	$\frac{1}{4}$	$\frac{1}{4}$	$\frac{1}{4}$									$\frac{4}{4}$
$\frac{1}{5}$	$\frac{1}{5}$	$\frac{1}{5}$	$\frac{1}{5}$	$\frac{1}{5}$								$\frac{5}{5}$
$\frac{1}{6}$	$\frac{1}{6}$	$\frac{1}{6}$	$\frac{1}{6}$	$\frac{1}{6}$	$\frac{1}{6}$							$\frac{6}{6}$
$\frac{1}{7}$	$\frac{1}{7}$	$\frac{1}{7}$	$\frac{1}{7}$	$\frac{1}{7}$	$\frac{1}{7}$	$\frac{1}{7}$						$\frac{7}{7}$
$\frac{1}{8}$	$\frac{1}{8}$	$\frac{1}{8}$	$\frac{1}{8}$	$\frac{1}{8}$	$\frac{1}{8}$	$\frac{1}{8}$	$\frac{1}{8}$					$\frac{8}{8}$
$\frac{1}{9}$	$\frac{1}{9}$	$\frac{1}{9}$	$\frac{1}{9}$	$\frac{1}{9}$	$\frac{1}{9}$	$\frac{1}{9}$	$\frac{1}{9}$	$\frac{1}{9}$				$\frac{9}{9}$
$\frac{1}{10}$	$\frac{1}{10}$	$\frac{1}{10}$	$\frac{1}{10}$	$\frac{1}{10}$	$\frac{1}{10}$	$\frac{1}{10}$	$\frac{1}{10}$	$\frac{1}{10}$	$\frac{1}{10}$			$\frac{10}{10}$
$\frac{1}{12}$	$\frac{1}{12}$	$\frac{1}{12}$	$\frac{1}{12}$	$\frac{1}{12}$	$\frac{1}{12}$	$\frac{1}{12}$	$\frac{1}{12}$	$\frac{1}{12}$	$\frac{1}{12}$	$\frac{1}{12}$	$\frac{1}{12}$	$\frac{12}{12}$

Name ______________________

What's the Error?

Dear Math Students,

My friend said, "If you catch 3 fish and then 2 more fish, how many fish will you have?" Of course, I know I will have 5 fish! She said, "This is the same problem, but you have fifths instead of fish!"

Can you help me understand what my friend meant and help me find the right answer?

Your friend,
Puzzled Penguin

$\frac{3}{5} + \frac{2}{5} = \frac{5}{10}$

28 Write a response to Puzzled Penguin.

____

____

____

Dear Math Students,

My friend said my answer for this problem is wrong too.

She said, "Think about fish again. If you have 4 fish and then eat 3, how many will you have?" What does she mean? What should the answer be?

Your friend,
Puzzled Penguin

$\frac{4}{5} - \frac{3}{5} = \frac{1}{0}$

29 Write a response to Puzzled Penguin.

____

____

____

Unit 6
Quick Quiz 1

Name ______________________________

Complete.

1. $\frac{5}{5} = \frac{1}{5} +$ ________

2. $\frac{6}{6} = \frac{2}{6} +$ ________

3. Write the fraction as a sum of unit fractions and as a product of a whole number and a unit fraction.

   $\frac{7}{8} =$ ______________________________ $=$ ______

Solve.

4. $\frac{3}{5} + \frac{1}{5} =$ ________

5. $\frac{7}{8} - \frac{2}{8} =$ ________

Fluency Check 17

Name ____________________

PATH to FLUENCY

Add or subtract.

1. $\begin{array}{r} 246 \\ +\ 313 \\ \hline \end{array}$

2. $\begin{array}{r} 487 \\ -\ 378 \\ \hline \end{array}$

3. $\begin{array}{r} 5{,}824 \\ +\ 1{,}355 \\ \hline \end{array}$

4. $\begin{array}{r} 7{,}896 \\ -\ 5{,}472 \\ \hline \end{array}$

5. $\begin{array}{r} 36{,}752 \\ +\ 15{,}417 \\ \hline \end{array}$

6. $\begin{array}{r} 56{,}008 \\ -\ \ 7{,}124 \\ \hline \end{array}$

7. $\begin{array}{r} 3{,}726 \\ +\ 4{,}469 \\ \hline \end{array}$

8. $\begin{array}{r} 8{,}034 \\ -\ 7{,}311 \\ \hline \end{array}$

9. $\begin{array}{r} 438 \\ +\ 621 \\ \hline \end{array}$

10. $\begin{array}{r} 765 \\ -\ 334 \\ \hline \end{array}$

11. $\begin{array}{r} 45{,}389 \\ -\ 28{,}685 \\ \hline \end{array}$

12. $\begin{array}{r} 51{,}386 \\ +\ \ 9{,}342 \\ \hline \end{array}$

13. $\begin{array}{r} 872{,}385 \\ -\ \ 49{,}817 \\ \hline \end{array}$

14. $\begin{array}{r} 428{,}595 \\ +\ 325{,}957 \\ \hline \end{array}$

15. $\begin{array}{r} 506{,}729 \\ -\ 388{,}214 \\ \hline \end{array}$

Name

Understand Fractions Greater Than 1 and Mixed Numbers

1 whole

$\frac{1}{8}$	$\frac{1}{8}$	$\frac{1}{8}$	$\frac{1}{8}$	$\frac{1}{8}$	$\frac{1}{8}$	$\frac{1}{8}$	$\frac{1}{8}$
$\frac{1}{8}$	$\frac{1}{8}$	$\frac{1}{8}$	$\frac{1}{8}$	$\frac{1}{8}$	$\frac{1}{8}$	$\frac{1}{8}$	$\frac{1}{8}$
$\frac{1}{8}$	$\frac{1}{8}$	$\frac{1}{8}$	$\frac{1}{8}$	$\frac{1}{8}$	$\frac{1}{8}$	$\frac{1}{8}$	$\frac{1}{8}$
$\frac{1}{8}$	$\frac{1}{8}$	$\frac{1}{8}$	$\frac{1}{8}$	$\frac{1}{8}$	$\frac{1}{8}$	$\frac{1}{8}$	$\frac{1}{8}$
$\frac{1}{8}$	$\frac{1}{8}$	$\frac{1}{8}$	$\frac{1}{8}$	$\frac{1}{8}$	$\frac{1}{8}$	$\frac{1}{8}$	$\frac{1}{8}$
$\frac{1}{8}$	$\frac{1}{8}$	$\frac{1}{8}$	$\frac{1}{8}$	$\frac{1}{8}$	$\frac{1}{8}$	$\frac{1}{8}$	$\frac{1}{8}$
$\frac{1}{8}$	$\frac{1}{8}$	$\frac{1}{8}$	$\frac{1}{8}$	$\frac{1}{8}$	$\frac{1}{8}$	$\frac{1}{8}$	$\frac{1}{8}$

$\frac{1}{5}$	$\frac{1}{5}$	$\frac{1}{5}$	$\frac{1}{5}$	$\frac{1}{5}$
$\frac{1}{5}$	$\frac{1}{5}$	$\frac{1}{5}$	$\frac{1}{5}$	$\frac{1}{5}$
$\frac{1}{5}$	$\frac{1}{5}$	$\frac{1}{5}$	$\frac{1}{5}$	$\frac{1}{5}$
$\frac{1}{5}$	$\frac{1}{5}$	$\frac{1}{5}$	$\frac{1}{5}$	$\frac{1}{5}$
$\frac{1}{5}$	$\frac{1}{5}$	$\frac{1}{5}$	$\frac{1}{5}$	$\frac{1}{5}$
$\frac{1}{5}$	$\frac{1}{5}$	$\frac{1}{5}$	$\frac{1}{5}$	$\frac{1}{5}$
$\frac{1}{5}$	$\frac{1}{5}$	$\frac{1}{5}$	$\frac{1}{5}$	$\frac{1}{5}$

Name ____________________

Understand Fractions Greater Than 1 and Mixed Numbers (continued)

1 whole

1 whole
1 whole
1 whole
1 whole
1 whole
1 whole
1 whole

1 whole
1 whole
1 whole
1 whole
1 whole
1 whole
1 whole

Name ______________________________

What's the Error?

Dear Math Students,

Here is a subtraction problem that I tried to solve.

Is my answer correct? If not, please help me understand why it is wrong.

Your friend,
Puzzled Penguin

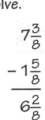

$$\begin{array}{r} 7\frac{3}{8} \\ -\,1\frac{5}{8} \\ \hline 6\frac{2}{8} \end{array}$$

?

18 Write a response to Puzzled Penguin.

____

____

____

____

Compare and Subtract

Compare each pair of mixed numbers using $>$ or $<$. Then subtract the lesser mixed number from the greater mixed number.

19 $3\frac{2}{5}$; $1\frac{4}{5}$ ______________

20 $1\frac{8}{9}$; $2\frac{2}{9}$ ______________

21 $1\frac{3}{11}$; $1\frac{6}{11}$ ______________

22 $4\frac{1}{8}$; $2\frac{7}{8}$ ______________

23 $3\frac{2}{6}$; $4\frac{3}{6}$ ______________

24 $10\frac{1}{3}$; $7\frac{2}{3}$ ______________

✔ **Check Understanding**
Represent your solution to Exercise 22 by drawing fraction bars.

Name ______________________________

Practice with Fractions and Mixed Numbers (continued)

Add or subtract.

23. $3\frac{1}{4} + 5\frac{2}{4}$

24. $4\frac{6}{8} - 3\frac{3}{8}$

25. $1\frac{3}{5} + 1\frac{2}{5}$

26. $4\frac{1}{3} - 1\frac{2}{3}$

27. $2\frac{5}{10} + 4\frac{9}{10}$

28. $10\frac{5}{8} - 3\frac{7}{8}$

What's the Error?

Dear Math Students,

This is a problem from my math homework. My friend says my answer is not correct, but I can't figure out what I did wrong. Can you help me find and fix my mistake?

Your friend,
Puzzled Penguin

$$\begin{array}{r} 4\frac{9}{8} \\ \cancel{4}\frac{1}{8} \\ -\ 1\frac{5}{8} \\ \hline 3\frac{4}{8} \end{array}$$

29. Write a response to Puzzled Penguin.

____

____

____

____

Name ______________________________

Make a Line Plot

36 Make a mark anywhere on this line segment.

37 Measure the distance from the left end of the segment to your mark to the nearest $\frac{1}{8}$ inch.

____

38 Collect measurements from your classmates and record them in the line plot below.

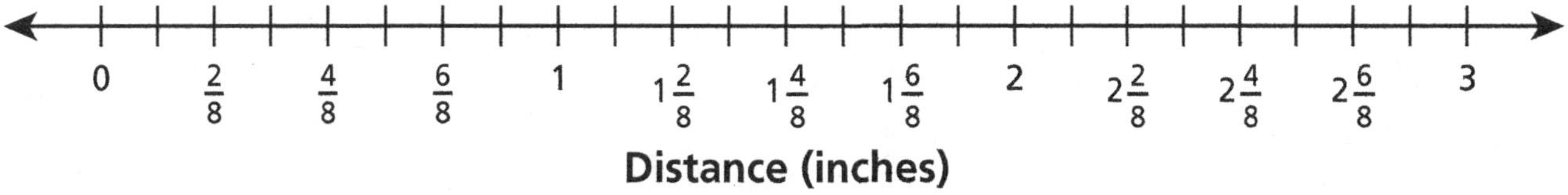
0
$\frac{2}{8}$
$\frac{4}{8}$
$\frac{6}{8}$
1
$1\frac{2}{8}$
$1\frac{4}{8}$
$1\frac{6}{8}$
2
$2\frac{2}{8}$
$2\frac{4}{8}$
$2\frac{6}{8}$
3
Distance (inches)

39 The range is the difference between the greatest value and the least value. What is the range of the data?

____

40 Which distance value occurred most often?

____

Check Understanding

For your line plot in Problem 38, suppose the greatest value is $1\frac{4}{8}$ and the least value is $\frac{6}{8}$. What is the range of the data?

____

Name ______________________________

Solve.

1 $\begin{array}{r} 3\frac{5}{6} \\ +\ 4\frac{5}{6} \\ \hline \end{array}$

2 $\begin{array}{r} 9\frac{3}{10} \\ -\ 2\frac{7}{10} \\ \hline \end{array}$

Write an equation. Then solve.

Show your work.

3 A caterer serves 8 pies at a banquet. The people at the banquet eat $5\frac{4}{6}$ pies. How many pies are left?

____

Solve.

4 The line plot shows the time Lina spent on homework during the past two weeks. What is the difference between the least amount of time and the greatest amount of time Lina spent on homework?

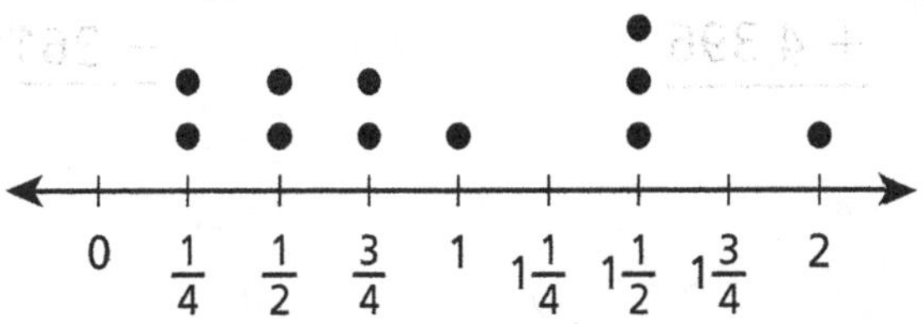
0
$\frac{1}{4}$
$\frac{1}{2}$
$\frac{3}{4}$
1
$1\frac{1}{4}$
$1\frac{1}{2}$
$1\frac{3}{4}$
2

Hours Spent on Homework

____

Write this fraction as a mixed number.

5 $\frac{23}{5}$

____

Fluency Check 18

Name ____________________

PATH to FLUENCY

Add or subtract.

1. $\begin{array}{r} 142 \\ +\ 557 \\ \hline \end{array}$

2. $\begin{array}{r} 6{,}703 \\ -\ 5{,}281 \\ \hline \end{array}$

3. $\begin{array}{r} 6{,}836 \\ +\ 742 \\ \hline \end{array}$

4. $\begin{array}{r} 76{,}294 \\ -\ 5{,}926 \\ \hline \end{array}$

5. $\begin{array}{r} 37{,}982 \\ +\ 31{,}856 \\ \hline \end{array}$

6. $\begin{array}{r} 486{,}793 \\ +\ 78{,}319 \\ \hline \end{array}$

7. $\begin{array}{r} 3{,}278 \\ +\ 4{,}396 \\ \hline \end{array}$

8. $\begin{array}{r} 742 \\ -\ 361 \\ \hline \end{array}$

9. $\begin{array}{r} 829 \\ +\ 155 \\ \hline \end{array}$

10. $\begin{array}{r} 60{,}508 \\ -\ 26{,}774 \\ \hline \end{array}$

11. $\begin{array}{r} 884 \\ -\ 371 \\ \hline \end{array}$

12. $\begin{array}{r} 87{,}314 \\ +\ 32{,}975 \\ \hline \end{array}$

13. $\begin{array}{r} 745{,}298 \\ -\ 51{,}889 \\ \hline \end{array}$

14. $\begin{array}{r} 5{,}976 \\ -\ 3{,}513 \\ \hline \end{array}$

15. $\begin{array}{r} 807{,}963 \\ -\ 348{,}279 \\ \hline \end{array}$

Name

Real World Problems (continued)

Write an equation. Then solve.

Show your work.

25 Ami has building bricks that are $\frac{5}{8}$ inch thick. She makes a stack of 15 bricks. How tall is the stack?

26 A crepe recipe calls for $\frac{3}{4}$ cup of flour. A bread recipe calls for four times this much flour. How much flour is in the bread recipe?

What's the Error?

Dear Math Students,

I have so much homework! I have assignments in math, science, and reading. I think each subject will take $\frac{1}{2}$ hour. I tried to multiply to find the total time.

$3 \cdot \frac{1}{2} = \frac{3}{6}$

That can't be right! I know $\frac{3}{6}$ is the same as $\frac{1}{2}$ so that is only $\frac{1}{2}$ hour.

What did I do wrong? How long will my homework really take?

Your friend,
Puzzled Penguin

?

27 Write a response to Puzzled Penguin.

Check Understanding

Draw a picture to show that $5 \cdot \frac{7}{12} = \frac{35}{12}$.

Unit 6
Quick Quiz 3

Name ______________________

Multiply.

1 $10 \cdot \frac{2}{10} =$ ______

2 $13 \cdot \frac{5}{8} =$ ______

3 Liam has two trophies. The first trophy weighs $\frac{3}{8}$ pound. The second trophy weighs 3 times as much as the first trophy. How much does the second trophy weigh?

Show your work.

____

Write an equation. Then solve.

4 Cassie works on her art project $\frac{3}{4}$ hour every day for 12 days. How many hours does Cassie work on her project altogether?

____

5 At a petting zoo, $\frac{2}{12}$ of the animals are sheep and $\frac{5}{12}$ are goats. What fraction of the animals at the petting zoo are sheep or goats?

____

Fluency Check 19 Name ______________________

PATH to FLUENCY

Add or subtract.

1. $\begin{array}{r} 6{,}894 \\ -\ 3{,}421 \\ \hline \end{array}$

2. $\begin{array}{r} 472 \\ -\ 368 \\ \hline \end{array}$

3. $\begin{array}{r} 7{,}086 \\ -\ 4{,}825 \\ \hline \end{array}$

4. $\begin{array}{r} 1{,}176 \\ +\ \ 483 \\ \hline \end{array}$

5. $\begin{array}{r} 345 \\ +\ 314 \\ \hline \end{array}$

6. $\begin{array}{r} 354{,}964 \\ -\ \ 46{,}379 \\ \hline \end{array}$

7. $\begin{array}{r} 76{,}429 \\ +\ \ 6{,}850 \\ \hline \end{array}$

8. $\begin{array}{r} 62{,}000 \\ -\ 51{,}752 \\ \hline \end{array}$

9. $\begin{array}{r} 205{,}782 \\ -\ 178{,}935 \\ \hline \end{array}$

10. $\begin{array}{r} 798 \\ -\ 340 \\ \hline \end{array}$

11. $\begin{array}{r} 45{,}284 \\ -\ \ 8{,}451 \\ \hline \end{array}$

12. $\begin{array}{r} 84{,}275 \\ +\ 17{,}682 \\ \hline \end{array}$

13. $\begin{array}{r} 725 \\ +\ 644 \\ \hline \end{array}$

14. $\begin{array}{r} 295{,}930 \\ +\ 357{,}392 \\ \hline \end{array}$

15. $\begin{array}{r} 8{,}312 \\ +\ 7{,}548 \\ \hline \end{array}$

Name ______________________________

1 Represent the shaded part of the fraction bar as the product of a whole number and a unit fraction.

1/8
1/8
1/8
1/8
1/8
1/8
1/8
1/8

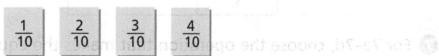

2 In the morning Naomi jumps rope for $\frac{1}{4}$ hour. After lunch she jumps rope for another $\frac{2}{4}$ hour. How long does Naomi jump rope? Write an equation. Then solve.

Equation: ______________

Solution: ______________ hour

3 For Exercises 3a–3d, write a fraction from the tiles to make a true equation.

$\frac{1}{10}$ $\frac{2}{10}$ $\frac{3}{10}$ $\frac{4}{10}$

3a. $\frac{10}{10} = \frac{5}{10} + \frac{3}{10} + \square$

3b. $1 = \frac{1}{10} + \frac{5}{10} + \square$

3c. $\frac{7}{10} = \frac{1}{10} + \frac{1}{10} + \frac{1}{10} + \frac{1}{10} + \square$

3d. $\frac{4}{10} = \frac{1}{10} + \frac{1}{10} + \frac{1}{10} + \square$

Name ______________________________

4 Caesar buys dog treats and cat treats. He buys $\frac{7}{8}$ pound of dog treats. This is $\frac{5}{8}$ pound more than the weight of the cat treats he buys. How many pounds of cat treats does Caesar buy? Write an equation. Then solve.

Equation: ____________

Solution: ____________ pound

5 A recipe calls for $\frac{2}{3}$ cup of mushrooms. Dae uses 3 times as many cups of mushrooms. Choose the number of cups of mushrooms he uses. Mark all that apply.

Ⓐ $\frac{5}{3}$ cups
Ⓑ $\frac{6}{3}$ cups
Ⓒ 2 cups
Ⓓ 3 cups

6 Complete the table to show the fraction as a product of a whole number and a unit fraction.

Fraction	Product
$\frac{5}{12}$	______
$\frac{2}{3}$	______
$\frac{4}{5}$	______

7 For 7a–7d, choose the operation that makes the equation true.

7a. 6 [+ / − / ×] $\frac{3}{4} = 4\frac{2}{4}$

7b. 3 [+ / − / ×] $\frac{2}{5} = 2\frac{3}{5}$

7c. 4 [+ / − / ×] $3\frac{3}{5} = 7\frac{3}{5}$

7d. 7 [+ / − / ×] $\frac{1}{3} = 2\frac{1}{3}$

Name ______________________________

8 Multiply the expression to complete the table.

Expression	Written as a Fraction	Written as a Mixed Number
$7 \cdot \frac{1}{6}$	____	____
$12 \cdot \frac{1}{5}$	____	$2\frac{2}{5}$
$3 \cdot \frac{5}{8}$	____	____

9 For Exercises 9a–9f, choose True or False for the equation.

9a. $\frac{2}{8} + \frac{1}{8} = \frac{3}{16}$ ○ True ○ False

9b. $\frac{4}{5} - \frac{1}{5} = \frac{3}{5}$ ○ True ○ False

9c. $\frac{9}{4} + \frac{2}{4} = 2\frac{3}{4}$ ○ True ○ False

9d. $\frac{5}{12} + \frac{4}{12} = \frac{9}{24}$ ○ True ○ False

9e. $8\frac{5}{6} - 6\frac{4}{6} = 2\frac{1}{6}$ ○ True ○ False

9f. $2\frac{7}{10} + 3\frac{3}{10} = 5\frac{10}{20}$ ○ True ○ False

10 Elias says this problem can be solved using addition. Vladimir says it can be solved using multiplication. Explain why both boys are correct.

Milo practices piano $\frac{3}{5}$ hour every day. How many hours does he practice in 5 days?

Name ____________________

11 For 11a and 11b, find the sum or difference. Write your answer as a mixed number or a whole number, when possible.

11a. $5\frac{2}{3} + 4\frac{2}{3} = \square$

11b. $9\frac{3}{8} - 3\frac{7}{8} = \square$

12 On Saturday morning, Jesse plays basketball for $\frac{2}{3}$ hour. In the afternoon, he plays some more. He plays $2\frac{1}{3}$ hours in all. How long did Jesse play basketball in the afternoon?

Part A

Draw a model to represent the problem. Then solve. Explain how your model helps you solve the problem.

Part B

On Sunday, Jesse played basketball for $1\frac{2}{3}$ hours. How many total hours did he play basketball on Saturday and Sunday? Show your work.

Name ______________________________

13 Rebecca's soup recipe calls for $\frac{3}{4}$ cup of milk. She needs 3 times as much milk to make a triple batch of soup. How many cups of milk does Rebecca need?

Part A

Draw a model for the problem.

Part B

Use your model to write two equations for the problem. Then solve.

14 For Exercises 14a–14e, choose Yes or No to tell whether the addition equation is true.

14a. $\frac{8}{10} = \frac{5}{10} + \frac{3}{10}$ ○ Yes ○ No

14b. $\frac{4}{5} = \frac{1}{5} + \frac{1}{5} + \frac{1}{5} + \frac{1}{5} + \frac{1}{5}$ ○ Yes ○ No

14c. $\frac{6}{11} = \frac{4}{6} + \frac{2}{5}$ ○ Yes ○ No

14d. $\frac{3}{8} = \frac{1}{8} + \frac{1}{8} + \frac{1}{8}$ ○ Yes ○ No

14e. $\frac{10}{12} = \frac{5}{12} + \frac{5}{12}$ ○ Yes ○ No

Name ______________________

15 The line plot shows the lengths of trails Andrea hiked last month at a state park.

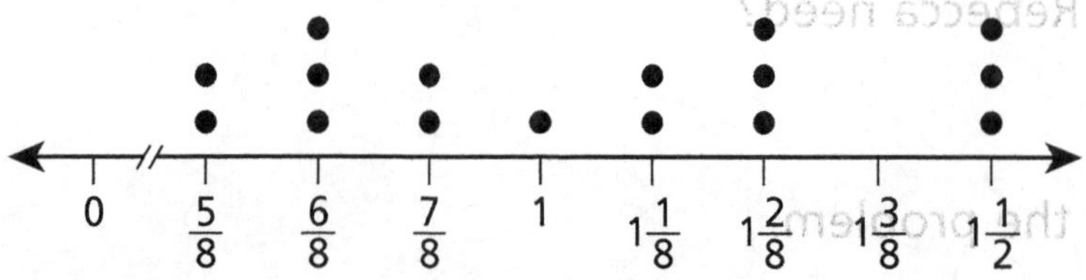
0
$\frac{5}{8}$
$\frac{6}{8}$
$\frac{7}{8}$
1
$1\frac{1}{8}$
$1\frac{2}{8}$
$1\frac{3}{8}$
$1\frac{1}{2}$

Trail Lengths (miles)

Andrea hiked 3 miles last week. She could have hiked two $1\frac{1}{2}$-mile trails. Describe two other combinations of trails she could have hiked.

16 Select the expression that is equivalent to $2\frac{2}{6}$. Mark all that apply.

Ⓐ $\frac{1}{6} + \frac{1}{6} + \frac{2}{6}$

Ⓑ $1 + 1 + \frac{2}{6}$

Ⓒ $\frac{2}{6} + \frac{2}{6} + \frac{2}{6}$

Ⓓ $\frac{6}{6} + \frac{6}{6} + \frac{1}{6} + \frac{1}{6}$

Ⓔ $\frac{20}{6} + \frac{2}{6}$

Ⓕ $\frac{6}{6} + \frac{3}{6} + \frac{3}{6} + \frac{2}{6}$

17 Explain how to change $\frac{11}{4}$ to a mixed number.

Name ____________________

Mixing Paint

Mr. Myers stores paint in equal-size jars in his classroom. The table shows the amount of each color he has.

Mr. Myers's Paint						
Color	Red	Orange	Yellow	Blue	Green	Purple
Amount of Jar Filled	1	$\frac{1}{8}$	$1\frac{2}{8}$	$\frac{4}{8}$	$\frac{3}{8}$	$\frac{7}{8}$

1. Janet's project requires $\frac{5}{8}$ of a jar of orange paint. To make more orange, she needs to combine equal parts of red and yellow. How much of each color does she need?

2. How much red paint is left? How much yellow paint is left?

3. Three students need purple paint. Show how Mr. Myers can divide all of the paint into three jars. If he wants the three jars to contain an equal amount of paint, how much will be in each jar? How much will be left over?

Name ______________________________

4. Emilio's project used all the green paint in the jar, but his project is not finished. Mr. Myers thinks that Emilio needs 3 times as much green paint as he started with to finish. To make green, equal parts of yellow and blue can be combined. Does Mr. Myers have enough paint to make the amount of green paint Emilio needs? Explain why or why not.

5. Mr. Myers decides to buy green paint instead of making it. How many full jars of green paint does he need to buy? Explain.

6. At the end of the class, Mr. Meyers has $\frac{4}{8}$ jar of red paint and $\frac{5}{8}$ jar of yellow paint, and no orange paint. He finds $\frac{6}{8}$ of another jar of red paint in the closet. He wants to combine both jars of red paint to make one full jar and use any remaining red paint to mix with an equal amount of yellow paint to make more orange paint. How much red, yellow, and orange paint will he have? Explain how you solved the problem.

Dear Family:

In Lessons 1 through 7 of Unit 7 of *Math Expressions*, your child will build on previous experience with fractions. Your child will use both physical models and numerical methods to recognize and to find fractions equivalent to a given fraction. Your child will also compare and order fractions and mixed numbers, including those with like and unlike numerators and denominators.

By using fraction strips students determine how to model and compare fractions, and to find equivalent fractions. Your child will also learn how to use multiplication and division to find equivalent fractions.

Examples of Fraction Bar Modeling:

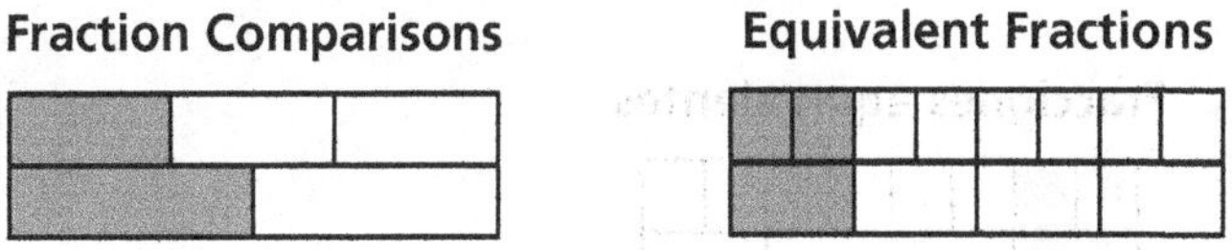
Fraction Comparisons
Equivalent Fractions

$\frac{1}{3} < \frac{1}{2}$ $\frac{2}{8} = \frac{1}{4}$

Your child will be introduced to the number-line model for fractions. Students name fractions corresponding to given lengths on the number line and identify lengths corresponding to given fractions. They also see that there are many equivalent fraction names for any given length.

Your child will apply this knowledge of fractions to word problems and in data displays.

If you have questions or problems, please contact me.

Thank you.

Sincerely,
Your child's teacher

Estimada familia:

En las lecciones 1 a 7 de la Unidad 7 de *Math Expressions,* el niño ampliará sus conocimientos previos acerca de las fracciones. Su niño usará modelos físicos y métodos numéricos para reconocer y hallar fracciones equivalentes para una fracción dada. También comparará y ordenará fracciones y números mixtos, incluyendo aquellos que tengan numeradores y denominadores iguales o diferentes.

Usando tiras de fracciones, los estudiantes determinarán cómo hacer modelos y comparar fracciones y cómo hallar fracciones equivalentes. Además, aprenderán cómo usar la multiplicación y división para hallar fracciones equivalentes.

Ejemplos de modelos con barras de fracciones:

Comparar fracciones

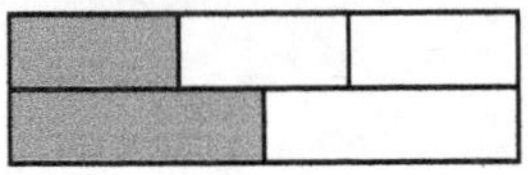

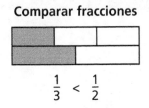

$\frac{1}{3} < \frac{1}{2}$

Fracciones equivalentes

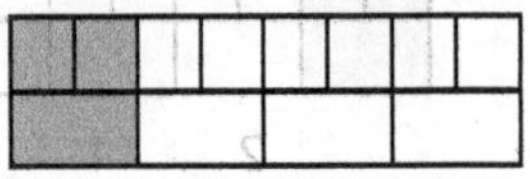

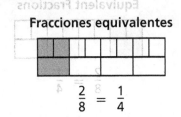

$\frac{2}{8} = \frac{1}{4}$

Su niño estudiará por primera vez el modelo de recta numérica para las fracciones. Los estudiantes nombrarán las fracciones que correspondan a determinadas longitudes en la recta numérica e identificarán longitudes que correspondan a fracciones dadas. También observarán que hay muchos nombres de fracciones equivalentes para una longitud determinada.

Su niño aplicará este conocimiento de las fracciones en problemas y en presentaciones de datos.

Si tiene alguna duda o algún comentario, por favor comuníquese conmigo.

Atentamente,
El maestro de su niño

common denominator

hundredth

decimal number

simplify a fraction

equivalent fractions

tenth

A unit fraction representing one of one hundred parts, written as 0.01 or $\frac{1}{100}$.

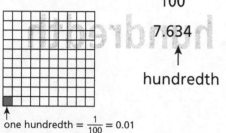

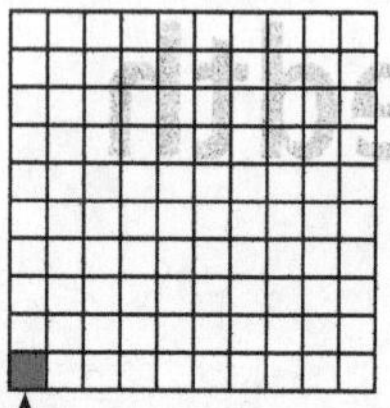

7.634

↑

hundredth

one hundredth = $\frac{1}{100}$ = 0.01

A common multiple of two or more denominators.

Example:

A common denominator of $\frac{1}{2}$ and $\frac{1}{3}$ is 6 because 6 is a multiple of 2 and 3.

Dividing the numerator and the denominator of a fraction by the same number to make an equivalent fraction made from fewer but larger unit fractions.

Example:

$\frac{5}{10} = \frac{5 \div 5}{10 \div 5} = \frac{1}{2}$

A representation of a number using the numerals 0 to 9, in which each digit has a value 10 times the digit to its right. A dot or **decimal point** separates the whole-number part of the number on the left from the fractional part on the right.

Examples:

1.23 and 0.3

A unit fraction representing one of ten equal parts of a whole, written as 0.1 or $\frac{1}{10}$.

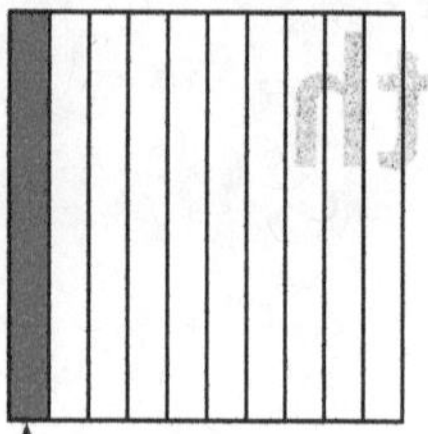

12.34

↑

tenth

one tenth = $\frac{1}{10}$ = 0.1

Two or more fractions that represent the same number.

Example:

$\frac{2}{4}$ and $\frac{4}{8}$ are equivalent because they both represent one half.

thousandth

A unit fraction representing one of one thousand equal parts of a whole, written as 0.001 or $\frac{1}{1,000}$.

1/1																				1/1
1/2	1/2																			2/2
1/3	1/3	1/3																		3/3
1/4	1/4	1/4	1/4																	4/4
1/5	1/5	1/5	1/5	1/5																5/5
1/6	1/6	1/6	1/6	1/6	1/6															6/6
1/7	1/7	1/7	1/7	1/7	1/7	1/7														7/7
1/8	1/8	1/8	1/8	1/8	1/8	1/8	1/8													8/8
1/9	1/9	1/9	1/9	1/9	1/9	1/9	1/9	1/9												9/9
1/10	1/10	1/10	1/10	1/10	1/10	1/10	1/10	1/10	1/10											10/10
1/11	1/11	1/11	1/11	1/11	1/11	1/11	1/11	1/11	1/11	1/11										11/11
1/12	1/12	1/12	1/12	1/12	1/12	1/12	1/12	1/12	1/12	1/12	1/12									12/12
1/13	1/13	1/13	1/13	1/13	1/13	1/13	1/13	1/13	1/13	1/13	1/13	1/13								13/13
1/14	1/14	1/14	1/14	1/14	1/14	1/14	1/14	1/14	1/14	1/14	1/14	1/14	1/14							14/14
1/15	1/15	1/15	1/15	1/15	1/15	1/15	1/15	1/15	1/15	1/15	1/15	1/15	1/15	1/15						15/15
1/16	1/16	1/16	1/16	1/16	1/16	1/16	1/16	1/16	1/16	1/16	1/16	1/16	1/16	1/16	1/16					16/16
1/17	1/17	1/17	1/17	1/17	1/17	1/17	1/17	1/17	1/17	1/17	1/17	1/17	1/17	1/17	1/17	1/17				17/17
1/18	1/18	1/18	1/18	1/18	1/18	1/18	1/18	1/18	1/18	1/18	1/18	1/18	1/18	1/18	1/18	1/18	1/18			18/18
1/19	1/19	1/19	1/19	1/19	1/19	1/19	1/19	1/19	1/19	1/19	1/19	1/19	1/19	1/19	1/19	1/19	1/19	1/19		19/19
1/20	1/20	1/20	1/20	1/20	1/20	1/20	1/20	1/20	1/20	1/20	1/20	1/20	1/20	1/20	1/20	1/20	1/20	1/20	1/20	20/20

Name ____________________

Practice Comparing Fractions

Circle the greater fraction. Use fraction strips if you need to.

1. $\frac{1}{12}$ or $\frac{1}{2}$
2. $\frac{3}{8}$ or $\frac{1}{8}$
3. $\frac{2}{5}$ or $\frac{2}{6}$
4. $\frac{1}{3}$ or $\frac{1}{5}$
5. $\frac{4}{12}$ or $\frac{5}{12}$
6. $\frac{7}{10}$ or $\frac{5}{10}$
7. $\frac{1}{3}$ or $\frac{2}{3}$
8. $\frac{3}{6}$ or $\frac{3}{8}$

Write > or < to make each statement true.

9. $\frac{3}{10} \bigcirc \frac{3}{8}$
10. $\frac{3}{6} \bigcirc \frac{3}{5}$
11. $\frac{8}{10} \bigcirc \frac{8}{12}$
12. $\frac{2}{6} \bigcirc \frac{3}{6}$
13. $\frac{7}{10} \bigcirc \frac{7}{8}$
14. $\frac{5}{100} \bigcirc \frac{4}{100}$

What's the Error?

Dear Math Students,

Yesterday, my family caught a large fish. We ate $\frac{2}{6}$ of the fish. Today, we ate $\frac{2}{4}$ of the fish. I told my mother that we ate more fish yesterday than today because 6 is greater than 4, so $\frac{2}{6}$ is greater than $\frac{2}{4}$. My mother told me I made a mistake. Can you help me to figure out what my mistake was?

Your friend,
Puzzled Penguin

15. Write a response to Puzzled Penguin.

____

____

____

____

Name ______________________________

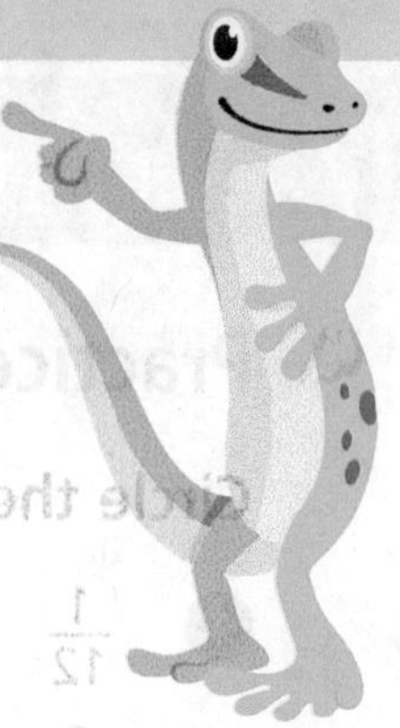

Discuss Number Lines

The number line below shows the fourths between 0 and 1. Discuss how the number line is like and unlike the fraction bar above it.

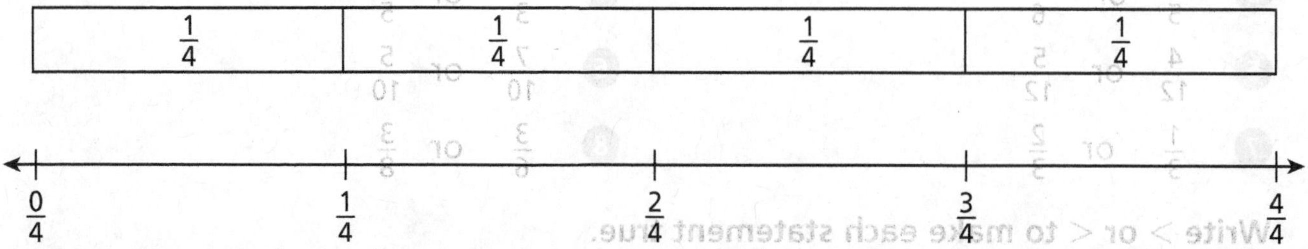

$\frac{1}{4}$ $\frac{1}{4}$ $\frac{1}{4}$ $\frac{1}{4}$
$\frac{0}{4}$ $\frac{1}{4}$ $\frac{2}{4}$ $\frac{3}{4}$ $\frac{4}{4}$

These number lines are divided to show different fractions.

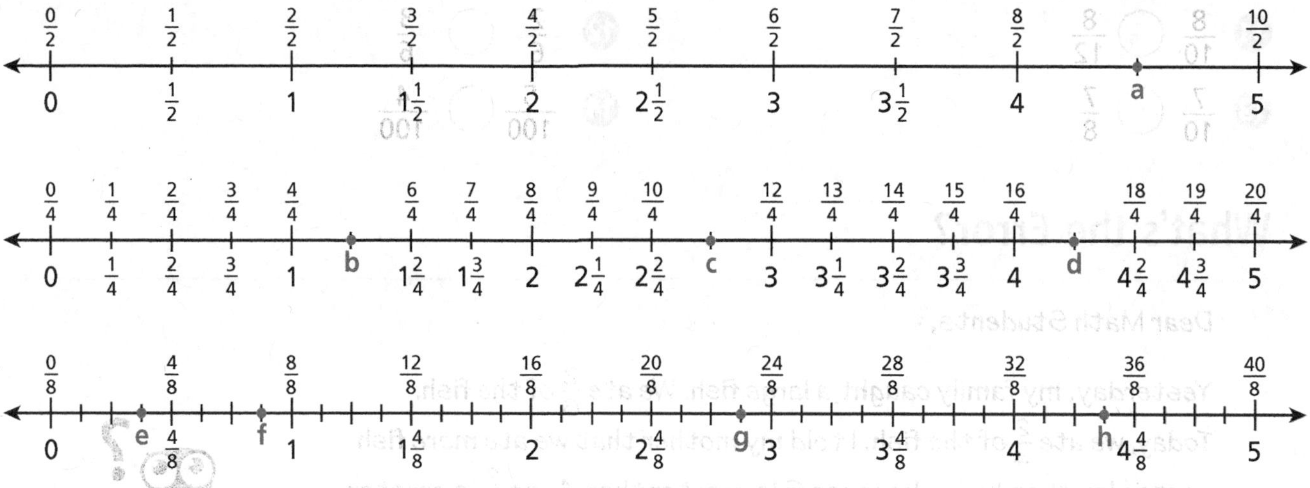

$\frac{0}{2}$ $\frac{1}{2}$ $\frac{2}{2}$ $\frac{3}{2}$ $\frac{4}{2}$ $\frac{5}{2}$ $\frac{6}{2}$ $\frac{7}{2}$ $\frac{8}{2}$ $\frac{10}{2}$
0 $\frac{1}{2}$ 1 $1\frac{1}{2}$ 2 $2\frac{1}{2}$ 3 $3\frac{1}{2}$ 4 a 5
$\frac{0}{4}$ $\frac{1}{4}$ $\frac{2}{4}$ $\frac{3}{4}$ $\frac{4}{4}$ $\frac{6}{4}$ $\frac{7}{4}$ $\frac{8}{4}$ $\frac{9}{4}$ $\frac{10}{4}$ $\frac{12}{4}$ $\frac{13}{4}$ $\frac{14}{4}$ $\frac{15}{4}$ $\frac{16}{4}$ $\frac{18}{4}$ $\frac{19}{4}$ $\frac{20}{4}$
0 $\frac{1}{4}$ $\frac{2}{4}$ $\frac{3}{4}$ 1 b $1\frac{2}{4}$ $1\frac{3}{4}$ 2 $2\frac{1}{4}$ $2\frac{2}{4}$ c 3 $3\frac{1}{4}$ $3\frac{2}{4}$ $3\frac{3}{4}$ 4 d $4\frac{2}{4}$ $4\frac{3}{4}$ 5
$\frac{0}{8}$ $\frac{4}{8}$ $\frac{8}{8}$ $\frac{12}{8}$ $\frac{16}{8}$ $\frac{20}{8}$ $\frac{24}{8}$ $\frac{28}{8}$ $\frac{32}{8}$ $\frac{36}{8}$ $\frac{40}{8}$
0 e $\frac{4}{8}$ f 1 $1\frac{4}{8}$ 2 $2\frac{4}{8}$ g 3 $3\frac{4}{8}$ 4 h $4\frac{4}{8}$ 5

Write > or < to make each statement true.

1. $\frac{3}{4}$ ◯ $\frac{5}{2}$
2. $\frac{15}{4}$ ◯ $\frac{20}{8}$
3. $\frac{10}{4}$ ◯ $\frac{24}{8}$
4. $2\frac{4}{8}$ ◯ $1\frac{3}{4}$

Identify Points

5. Write the fraction or mixed number for each lettered point on the number lines above.

a. ______ b. ______ c. ______ d. ______

e. ______ f. ______ g. ______ h. ______

Name ______________________

Number Lines for Thirds and Sixths

Tell how many equal parts are between 0 and 1. Then write fraction labels above the equal parts.

6 ______

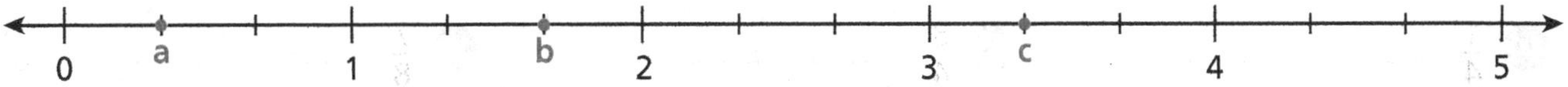

0
a
1
b
2
3
c
4
5

7 ______

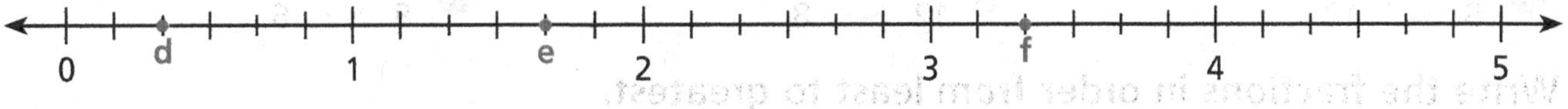

0
d
1
e
2
3
f
4
5

8 ______

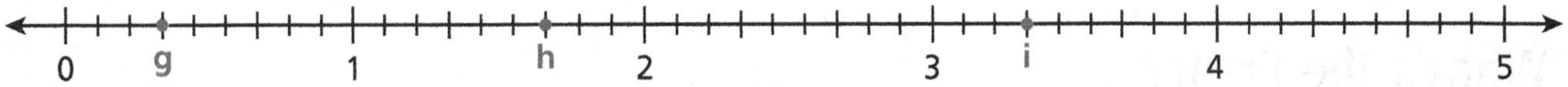

0
g
1
h
2
3
i
4
5

Write > or < to make each statement true.

9 $\frac{4}{3}$ ◯ $\frac{7}{6}$

10 $\frac{8}{3}$ ◯ $\frac{18}{6}$

11 $3\frac{5}{6}$ ◯ $3\frac{2}{3}$

Identify Points

12 Write the fraction or mixed number for each lettered point above. Describe any patterns you see with the class.

a. ______ b. ______ c. ______

d. ______ e. ______ f. ______

g. ______ h. ______ i. ______

Mark and label the letter of each fraction or mixed number on the number line.

13 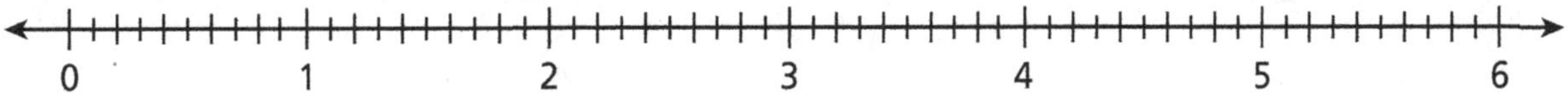

0
1
2
3
4
5
6

a. $\frac{1}{5}$ b. $\frac{7}{10}$ c. $1\frac{2}{5}$ d. $2\frac{1}{2}$

e. $3\frac{3}{10}$ f. $4\frac{2}{5}$ g. $4\frac{9}{10}$ h. $5\frac{1}{2}$

Name ______________________

Fractions and Benchmarks

Decide if each fraction is closer to 0 or closer to 1.
Write *closer to 0* or *closer to 1*.

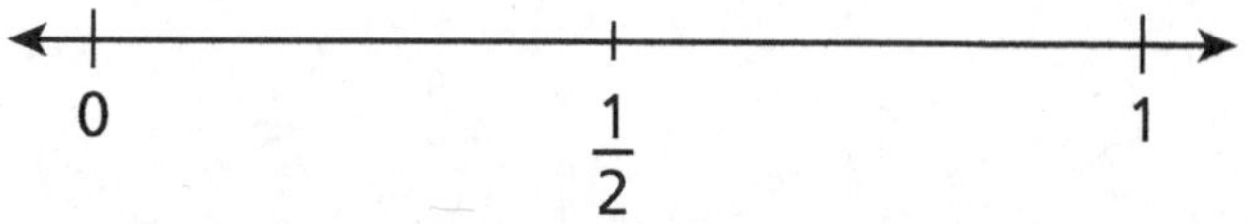
0
1/2
1

14 $\frac{1}{4}$ ______________ **15** $\frac{3}{4}$ ______________ **16** $\frac{7}{8}$ ______________

Write > or < to make each statement true.

17 $\frac{5}{8} \bigcirc \frac{11}{12}$ **18** $\frac{7}{12} \bigcirc \frac{1}{8}$ **19** $\frac{3}{8} \bigcirc \frac{1}{6}$

Write the fractions in order from least to greatest.

20 $\frac{5}{12}, \frac{1}{8}, \frac{4}{6}$ ______________ **21** $\frac{3}{6}, \frac{3}{4}, \frac{2}{9}$ ______________

What's the Error?

Dear Math Students,

I am baking cookies. My recipe calls for $\frac{5}{8}$ pound of walnuts. Walnuts come in $\frac{1}{2}$-pound bags and 1-pound bags. My friend says that $\frac{5}{8}$ is closer to $\frac{1}{2}$ than it is to 1, so I should buy a $\frac{1}{2}$-pound bag. I think my friend is wrong.

Do you agree with me or with my friend? Can you help me decide what size bag of walnuts I should buy?

Your friend,
Puzzled Penguin

?

22 Write a response to Puzzled Penguin.

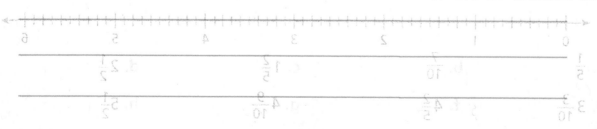

____

____

Name ______________________________

Write >, <, or = to make the statement true.

1. $\frac{3}{5} \bigcirc \frac{3}{8}$

2. $\frac{3}{8} \bigcirc \frac{5}{8}$

3. Label the point for each fraction or mixed number with the corresponding letter.

0
1
2
3
4
5
6

a. $3\frac{1}{2}$ b. $2\frac{1}{3}$ c. $\frac{2}{3}$ d. $5\frac{5}{6}$ e. $1\frac{1}{6}$

Which fraction or mixed number is closest to 1?

____

Solve. *Show your work.*

4. Cory ships two paperback books. One weighs $\frac{3}{8}$ pound and the other weighs $\frac{3}{4}$ pound. Which weight is greater than $\frac{1}{2}$ pound?

____

5. A farmer has 8 horses and 12 cows. He put $\frac{1}{4}$ of the horses in the barn and $\frac{1}{4}$ of the cows in the barn. Did he put more horses or cows in the barn? Explain.

____

____

Fluency Check 20

Name ______________________

PATH to FLUENCY

Add or subtract.

1. $\begin{array}{r} 2{,}156 \\ +\ 4{,}869 \\ \hline \end{array}$

2. $\begin{array}{r} 478 \\ -\ 386 \\ \hline \end{array}$

3. $\begin{array}{r} 3{,}742 \\ +\ 823 \\ \hline \end{array}$

4. $\begin{array}{r} 7{,}968 \\ -\ 3{,}526 \\ \hline \end{array}$

5. $\begin{array}{r} 54{,}683 \\ +\ 23{,}574 \\ \hline \end{array}$

6. $\begin{array}{r} 475{,}498 \\ -\ 88{,}532 \\ \hline \end{array}$

7. $\begin{array}{r} 605{,}748 \\ -\ 349{,}582 \\ \hline \end{array}$

8. $\begin{array}{r} 537 \\ -\ 315 \\ \hline \end{array}$

9. $\begin{array}{r} 836 \\ +\ 753 \\ \hline \end{array}$

10. $\begin{array}{r} 86{,}334 \\ -\ 3{,}782 \\ \hline \end{array}$

11. $\begin{array}{r} 145 \\ +\ 232 \\ \hline \end{array}$

12. $\begin{array}{r} 47{,}542 \\ +\ 8{,}750 \\ \hline \end{array}$

13. $\begin{array}{r} 80{,}000 \\ -\ 34{,}689 \\ \hline \end{array}$

14. $\begin{array}{r} 586{,}456 \\ +\ 56{,}967 \\ \hline \end{array}$

15. $\begin{array}{r} 7{,}603 \\ -\ 4{,}421 \\ \hline \end{array}$

Name ______________________________

Use Fraction Bars to Find Equivalent Fractions

3 How do these fraction bars show equivalent fractions for $\frac{1}{3}$?

____

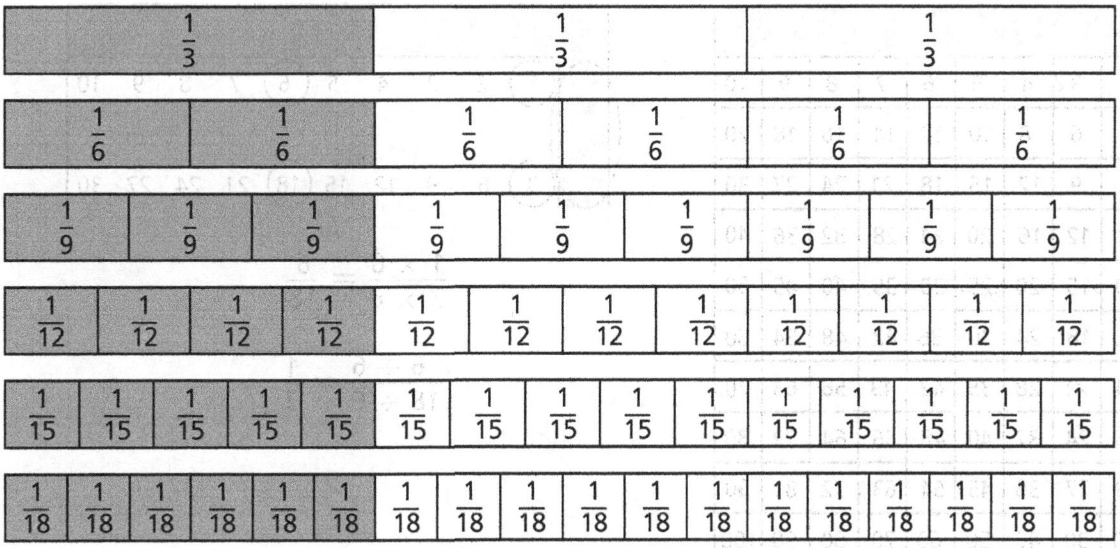

1/3 1/3 1/3
1/6 1/6 1/6 1/6 1/6 1/6
1/9 1/9 1/9 1/9 1/9 1/9 1/9 1/9 1/9
1/12 1/12 1/12 1/12 1/12 1/12 1/12 1/12 1/12 1/12 1/12 1/12
1/15 1/15 1/15 1/15 1/15 1/15 1/15 1/15 1/15 1/15 1/15 1/15 1/15 1/15 1/15
1/18 1/18 1/18 1/18 1/18 1/18 1/18 1/18 1/18 1/18 1/18 1/18 1/18 1/18 1/18 1/18 1/18 1/18

4 You can show how to find fractions equivalent to $\frac{1}{3}$ numerically. Fill in the blanks and finish the equations. Then explain how these fraction equations show equivalent fractions.

2 equal parts	3 equal parts	4 equal parts	__ equal parts	__ equal parts
× 2	× 3	× __	× __	× __
$\frac{1 \times 2}{3 \times 2} = \frac{2}{6}$	$\frac{1 \times \_}{3 \times \_} = \frac{\_}{9}$	$\frac{1 \times \_}{3 \times \_} = \frac{\_}{12}$	$\frac{1 \times \_}{3 \times \_} = \frac{\_}{15}$	$\frac{1 \times \_}{3 \times \_} = \frac{\_}{18}$

____

____

5 Tell whether the fractions are equivalent.

a. $\frac{1}{6}$ and $\frac{2}{12}$ ________ b. $\frac{3}{6}$ and $\frac{5}{9}$ ________ c. $\frac{6}{12}$ and $\frac{8}{15}$ ________

Name ______________________

Use a Multiplication Table to Find Equivalent Fractions

The table on the right shows part of the multiplication table at the left. You can find fractions equivalent to $\frac{1}{3}$ by using the products in the rows for the factors 1 and 3.

×	1	2	3	4	5	6	7	8	9	10
1	1	2	3	4	5	6	7	8	9	10
2	2	4	6	8	10	12	14	16	18	20
3	3	6	9	12	15	18	21	24	27	30
4	4	8	12	16	20	24	28	32	36	40
5	5	10	15	20	25	30	35	40	45	50
6	6	12	18	24	30	36	42	48	54	60
7	7	14	21	28	35	42	49	56	63	70
8	8	16	24	32	40	48	56	64	72	80
9	9	18	27	36	45	54	63	72	81	90
10	10	20	30	40	50	60	70	80	90	100

× 6

×	1	2	3	4	5	6	7	8	9	10
1	(1)	2	3	4	5	(6)	7	8	9	10
3	(3)	6	9	12	15	(18)	21	24	27	30

$$\frac{1 \times 6}{3 \times 6} = \frac{6}{18}$$

$$\frac{6 \div 6}{18 \div 6} = \frac{1}{3}$$

$\frac{1}{3}$	$\frac{1}{3}$	$\frac{1}{3}$

$\frac{1}{18}$	$\frac{1}{18}$	$\frac{1}{18}$	$\frac{1}{18}$	$\frac{1}{18}$	$\frac{1}{18}$	$\frac{1}{18}$	$\frac{1}{18}$	$\frac{1}{18}$	$\frac{1}{18}$	$\frac{1}{18}$	$\frac{1}{18}$	$\frac{1}{18}$	$\frac{1}{18}$	$\frac{1}{18}$	$\frac{1}{18}$	$\frac{1}{18}$	$\frac{1}{18}$

Complete each fraction equation. Look in the top row of the table above to find the multiplier.

6. $\frac{1 \times \quad}{3 \times \quad} = \frac{4}{12}$

7. $\frac{1 \times \quad}{3 \times \quad} = \frac{9}{27}$

8. $\frac{1 \times \quad}{3 \times \quad} = \frac{2}{6}$

9. $\frac{1 \times \quad}{4 \times \quad} = \frac{3}{12}$

10. $\frac{3 \times \quad}{10 \times \quad} = \frac{30}{100}$

11. $\frac{5 \times \quad}{8 \times \quad} = \frac{30}{48}$

12. Tell whether the fractions are equivalent.

a. $\frac{3}{4}$ and $\frac{12}{16}$ ______

b. $\frac{1}{2}$ and $\frac{5}{12}$ ______

c. $\frac{9}{10}$ and $\frac{90}{100}$ ______

Name ______________________________

What's the Error?

Dear Students,

I tried to find a fraction equivalent to $\frac{2}{3}$. Here's what I wrote.

$$\frac{2}{3} = \frac{5}{6}$$

Is my answer correct? If not, please help me understand why it is wrong.

Thank you.
Puzzled Penguin

?

13 Write a response to Puzzled Penguin.

____

____

____

Practice

Find a fraction equivalent to the given fraction.

14 $\frac{1}{4}$ $\frac{1 \times 2}{4 \times 2} = \frac{2}{\square}$

15 $\frac{3}{8}$ $\frac{3 \times 3}{8 \times 3} = \frac{9}{\square}$

16 $\frac{3}{10}$ ______________

17 $\frac{3}{4}$ ______________

18 $\frac{4}{5}$ ______________

19 $\frac{7}{12}$ ______________

20 $\frac{5}{6}$ ______________

21 $\frac{7}{8}$ ______________

Check Understanding

Write two fractions with the denominator 20: one equivalent to $\frac{1}{4}$ and one equivalent to $\frac{7}{10}$.

____

Name ______________________________

VOCABULARY
simplify a fraction

Simplify Fractions

Maria had 12 boxes of apricots. She sold 10 of the boxes. Then Maria said that she sold $\frac{5}{6}$ of the boxes. She made this drawing to show that $\frac{10}{12}$ and $\frac{5}{6}$ are equivalent fractions.

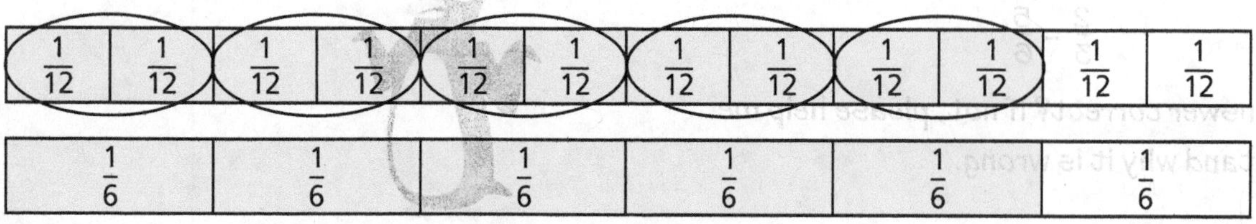

1/12 1/12 1/12 1/12 1/12 1/12 1/12 1/12 1/12 1/12 1/12 1/12
1/6 1/6 1/6 1/6 1/6 1/6

1 Do you agree that $\frac{10}{12}$ and $\frac{5}{6}$ are equivalent? Why?

____

2 Maria formed groups of twelfths to get a greater unit fraction. What is that unit fraction?

____

3 How many twelfths did she put in each group? In other words, what was the group size? ____________

4 Show how you can find the equivalent fraction by dividing the numerator and denominator by the group size.

$$\frac{10}{12} = \frac{10 \div \square}{12 \div \square} = \frac{\square}{\square}$$

To **simplify a fraction,** divide the numerator and denominator of a fraction by the same number to make an equivalent fraction made from fewer but larger unit fractions.

Use what you know to simplify each fraction to make an equivalent fraction with a unit fraction of $\frac{1}{6}$.

5 $\frac{8}{12} = \frac{8 \div \square}{12 \div \square} = \frac{\square}{6}$

6 $\frac{14}{12} = \frac{14 \div \square}{12 \div \square} = \frac{\square}{6} = \square\frac{\square}{6}$

Name ______________________________

Divide to Find Equivalent Fractions

7 Look at the thirds bar. Circle enough unit fractions on each of the other bars to equal $\frac{1}{3}$.

$\frac{1}{18}$	$\frac{1}{18}$	$\frac{1}{18}$	$\frac{1}{18}$	$\frac{1}{18}$	$\frac{1}{18}$	$\frac{1}{18}$	$\frac{1}{18}$	$\frac{1}{18}$	$\frac{1}{18}$	$\frac{1}{18}$	$\frac{1}{18}$	$\frac{1}{18}$	$\frac{1}{18}$	$\frac{1}{18}$	$\frac{1}{18}$	$\frac{1}{18}$	$\frac{1}{18}$

$\frac{1}{15}$	$\frac{1}{15}$	$\frac{1}{15}$	$\frac{1}{15}$	$\frac{1}{15}$	$\frac{1}{15}$	$\frac{1}{15}$	$\frac{1}{15}$	$\frac{1}{15}$	$\frac{1}{15}$	$\frac{1}{15}$	$\frac{1}{15}$	$\frac{1}{15}$	$\frac{1}{15}$	$\frac{1}{15}$

$\frac{1}{12}$	$\frac{1}{12}$	$\frac{1}{12}$	$\frac{1}{12}$	$\frac{1}{12}$	$\frac{1}{12}$	$\frac{1}{12}$	$\frac{1}{12}$	$\frac{1}{12}$	$\frac{1}{12}$	$\frac{1}{12}$	$\frac{1}{12}$

$\frac{1}{9}$	$\frac{1}{9}$	$\frac{1}{9}$	$\frac{1}{9}$	$\frac{1}{9}$	$\frac{1}{9}$	$\frac{1}{9}$	$\frac{1}{9}$	$\frac{1}{9}$

$\frac{1}{6}$	$\frac{1}{6}$	$\frac{1}{6}$	$\frac{1}{6}$	$\frac{1}{6}$	$\frac{1}{6}$

$\frac{1}{3}$	$\frac{1}{3}$	$\frac{1}{3}$

8 Discuss how the parts of the fraction bars you circled show this chain of equivalent fractions. Explain how each different group of unit fractions is equal to $\frac{1}{3}$.

$$\frac{6}{18} = \frac{5}{15} = \frac{4}{12} = \frac{3}{9} = \frac{2}{6} = \frac{1}{3}$$

____

____

9 Write the group size for each fraction in the chain of equivalent fractions. The first one is done for you.

6 ______ ______ ______ ______ ______

10 Complete each equation by showing how you use group size to simplify. The first one is done for you.

$\frac{6 \div 6}{18 \div 6} = \frac{1}{3}$ $\frac{5 \div \square}{15 \div \square} = \frac{1}{3}$ $\frac{4 \div \square}{12 \div \square} = \frac{1}{3}$

$\frac{3 \div \square}{9 \div \square} = \frac{1}{3}$ $\frac{2 \div \square}{6 \div \square} = \frac{1}{3}$

Name ______________________

What's the Error?

Dear Math Students,

My brother had a bowl of cherries to share.
My brother ate $\frac{3}{8}$ of the cherries. I ate $\frac{2}{5}$ of the cherries. I wrote two fractions with a common denominator and compared them.

$\frac{3}{8 \times 5} = \frac{3}{40}$ and $\frac{2}{5 \times 8} = \frac{2}{40}$

$\frac{3}{40} > \frac{2}{40}$, so $\frac{3}{8} > \frac{2}{5}$.

I don't think my brother was fair. He had more than I did! Do you agree?

Your friend,
Puzzled Penguin

15 Write a response to Puzzled Penguin.

____

____

____

____

____

Practice

Compare.

16 $\frac{3}{6}$ ◯ $\frac{5}{10}$

17 $\frac{10}{12}$ ◯ $\frac{7}{8}$

18 $\frac{2}{6}$ ◯ $\frac{1}{5}$

19 $\frac{3}{8}$ ◯ $\frac{1}{4}$

20 $\frac{3}{10}$ ◯ $\frac{25}{100}$

21 $\frac{6}{12}$ ◯ $\frac{2}{3}$

22 $\frac{2}{5}$ ◯ $\frac{35}{100}$

23 $\frac{5}{12}$ ◯ $\frac{9}{10}$

24 $\frac{45}{100}$ ◯ $\frac{5}{10}$

25 $\frac{4}{5}$ ◯ $\frac{11}{12}$

26 $\frac{3}{12}$ ◯ $\frac{6}{8}$

27 $\frac{11}{12}$ ◯ $\frac{9}{10}$

Name ____________________

Make a Line Plot

Mai cut up strips of color paper to make a collage. The lengths of the unused pieces are shown in the table.

Length (in inches)	Number of Pieces
$\frac{1}{2}$	4
$\frac{5}{8}$	2
$\frac{3}{4}$	2
$\frac{7}{8}$	3
$1\frac{1}{4}$	2

7 Make a line plot to display the data.

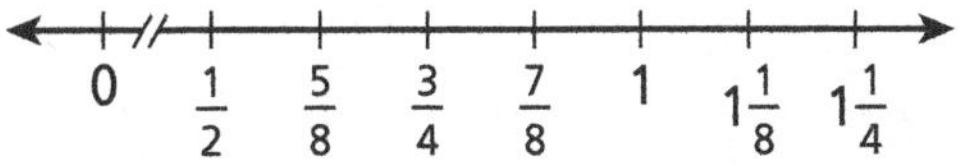

0
$\frac{1}{2}$
$\frac{5}{8}$
$\frac{3}{4}$
$\frac{7}{8}$
1
$1\frac{1}{8}$
$1\frac{1}{4}$

Paper Lengths (in inches)

8 Mai placed the shortest pieces in a row end to end.

How long was the row? ____________________

A group of students measured the widths of their hands. The measurements are shown in the table.

Width (in inches)	Number of Students
$2\frac{1}{4}$	1
$2\frac{3}{8}$	2
$2\frac{1}{2}$	2
$2\frac{5}{8}$	4
$2\frac{3}{4}$	2
$2\frac{7}{8}$	1

9 Make a line plot to display the data.

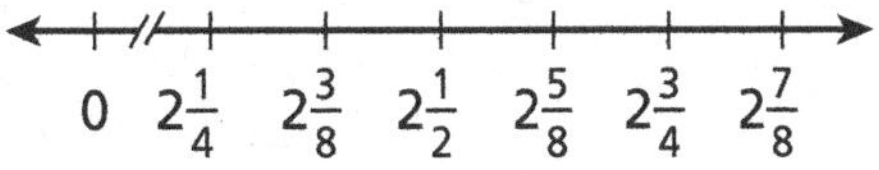

0
$2\frac{1}{4}$
$2\frac{3}{8}$
$2\frac{1}{2}$
$2\frac{5}{8}$
$2\frac{3}{4}$
$2\frac{7}{8}$

Hand Width (in inches)

10 What is the difference between the width of the widest hand and the most common hand width? ____________________

11 Write a problem you could solve by using the line plot.

____

____

Check Understanding

Describe the parts of a line plot.

____

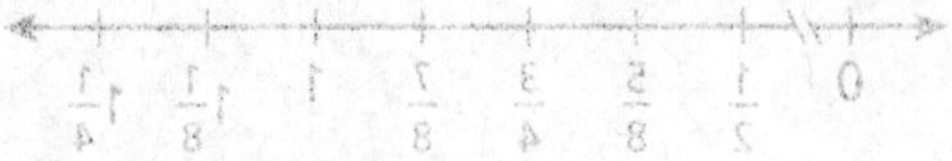

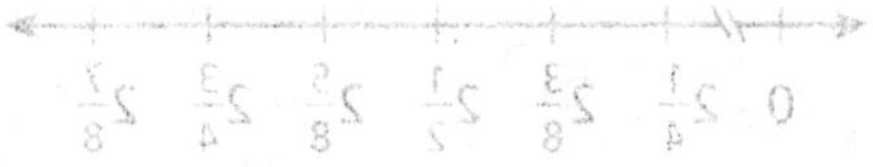

Unit 7
Quick Quiz 2

Name ______________________________

1. Write 5 fractions that are equivalent to $\frac{1}{4}$.

____

2. Simplify the fraction.

$\frac{10}{25} =$ ______

3. Use the fraction strips to compare the fractions $\frac{5}{8}$ and $\frac{7}{12}$. Write a true statement using one of the symbols >, <, or =.

$\frac{1}{8}$	$\frac{1}{8}$	$\frac{1}{8}$	$\frac{1}{8}$	$\frac{1}{8}$	$\frac{1}{8}$	$\frac{1}{8}$	$\frac{1}{8}$

$\frac{1}{12}$	$\frac{1}{12}$	$\frac{1}{12}$	$\frac{1}{12}$	$\frac{1}{12}$	$\frac{1}{12}$	$\frac{1}{12}$	$\frac{1}{12}$	$\frac{1}{12}$	$\frac{1}{12}$	$\frac{1}{12}$	$\frac{1}{12}$

____

Show your work.

4. Ethan plans for $\frac{3}{10}$ of the plants in his garden to be tomatoes. He wants $\frac{2}{5}$ of the plants to be peppers. Will Ethan plant more tomato plants or pepper plants?

____

5. The line plot shows the numbers of cups of cornmeal used in different cornbread recipes.

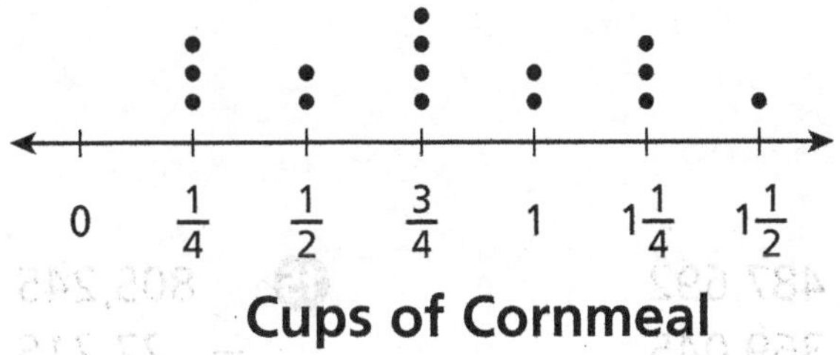

0
1/4
1/2
3/4
1
1 1/4
1 1/2
Cups of Cornmeal

How much less cornmeal is in a recipe with the least cornmeal than in a recipe with the most cornmeal?

____

Name ______________________

PATH to FLUENCY

Add or subtract.

1. 112 + 465

2. 412 − 381

3. 7,387 + 372

4. 543,582 − 451,866

5. 34,985 + 9,077

6. 60,056 − 34,163

7. 8,309 + 6,582

8. 6,478 − 5,116

9. 745 + 619

10. 799 − 476

11. 31,178 − 8,636

12. 4,708 − 3,647

13. 55,268 + 27,654

14. 487,692 + 369,045

15. 805,245 − 27,716

Dear Family:

In Lessons 8 through 16 of Unit 7 of *Math Expressions*, your child will be introduced to decimal numbers. Students will begin by using what they already know about pennies, dimes, and dollars to see connections between fractions and decimals.

Students will explore decimal numbers by using bars divided into tenths and hundredths. They will relate decimals to fractions, which are also used to represent parts of a whole.

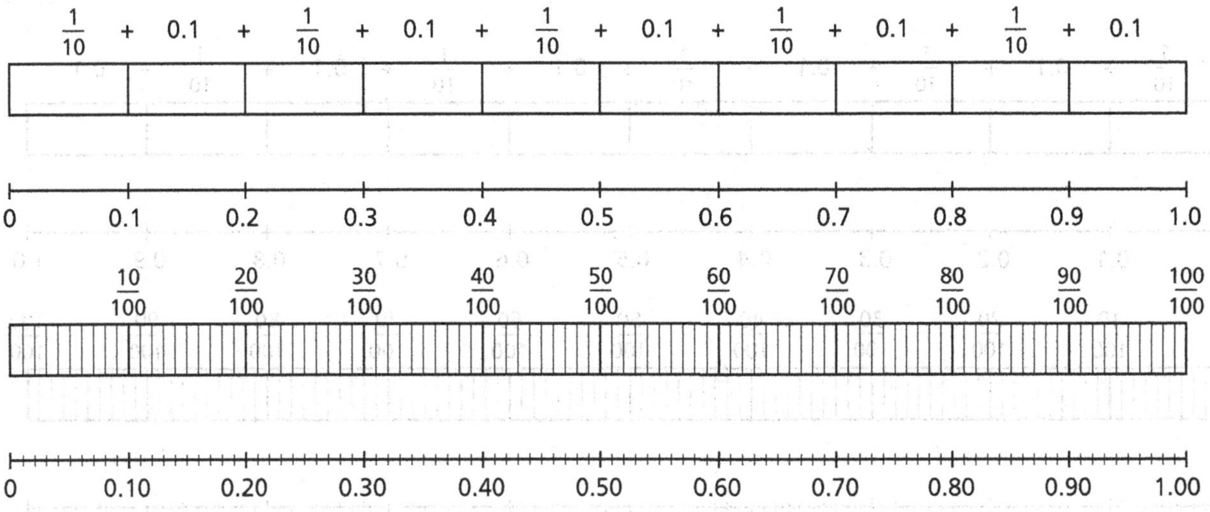

1/10 + 0.1 + 1/10 + 0.1 + 1/10 + 0.1 + 1/10 + 0.1 + 1/10 + 0.1
0 0.1 0.2 0.3 0.4 0.5 0.6 0.7 0.8 0.9 1.0
10/100 20/100 30/100 40/100 50/100 60/100 70/100 80/100 90/100 100/100
0 0.10 0.20 0.30 0.40 0.50 0.60 0.70 0.80 0.90 1.00

Students will read, write, and model decimal numbers. They will learn to combine whole numbers with decimals. They will work with numbers such as 9.001, 1.72, and 12.9. Students will compare decimal numbers with other decimal numbers. They will also order decimals from least to greatest or greatest to least.

Students will apply their understanding of decimal concepts when they compare and order decimals.

Comparing Decimals

6.8 ◯ 3.42   6.80 (>) 3.42

Adding a zero makes the numbers easier to compare.

Please contact me if you have any questions or comments.

Thank you.

Sincerely,
Your child's teacher

Estimada familia:

En las Lecciones 8 a 16 de la Unidad 7 de Expresiones en matemáticas, se presentarán los números decimales. Para comenzar, los estudiantes usarán lo que ya saben acerca de las monedas de un centavo, de las monedas de diez y de los dólares, para ver cómo se relacionan las fracciones y los decimales.

Los estudiantes estudiarán los números decimales usando barras divididas en décimos y centésimos. Relacionarán los decimales con las fracciones que también se usan para representar partes del entero.

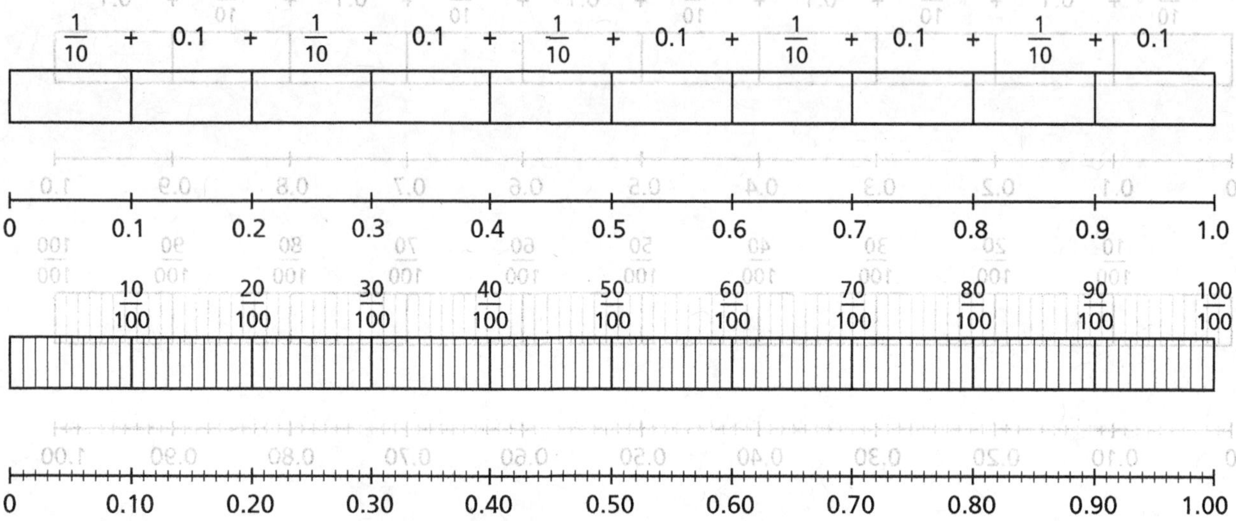
1/10 + 0.1 + 1/10 + 0.1 + 1/10 + 0.1 + 1/10 + 0.1 + 1/10 + 0.1
0 0.1 0.2 0.3 0.4 0.5 0.6 0.7 0.8 0.9 1.0
10/100 20/100 30/100 40/100 50/100 60/100 70/100 80/100 90/100 100/100
0 0.10 0.20 0.30 0.40 0.50 0.60 0.70 0.80 0.90 1.00

Los estudiantes leerán, escribirán y representarán números decimales. Aprenderán a combinar números enteros con decimales. Trabajarán con números tales como 9.001, 1.72 y 12.9. Compararán números decimales con otros números decimales. También ordenarán decimales de menor a mayor o mayor a menor.

Al comparar y ordenar decimales, los estudiantes aplicarán los conceptos decimales que ya conozcan.

Comparar decimales

6.8 ◯ 3.42 6.80 (>) 3.42

Añadir un cero facilita la comparación de números.

Si tiene alguna duda o algún comentario, por favor comuníquese conmigo.

Gracias.

Atentamente,
El maestro de su niño

Name ______________________________

Model Equivalent Fractions and Decimals

Write a fraction and a decimal to represent the shaded part of each whole.

15 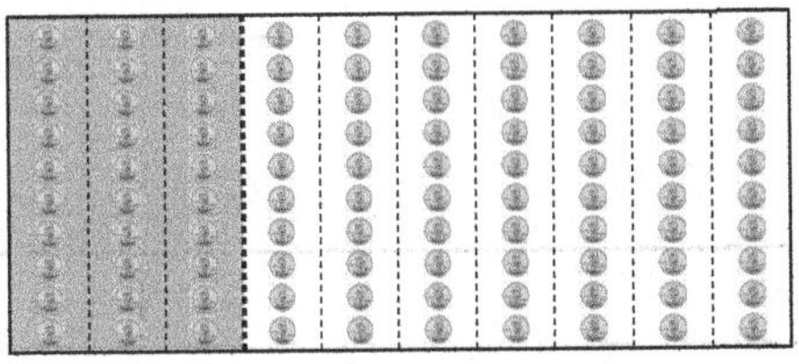

____

16 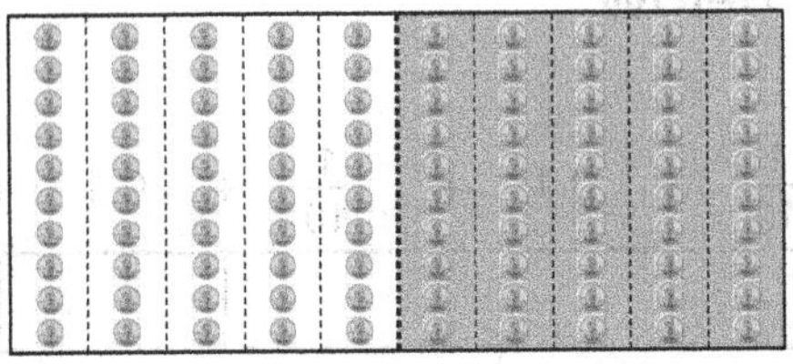

____

Divide each whole and use shading to show the given fraction or decimal.

17 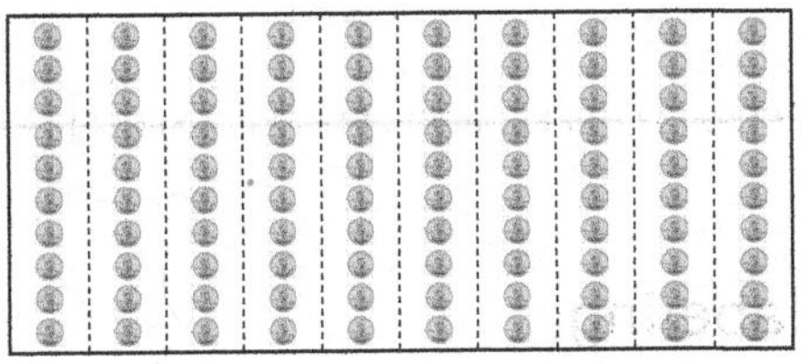 0.75

18 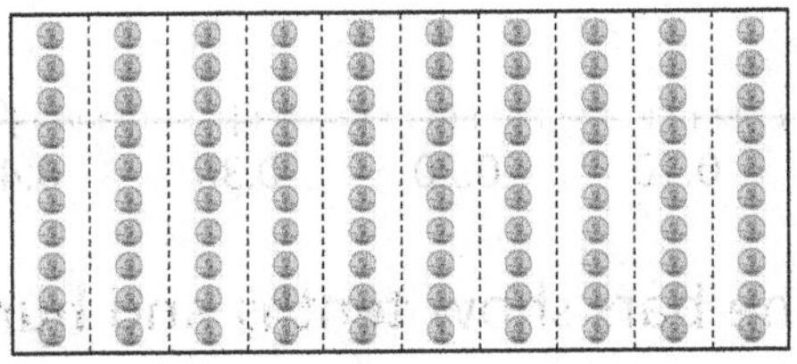 $\frac{9}{10}$

Shade these grids to show that $\frac{3}{2} = 1\frac{1}{2}$.

19 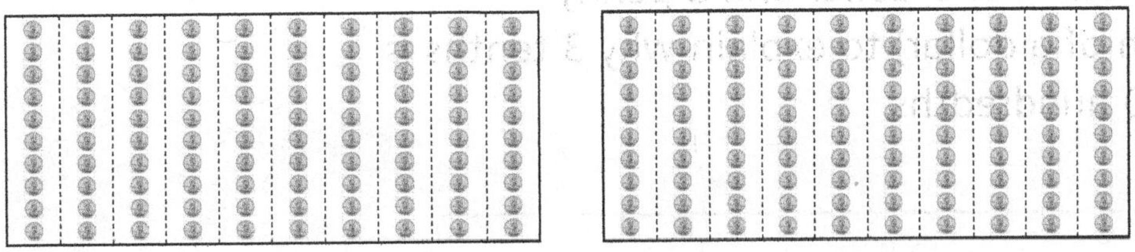

Check Understanding

Name a fraction and a decimal that represents 60 cents as part of 1 dollar. Draw a diagram to support your answer.

____

Name ____________________

Understand Tenths and Hundredths

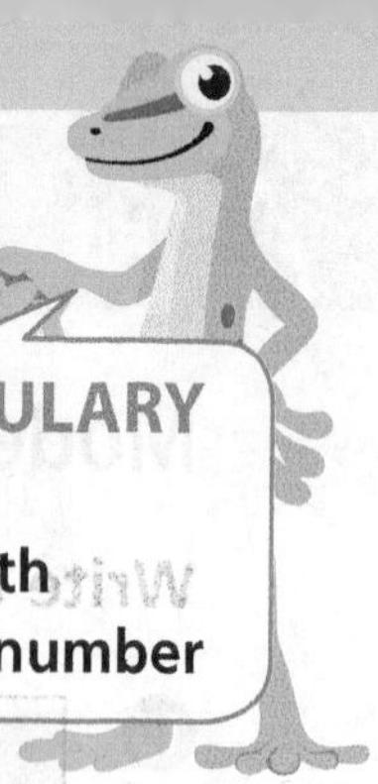

VOCABULARY
tenth
hundredth
decimal number

Answer the questions about the bars and number lines below.

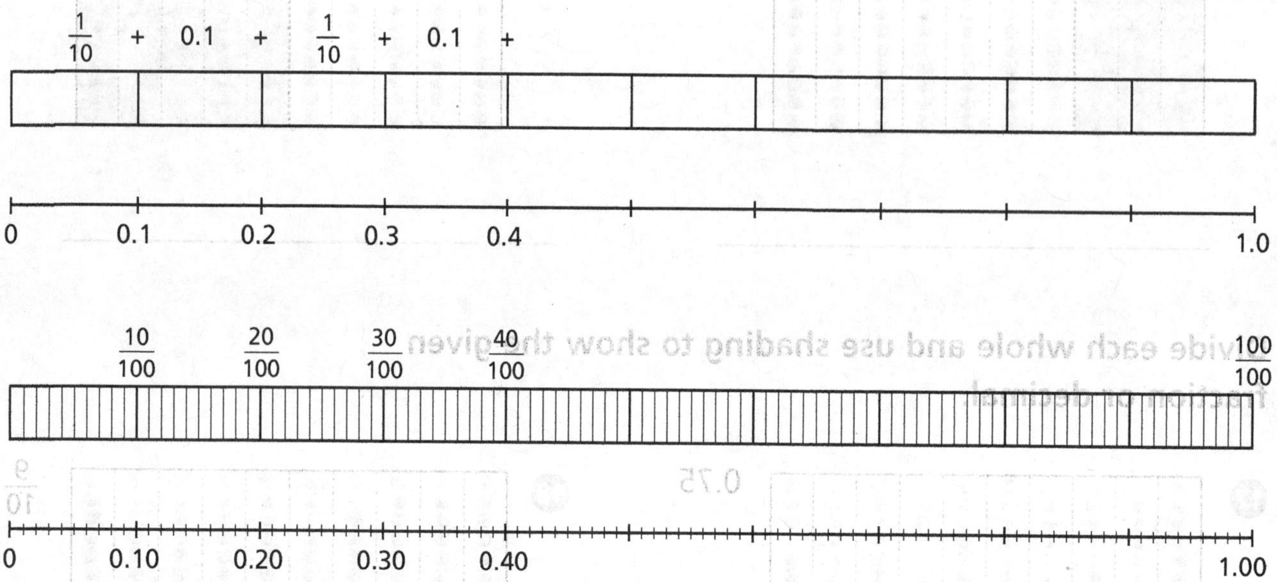

$\frac{1}{10}$ + 0.1 + $\frac{1}{10}$ + 0.1 +
0 0.1 0.2 0.3 0.4 1.0
$\frac{10}{100}$ $\frac{20}{100}$ $\frac{30}{100}$ $\frac{40}{100}$ $\frac{100}{100}$
0 0.10 0.20 0.30 0.40 1.00

1. The bars show **tenths** and **hundredths**. Finish labeling the bars and number lines using fractions and **decimal numbers**.

2. Use what you know about fractions and about money (a dime = one tenth of a dollar and a penny = one hundredth of a dollar) to explain why 3 tenths is the same as 30 hundredths.

____

____

____

3. One tenth is greater than one hundredth even though 10 is less than 100. Explain why this is true.

____

____

Name ____________________

Practice Writing Decimal Numbers

Write these numbers in decimal form.

4. 8 tenths ______
5. 6 hundredths ______
6. 35 hundredths ______
7. $\frac{92}{100}$ ______
8. $\frac{2}{10}$ ______
9. $\frac{9}{100}$ ______

Answer the questions below.

In the little town of Silver there are 100 people. Four are left-handed.

10. What decimal number shows the fraction of the people who are left-handed?

______

11. What decimal number shows the fraction of the people who are right-handed?

______

There are 10 children playing volleyball, and 6 of them are boys.

12. What decimal number shows the fraction of the players who are boys?

______

13. What decimal number shows the fraction of the players who are girls?

______

Complete the table.

	Name of Coin	Fraction of a Dollar	Decimal Part of a Dollar
14	Penny	$\frac{\quad}{100}$	
15	Nickel	$\frac{\quad}{100} =$	
16	Dime	$\frac{\quad}{100} =$	
17	Quarter	$\frac{\quad}{100} =$	

Check Understanding

Explain why 0.7 = 0.70.

0.1 — 0.1	0.01 — 0.0 1
0.2 — 0.2	0.02 — 0.0 2
0.3 — 0.3	0.03 — 0.0 3
0.4 — 0.4	0.04 — 0.0 4
0.5 — 0.5	0.05 — 0.0 5
0.6 — 0.6	0.06 — 0.0 6
0.7 — 0.7	0.07 — 0.0 7
0.8 — 0.8	0.08 — 0.0 8
0.9 — 0.9	0.09 — 0.0 9

.0 0	
.0 0	
.0 0	
.0 0	
>	<

> <

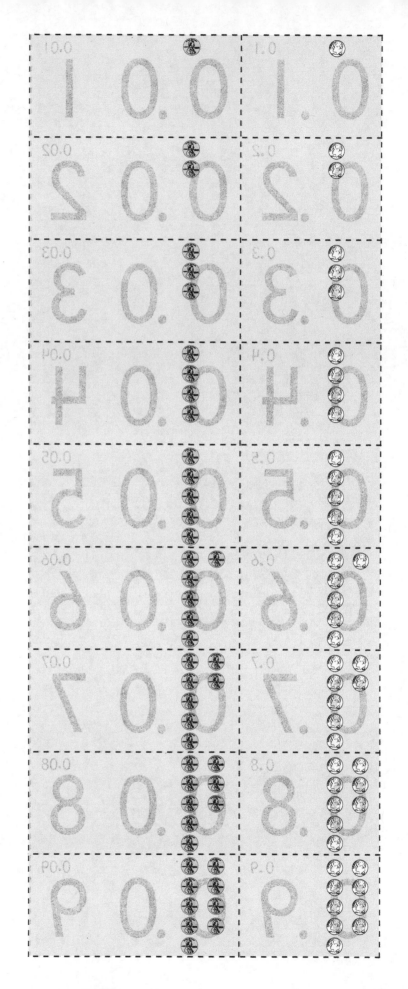

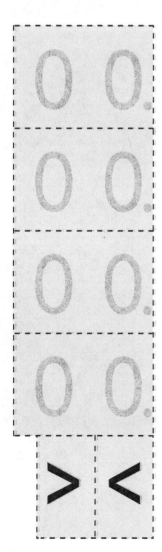

100 100	10 10	1 1
200 200	20 20	2 2
300 300	30 30	3 3
400 400	40 40	4 4
500 500	50 50	5 5
600 600	60 60	6 6
700 700	70 70	7 7
800 800	80 80	8 8
900 900	90 90	9 9

$1	$10	$100
$1 $1	$10 $10	$100 $100
$1 $1 $1	$10 $10 $10	$100 $100 $100
$1 $1 $1 $1	$10 $10 $10 $10	$100 $100 $100 $100
$1 $1 $1 $1 $1	$10 $10 $10 $10 $10	$100 $100 $100 $100 $100
$1 $1 $1 $1 $1 $1	$10 $10 $10 $10 $10 $10	$100 $100 $100 $100 $100 $100
$1 $1 $1 $1 $1 $1 $1	$10 $10 $10 $10 $10 $10 $10	$100 $100 $100 $100 $100 $100 $100
$1 $1 $1 $1 $1 $1 $1 $1	$10 $10 $10 $10 $10 $10 $10 $10	$100 $100 $100 $100 $100 $100 $100 $100
$1 $1 $1 $1 $1 $1 $1 $1 $1	$10 $10 $10 $10 $10 $10 $10 $10 $10	$100 $100 $100 $100 $100 $100 $100 $100 $100

Unit 7
Quick Quiz 3

Name ______________________

Write the correct answer.

1. Mark has 100 marbles. Eight are bumblebee marbles. What decimal number shows the fraction of marbles that are bumblebees?

____

2. An insect egg can be as small as two hundredths of a millimeter long. What is this number written as a decimal?

____

3. On a tree farm, 0.28 of the trees are oak. Write this decimal as a fraction.

____

4. James ran a race in 2.2 hours. Casey ran the same race in 2.25 hours. Who took less time to run the race?

____

5. Traci rode her mountain bike 2.8 miles on Monday. She rode 2.7 miles on Tuesday. On which day did she ride a longer distance? Write the comparison using >, <, or =.

____

Fluency Check 22

Name

PATH to FLUENCY

Add or subtract.

1. 512 + 436

2. 38,923 + 35,468

3. 782,465 − 447,869

4. 674 − 338

5. 128,492 + 56,932

6. 2,492 + 455

7. 76,829 + 2,457

8. 32,589 − 3,741

9. 935 + 562

10. 8,241 + 4,976

11. 40,670 − 19,843

12. 9,945 − 3,831

13. 3,280 − 1,159

14. 506 − 305

15. 670,834 − 88,560

1,000 1,000	0.001 0.001
2,000 2,000	0.002 0.002
3,000 3,000	0.003 0.003
4,000 4,000	0.004 0.004
5,000 5,000	0.005 0.005
6,000 6,000	0.006 0.006
7,000 7,000	0.007 0.007
8,000 8,000	0.008 0.008
9,000 9,000	0.009 0.009

.000

.000

.000

.000

$1,000

$1,000
$1,000

$1,000
$1,000
$1,000

$1,000
$1,000
$1,000
$1,000

$1,000
$1,000
$1,000
$1,000
$1,000

$1,000 $1,000
$1,000
$1,000
$1,000
$1,000

$1,000 $1,000
$1,000 $1,000
$1,000
$1,000
$1,000

$1,000 $1,000
$1,000 $1,000
$1,000 $1,000
$1,000
$1,000

$1,000 $1,000
$1,000 $1,000
$1,000 $1,000
$1,000 $1,000
$1,000

Name ____________________

Use a Number Line

You can use a number line to compare and order decimal numbers.

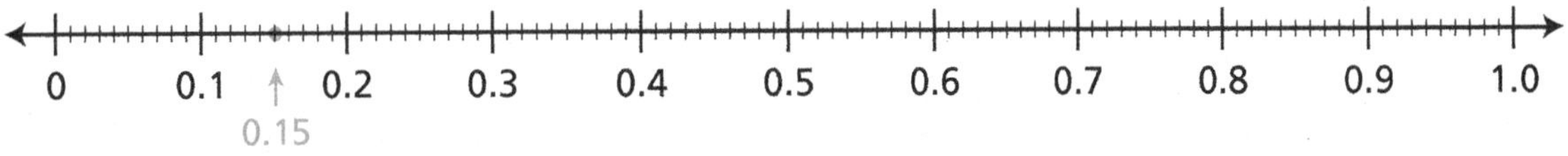
0
0.1
0.15
0.2
0.3
0.4
0.5
0.6
0.7
0.8
0.9
1.0

1. Label points on the number line above to show 0.09, 0.23, and 0.17.
2. Write the numbers in Exercise 1 in order from least to greatest.

   ____

3. How could you use the number line to compare 0.59 and 0.83?

   ____

Order the decimals from least to greatest.

4. 0.5, 0.2, 0.1 ____________
5. 0.13, 0.08, 0.2 ____________
6. 0.12, 0.3, 0.04 ____________
7. 1.0, 0.1, 0.11 ____________

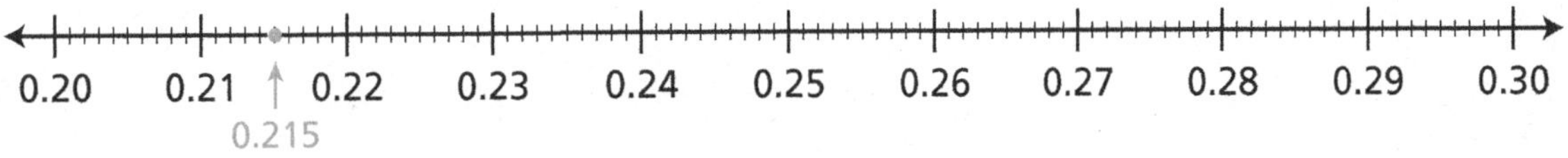
0.20
0.21
0.215
0.22
0.23
0.24
0.25
0.26
0.27
0.28
0.29
0.30

8. Label points on the number line above to show 0.250, 0.271, and 0.225.
9. Write the numbers in Exercise 8 in order from greatest to least.

   ____

10. Explain how you know 0.310 is greater than 0.269.

    ____

Use the number line to order the decimals from greatest to least.

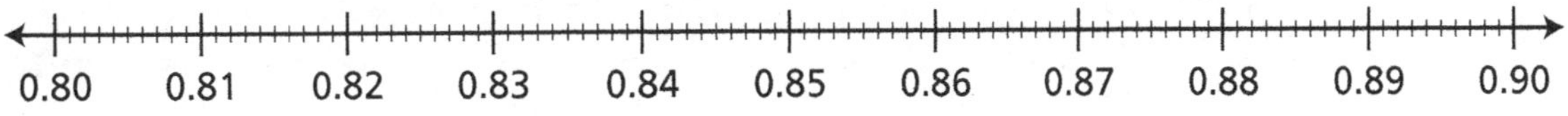
0.80
0.81
0.82
0.83
0.84
0.85
0.86
0.87
0.88
0.89
0.90

11. 0.815, 0.85, 0.891 ____________
12. 0.882, 0.808, 0.822 ____________

Name ____________________

Write the correct answer.

1. Read and write the mixed number as a decimal.

$21\frac{206}{1,000}$

____

2. Write the number in expanded form.

302.651

____

3. The table shows scores in a gymnastics competition. List the competitors in order from the highest score to the lowest score.

Competitor	Score
Rahul	8.950
Andrei	7.895
Saul	8.595
Alberto	8.095

____

4. Use the number line. What is 0.273 rounded to the nearest tenth?

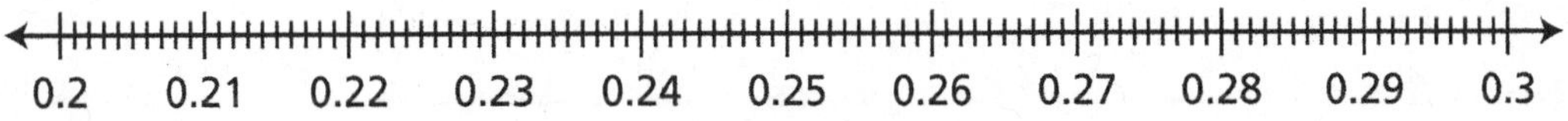
0.2
0.21
0.22
0.23
0.24
0.25
0.26
0.27
0.28
0.29
0.3

____

5. There are 1,000 seats in a theater. 455 seats are in the lower level. What decimal number represents the number of seats in the lower level?

____

Fluency Check 23

Name ________________________

PATH to FLUENCY

Multiply.

1. 1 × 3 = ☐
2. 3 × 2 = ☐
3. 4 × 3 = ☐
4. 4 × 1 = ☐
5. 2 × 5 = ☐
6. 6 × 1 = ☐
7. 6 × 6 = ☐
8. 8 × 4 = ☐
9. 5 × 7 = ☐
10. 9 × 3 = ☐
11. 8 × 8 = ☐
12. 6 × 9 = ☐
13. 7 × 10 = ☐
14. 10 × 10 = ☐
15. 8 × 9 = ☐

Name ______________________

1 For Exercises 1a–1d, write > or < to make the inequality true.

1a. $\frac{3}{5}$ ◯ $\frac{1}{5}$

1c. $\frac{9}{10}$ ◯ $\frac{9}{12}$

1b. $\frac{2}{8}$ ◯ $\frac{2}{3}$

1d. $\frac{5}{8}$ ◯ $\frac{7}{8}$

2 Choose numbers from the tiles to make an equivalent fraction with the least possible denominator.

2 | 3 | 4 | 6

$\frac{8}{12} = \frac{\square}{\square}$

3 Farid measures the masses of four books in kilograms. He records the data in the table. Which two books have the same mass?

Masses of Books

Book	1	2	3	4
Mass (kg)	1.12	1.20	1.02	1.2

Ⓐ Books 1 and 3

Ⓑ Books 2 and 3

Ⓒ Books 3 and 4

Ⓓ Books 2 and 4

4 In a survey, $\frac{7}{10}$ of the students said they watched the news last week. Complete the fraction equation.

$$\frac{7}{10} = \frac{\square}{100}$$

Name ____________________

5 A trail is $\frac{7}{12}$ mile long. Select the trail length that is shorter than $\frac{7}{12}$ mile. Mark all that apply.

Ⓐ $\frac{3}{8}$ mile　Ⓑ $\frac{2}{3}$ mile　Ⓒ $\frac{3}{4}$ mile　Ⓓ $\frac{1}{2}$ mile

6 On average, a chimpanzee spends about $\frac{2}{5}$ of the day sleeping. A squirrel spends about $\frac{5}{8}$ of the day sleeping. A three-toed sloth spends about $\frac{5}{6}$ of the day sleeping. For Exercises 6a–6d, choose True or False to best describe the statement.

6a. A chimpanzee spends more of the day sleeping than a three-toed sloth. ○ True ○ False

6b. A squirrel spends more of the day sleeping than a chimpanzee. ○ True ○ False

6c. A three-toed sloth spends more of the day sleeping than a squirrel. ○ True ○ False

6d. A chimpanzee sleeps more than the other two types of animals. ○ True ○ False

7 Emily and Leah each brought a full water bottle to practice. Their bottles were the same shape, but Leah's bottle was taller than Emily's. Each girl drank $\frac{1}{2}$ of her water.

Part A

Draw a picture to show Emily and Leah's water bottles. Shade the bottles to show how much water each girl originally had. Then cross out the amount each girl drank.

Part B

Did each girl drink the same amount of water? Explain.

Name ______________________________

8 Locate and draw a point on the number line for the fraction or mixed number. Then label it with its corresponding letter.

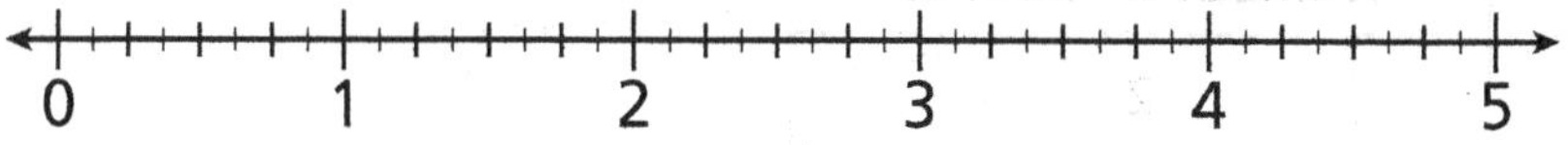
0
1
2
3
4
5

a. $4\frac{1}{2}$ b. $\frac{7}{8}$ c. $1\frac{3}{4}$ d. $3\frac{1}{4}$ e. $2\frac{3}{8}$

9 For Exercises 9a–9c, complete the chain of equivalent fractions.

9a. $\frac{2}{5} = \frac{\square}{10} = \frac{\square}{15} = \frac{\square}{20}$

9b. $\frac{6}{12} = \frac{\square}{6} = \frac{1}{\square}$

9c. $\frac{5}{8} = \frac{\square}{16} = \frac{\square}{24} = \frac{20}{\square}$

10 Write five fractions that are equivalent to $\frac{1}{6}$.

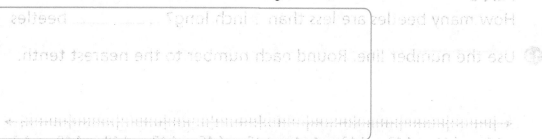

11 A lizard has a length of $\frac{43}{100}$ meter. Write $\frac{43}{100}$ in decimal form. $\square$

Name ______________________________

12 Tione is researching beetles. She records the lengths of some beetles in the table.

Length (in inches)	Number of Beetles
$\frac{1}{4}$	2
$\frac{1}{2}$	3
$\frac{3}{4}$	6
1	1
$1\frac{1}{4}$	4
$1\frac{1}{2}$	2

Part A

Make a line plot to display the data.

Part B

How many beetles are less than 1 inch long? __________ beetles

13 Use the number line. Round each number to the nearest tenth.

4.1
4.11
4.12
4.13
4.14
4.15
4.16
4.17
4.18
4.19
4.2

13a. 4.125 ______ **13b.** 4.156 ______ **13c.** 4.182 ______

Name ____________________

14 Write a decimal to make the statement true.

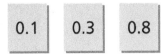

0.1	0.3	0.8

☐ > 0.650 0.15 > ☐ ☐ = 0.30

15 A forest ranger saw 10 deer. There were 2 male and 8 female deer. What fraction or decimal number shows the part of the deer that were female? Mark all that apply.

Ⓐ $\frac{2}{10}$ Ⓒ 0.80 Ⓔ $\frac{8}{10}$

Ⓑ 0.2 Ⓓ 0.08 Ⓕ 0.8

16 Each model represents 1 whole dollar. The shaded part represents the part of a dollar Loren took to the bank.

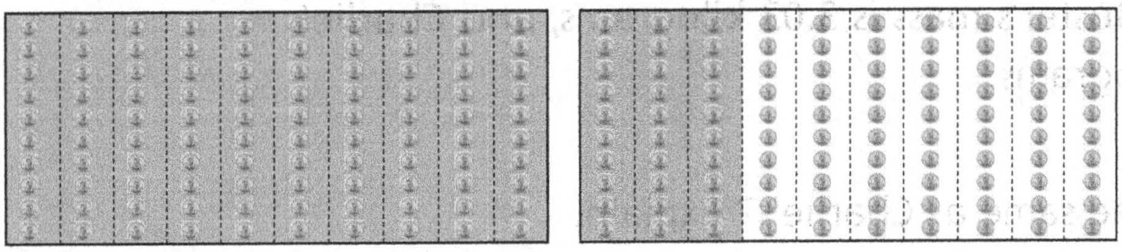

Part A

Write a mixed number to represent the part of a dollar Loren took to the bank.

☐

Part B

Loren says she can represent the part of a dollar she took to the bank as 1.3 but not as 1.30. Do you agree? Why or why not?

Name

17 Beth wrote the number sixty-one and five hundred eight thousandths in decimal form.

What did Beth write? ☐

18 Trading cards come in packs of 1,000. Becca has 3 full packs and 7 more cards. For Exercises 18a–18d, choose Yes or No to tell whether the number represents the number of packs Becca has.

18a. 3.007	○ Yes	○ No
18b. 3 and 7 thousandths	○ Yes	○ No
18c. three and one seventh	○ Yes	○ No
18d. 3.7	○ Yes	○ No

19 A vet measures the mass of three puppies. Suzy's mass is 3.3 kilograms. Buster's mass is 3.03 kilograms, and Charlie's mass is 3.30 kilograms.

Part A

Is Suzy's mass the same as Charlie's? Explain.

Part B

A fourth puppy, Pluto, has a mass of 3.33 kilograms. Which of the four puppies has the least mass? Explain how you found your answer.

Name

Bicycle Parking Only

Jacob rides his bike to school and parks it in the bicycle rack near the front entrance. He counted the number of bicycles in the rack each school day for a week and recorded his count in this table.

Bicycles in the Front Entrance Rack					
Day	**Monday**	**Tuesday**	**Wednesday**	**Thursday**	**Friday**
Number of Bicycles	3	7	4	8	10

1. The rack can hold up to 10 bicycles. What fraction of the bicycle rack was used each day?

2. Jenny thinks that on Tuesday, about $\frac{1}{2}$ of the bicycle rack was used. Jacob thinks about $\frac{1}{2}$ of the rack was used on Wednesday. Who is correct? Use a diagram or number line to justify your answer.

3. What decimal number shows the part of the bicycle rack that was used each day?

4. Jacob thinks it is easier to write decimals than fractions to describe how much of the rack was used each day. Do you think he would feel the same if the rack had spaces for 12 bikes? Explain your reasoning.

 Name

Jacob counted the number of bicycles at the back entrance for the same week. The back entrance bicycle rack also holds 10 bicycles. His results are in the table below.

Bicycles in the Back Entrance Rack					
Day	Monday	Tuesday	Wednesday	Thursday	Friday
Number of Bicycles	7	4	8	7	2

5 What fraction of the spaces was used in the back entrance rack on Friday?

6 On which day of the week were $\frac{4}{5}$ of the spaces in the back entrance rack used? Explain how you solved the problem.

7 What decimal number shows the part of the back entrance rack that was not used each day?

8 On the following Monday, $\frac{3}{5}$ of the front entrance rack was used and 0.3 of the back entrance rack was used. Were there more bikes in the front rack or the back rack? Explain.

Dear Family:

In the first half of Unit 8, your child will be learning to recognize and describe geometric figures. One type of figure is an angle. Your child will use a protractor to find the measures of angles.

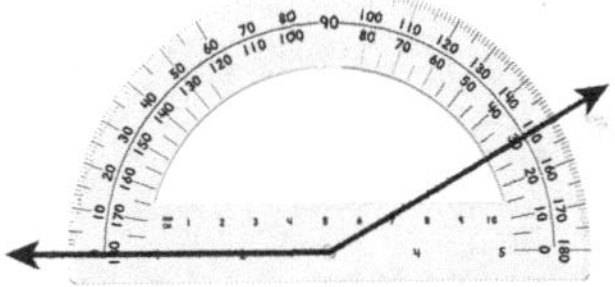

Other figures, such as triangles, may be named based on their angles and sides.

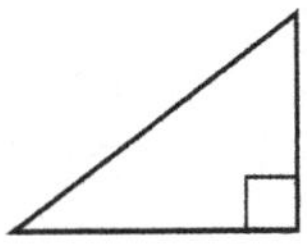

Right triangle

One right angle (90°)

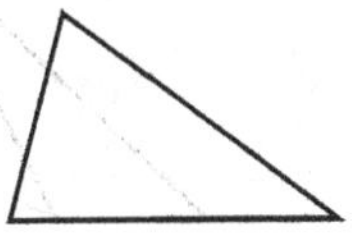

Acute triangle

All angles less than 90°

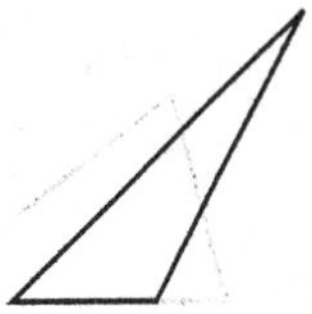

Obtuse triangle

One angle greater than 90°

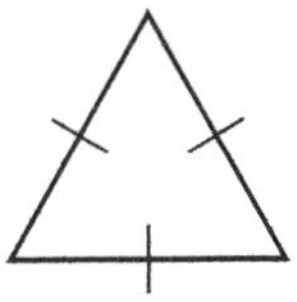

Equilateral triangle

all three sides of equal length

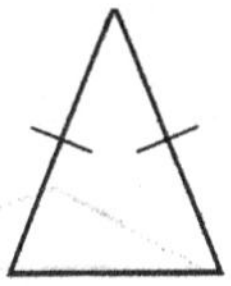

Isosceles triangle

two sides of equal length

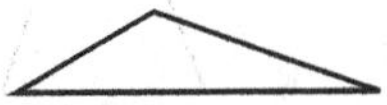

Scalene triangle

three sides of different lengths

Be sure that your child continues to review and practice the basics of multiplication and division. A good understanding of the basics will be very important in later math courses when students learn more difficult concepts in multiplication and division.

If you have any questions or comments, please contact me.

Thank you.

Sincerely,
Your child's teacher

Estimada familia:

En la primera parte de la Unidad 8, su niño aprenderá a reconocer y a describir figuras geométricas. Un ángulo es un tipo de figura. Su niño usará un transportador para hallar las medidas de los ángulos.

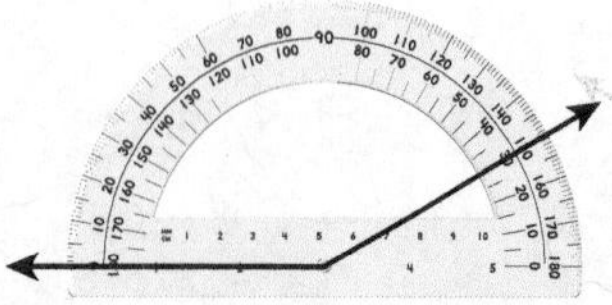

Otras figuras, tales como los triángulos, se nombran según sus ángulos y lados.

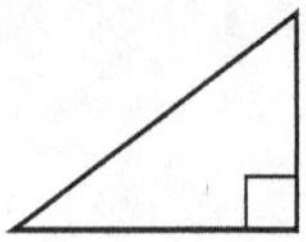

Triángulo rectángulo

Tiene un ángulo recto (90°)

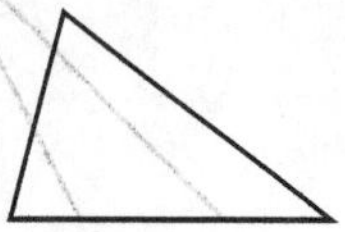

Triángulo acutángulo

Todos los ángulos son menores que 90°

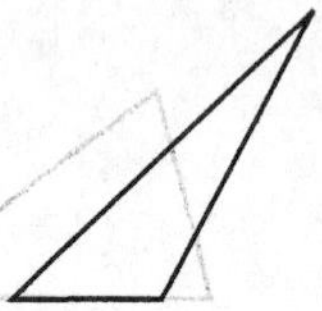

Triángulo obtusángulo

Tiene un ángulo mayor que 90°

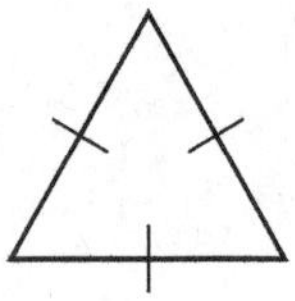

Triángulo equilátero

los tres lados tienen la misma longitud

Triángulo isósceles

dos lados tienen la misma longitud

Triángulo escaleno

los tres lados tienen diferente longitud

Asegúrese de que su niño siga repasando y practicando las multiplicaciones y divisiones básicas. Es importante que domine las operaciones básicas para que, en los cursos de matemáticas de más adelante, pueda aprender conceptos de multiplicación y división más difíciles.

Si tiene alguna pregunta o algún comentario, por favor comuníquese conmigo.

Gracias.

Atentamente,
El maestro de su niño

acute angle

angle

acute triangle

circle

adjacent sides

congruent

A figure formed by two rays with the same endpoint.

An angle smaller than a right angle.

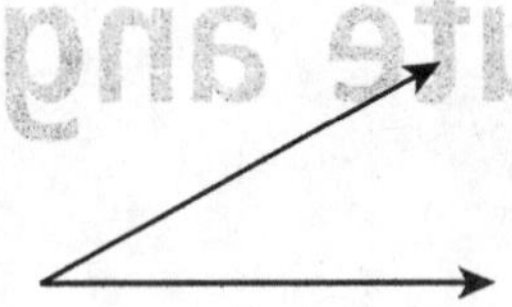

A plane figure that forms a closed path so that all the points on the path are the same distance from a point called the center.

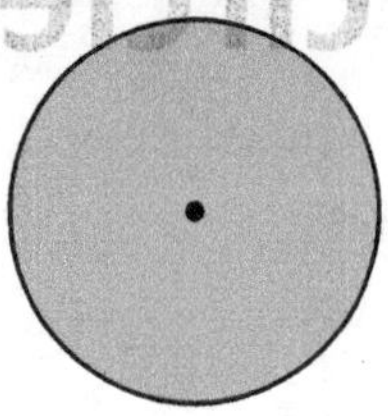

A triangle with three acute angles.

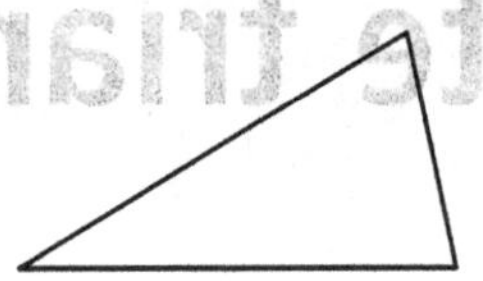

Figures that are the same size and shape.

Two sides that meet at a point.

Example:
Sides *a* and *b* are adjacent.

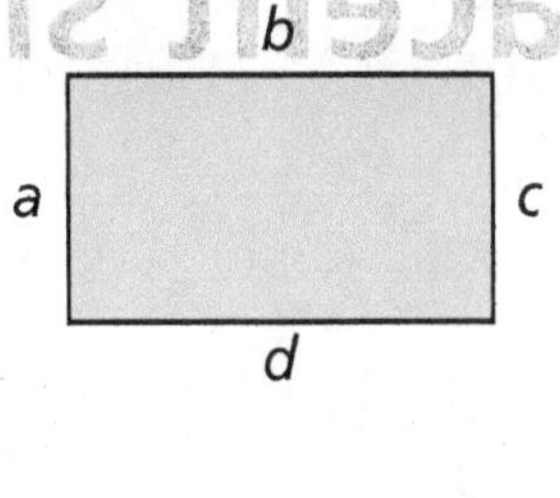
b
a
c
d

degree (°)

equilateral triangle

diagonal of a quadrilateral

intersecting lines

endpoint

isosceles triangle

A triangle with three sides of equal length.

A unit for measuring angles.

Lines that meet at a point.

Examples:

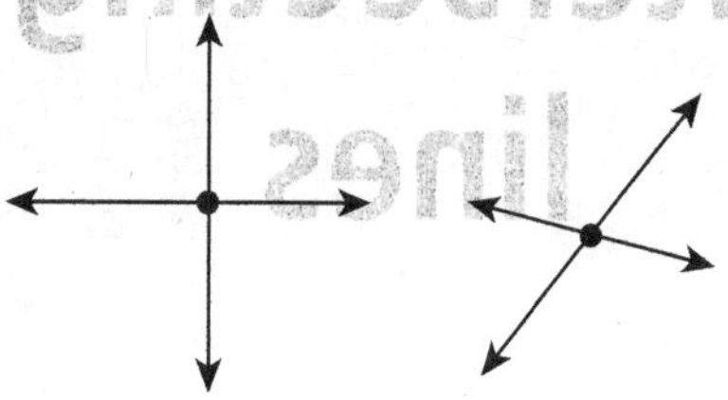

A line segment that connects two opposite corners (vertices).

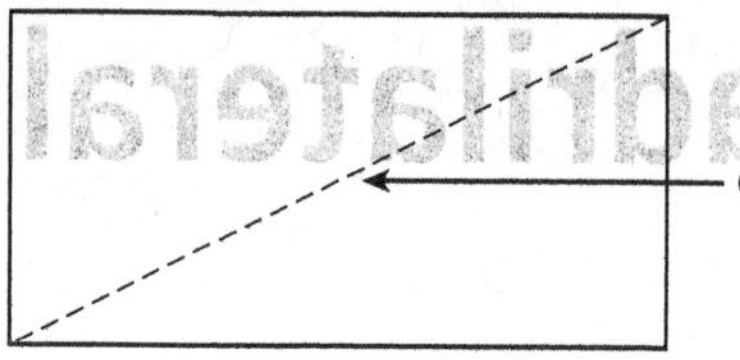
diagonal

A triangle with at least two sides of equal length.

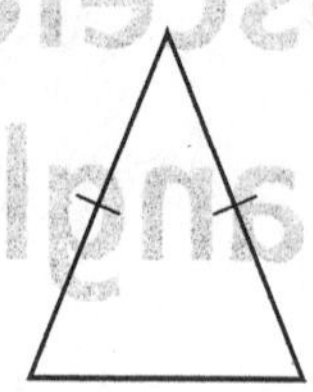

The point at either end of a line segment or the beginning point of a ray.

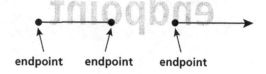
endpoint
endpoint
endpoint

kite

line segment

line

line symmetry

line of symmetry

obtuse angle

Part of a line that has two endpoints.

A quadrilateral with two pairs of equal adjacent sides.

Examples:

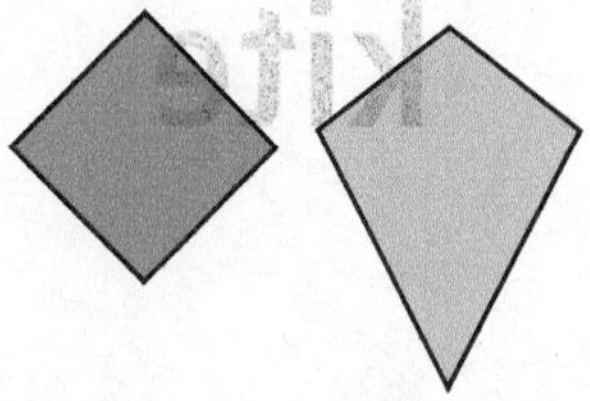

A figure has line symmetry if it can be folded along a line to create two halves that match exactly.

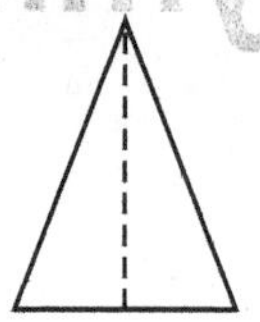

A straight path that goes on forever in opposite directions.

Example:
line *AB*

A
B

An angle greater than a right angle and less than a straight angle.

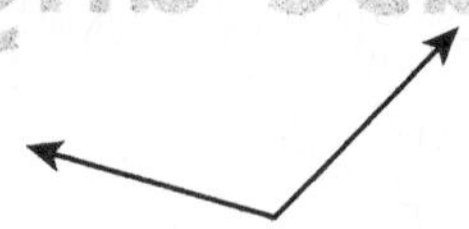

A line on which a figure can be folded so that the two halves match exactly.

line of symmetry

obtuse triangle

parallelogram

opposite sides

perpendicular lines

parallel lines

point

A quadrilateral with both pairs of opposite sides parallel.

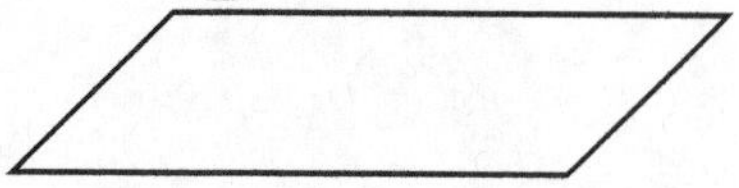

A triangle with one obtuse angle.

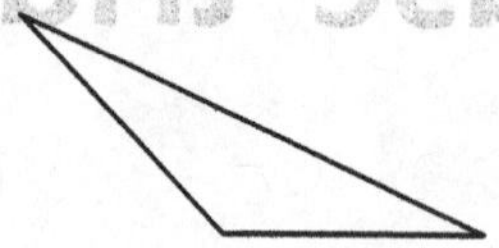

Lines, line segments, or rays are perpendicular if they form right angles.

Example:
These two lines are perpendicular.

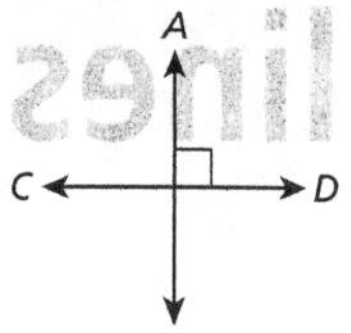
A
C
D
B

Sides that are across from each other; they do not meet at a point.

Example:
Sides *a* and *c* are opposite.

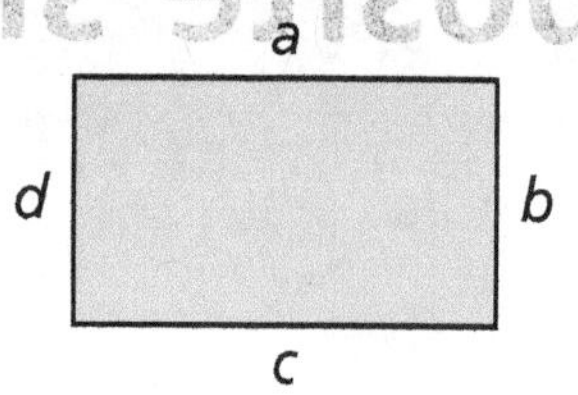
a
d
b
c

A location in a plane. It is usually shown by a dot.

Lines in the same plane that never intersect are parallel. Line segments and rays that are part of parallel lines are also parallel.

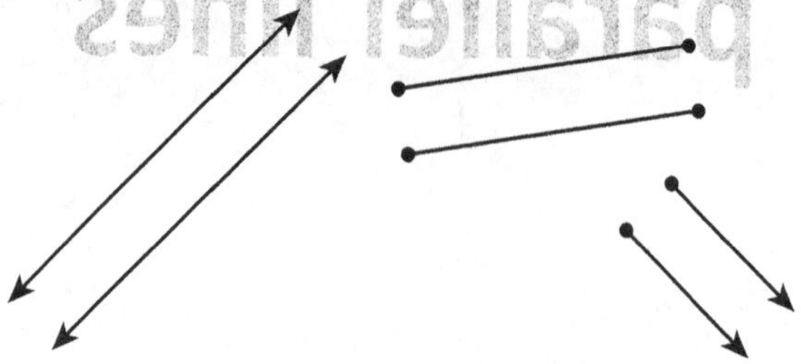

polygon	**ray**
protractor	**reflection**
quadrilateral	**reflex angle**

Part of a line that has one endpoint and extends without end in one direction.

A closed plane figure with sides made of straight line segments.

A flip of a figure across a line, which is called the line of reflection.

Example:

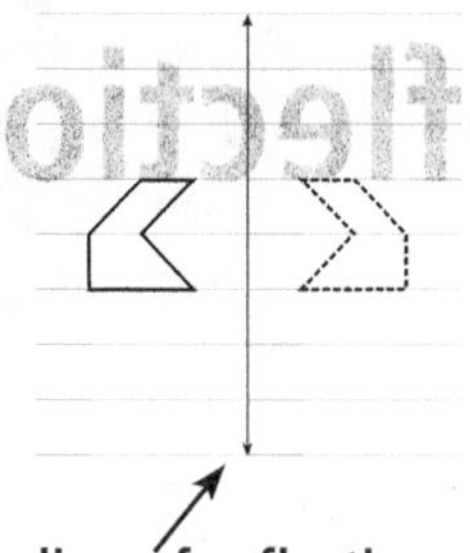
line of reflection

A semicircular tool for measuring and constructing angles.

An angle with a measure that is greater than 180° and less than 360°.

A polygon with four sides.

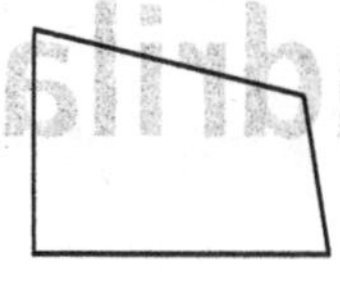

rhombus

rotation

right angle

scalene triangle

right triangle

straight angle

A turn of a figure in degrees (°), either clockwise or counterclockwise.

Example:

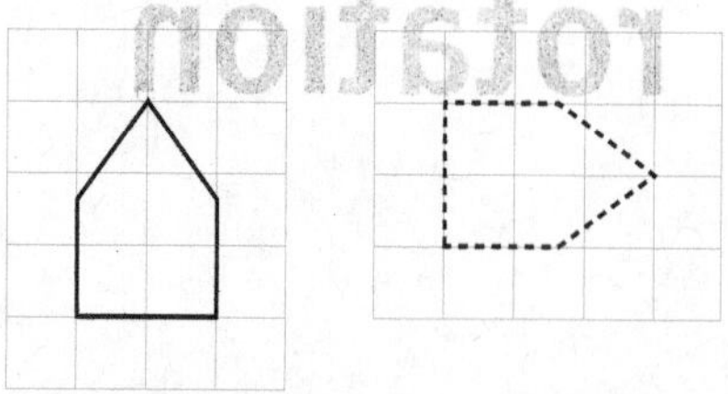

A parallelogram with sides of equal length.

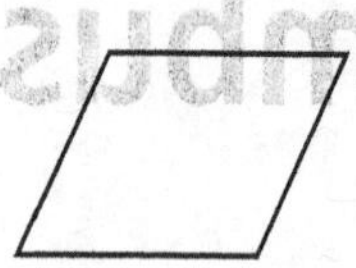

A triangle with no equal sides.

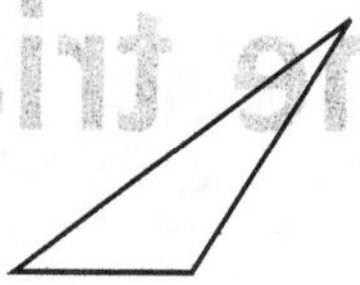

An angle that measures 90°.

An angle that measures 180°.

A triangle with one right angle.

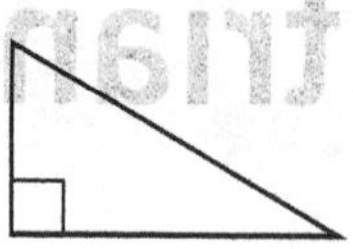

transformation	**Venn diagram**
translation	**vertex of an angle**
trapezoid	**vertex of a polygon**

A diagram that uses circles or other shapes to show how sets are related.

Example:

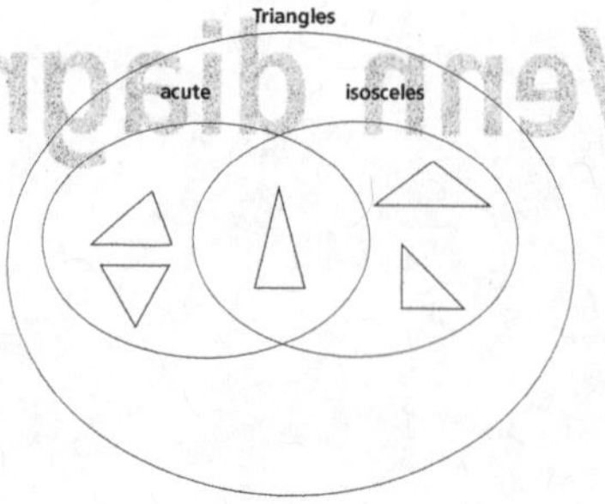
Triangles
acute
isosceles

A change in the position of a figure. Rotations, reflections, and translations are types of transformations.

A point that is shared by two sides of an angle.

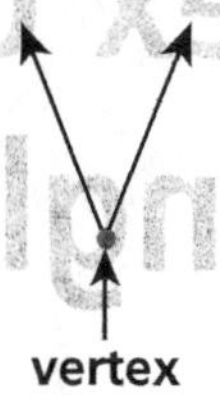
vertex

A slide of a figure. Each point of the figure moves the same distance in the same direction.

Example:

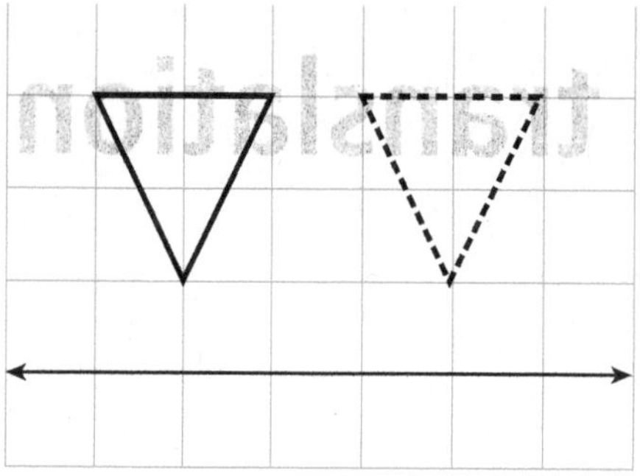

A point that is shared by two sides of a polygon.

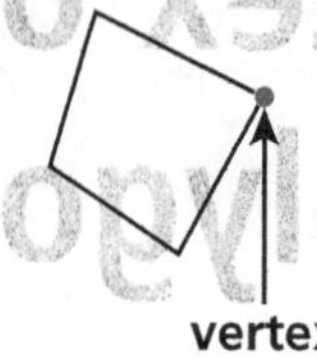
vertex

A quadrilateral with exactly one pair of parallel sides.

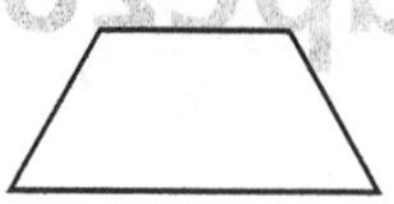

Name ______________________________

Classify Angles

Use the letters to name each angle. Then write *acute, right,* or *obtuse* to describe each angle.

10

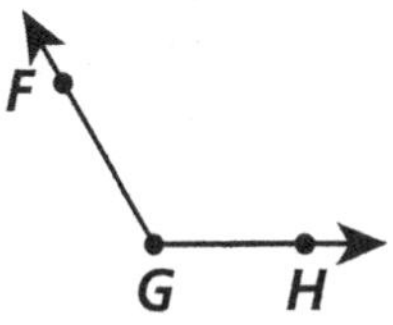
F
G
H

____

____

11

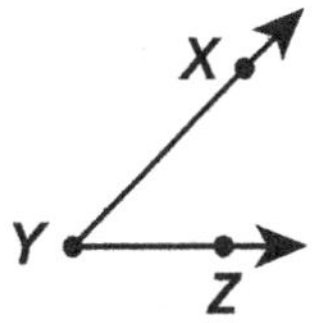
X
Y
Z

____

____

12

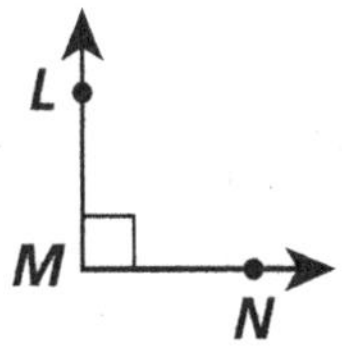
L
M
N

____

____

13 Use the letters to name two acute and two obtuse angles in this figure. Write *acute* or *obtuse* to describe each angle.

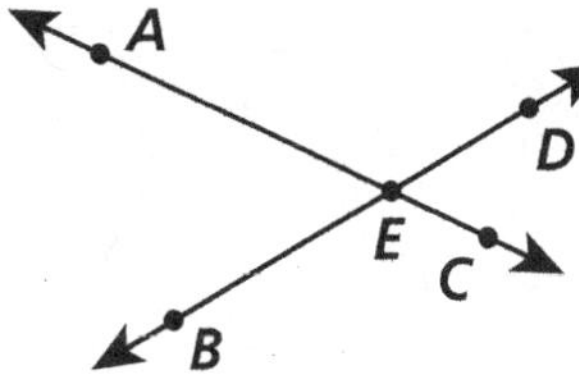
A
D
E
C
B

____

____

____

____

14 Draw and label a right angle, an acute angle, and an obtuse angle.

Check Understanding

Draw and label a line, a line segment, and a ray.

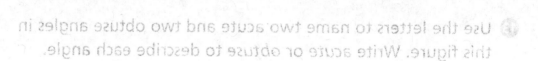

Name ______________________

Sort Angles

Cut along the dashed lines.

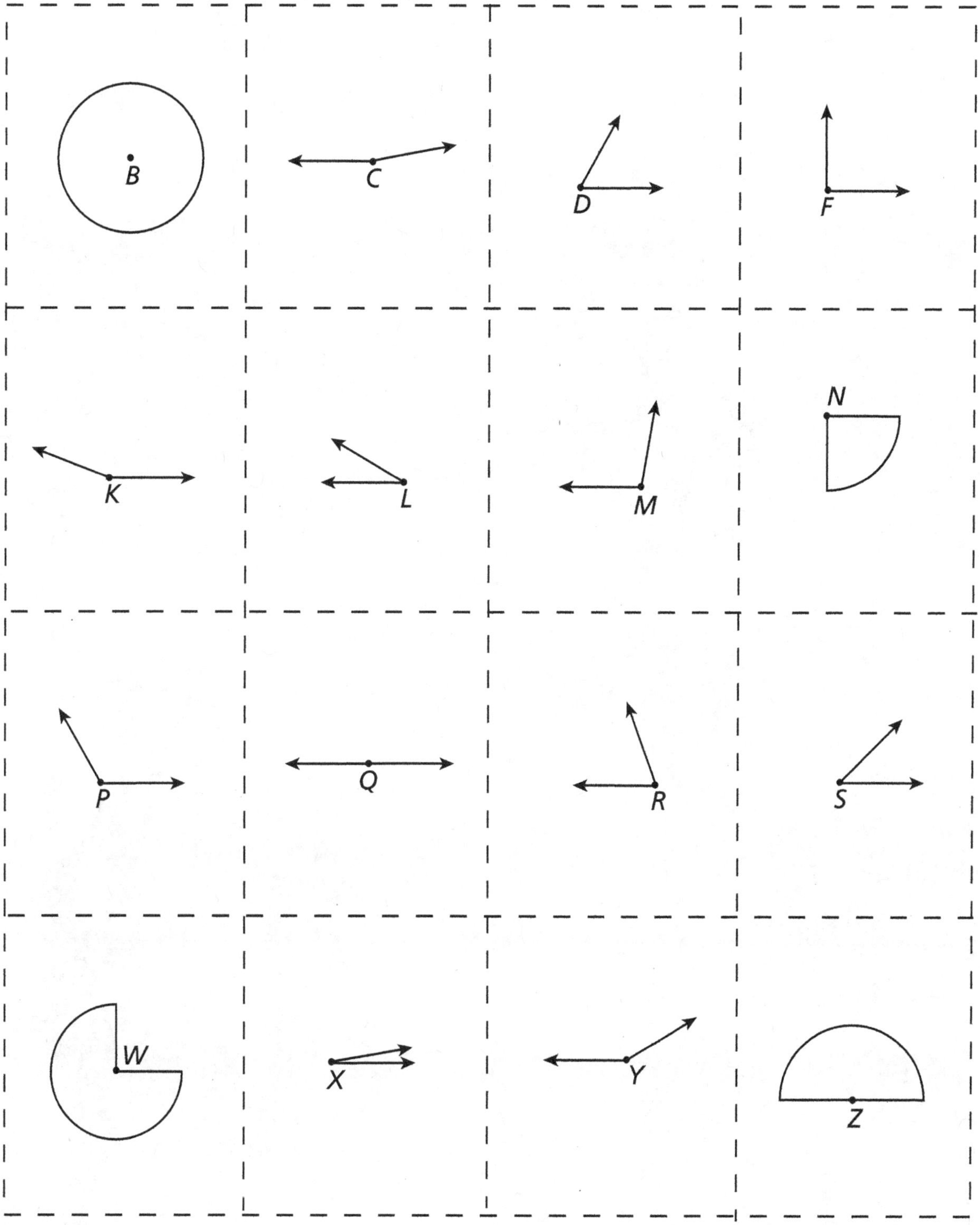
B
C
D
F
K
L
M
N
P
Q
R
S
W
X
Y
Z

Name ________________________________

Sketch Angles

Sketch each angle, or draw it using a protractor.

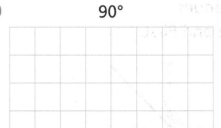

5 90°

6 45°

7 180°

8 360°

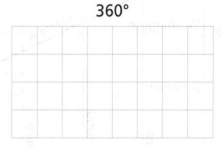

Use Reasoning

Use the figures at the right to answer the following questions.

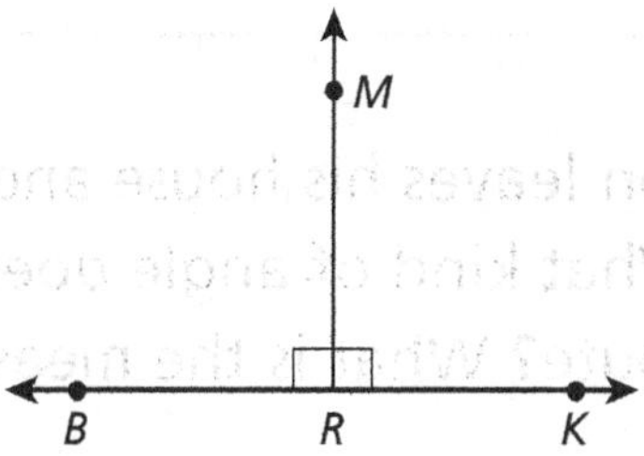

M
B
R
K

9 Name one right angle in each figure.

____

10 Name one straight angle in each figure.

____

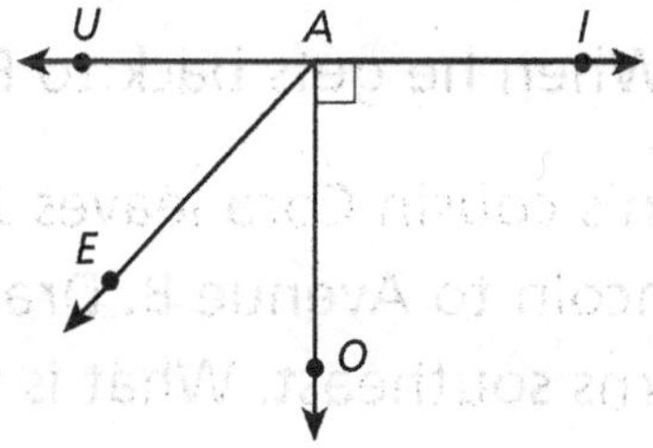

U
A
I
E
O

11 How much greater is the measure of ∠*KRB* than the measure of ∠*IAO*?

____

12 Which angle appears to be a 45° angle?

____

13 The measure of ∠*IAE* is 135°.

What is the measure of ∠*OAE*? ______

What is the measure of ∠*UAE*? ______

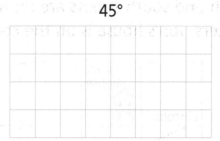

Name

Angles in the Real World

Here is a map of Jon's neighborhood. The east and west streets are named for presidents of the United States. The north and south streets are numbered. The avenues have letters. Jon's house is on the corner of Lincoln and First.

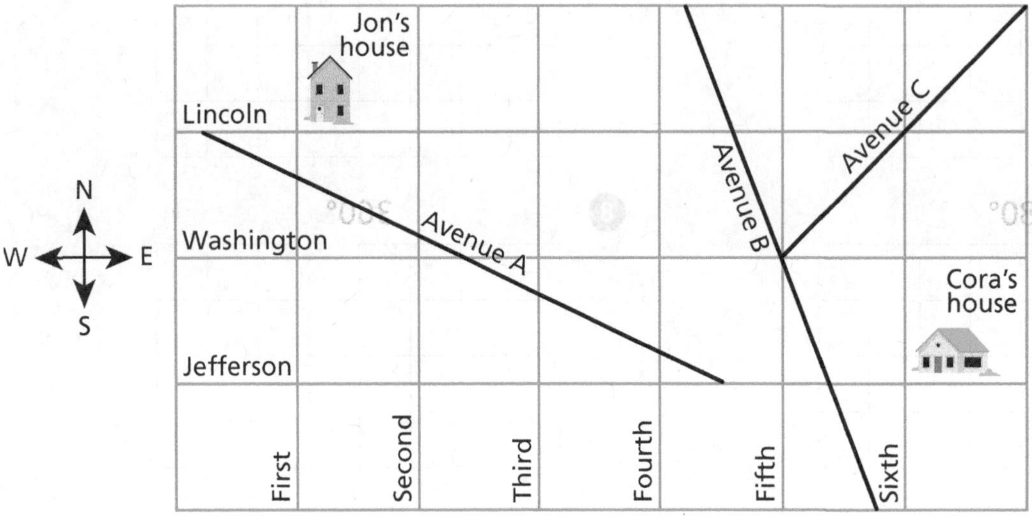

Jon's house
Lincoln
Washington
Jefferson
Avenue A
Avenue B
Avenue C
Cora's house
N
W
E
S
First
Second
Third
Fourth
Fifth
Sixth

14 What do the arrows to the left of the map tell you?

15 Jon leaves his house and rides his bike south on First. What kind of angle does he make for each turn in this route? What is the measure of each angle?

- Jon turns southeast onto Avenue A.
- When he reaches Washington, he turns west.
- When he gets back to First, he turns south.

16 Jon's cousin Cora leaves Jon's house and rides east on Lincoln to Avenue B. Draw the angle Cora makes if she turns southeast. What is the measure of the angle?

Check Understanding

Draw a 90° angle, a 135° angle, and a 180° angle.

Name ____________________

Draw Angles in a Circle

Use a straightedge and a protractor to draw and shade an angle of each type. Measure and label each angle.

1. obtuse angle

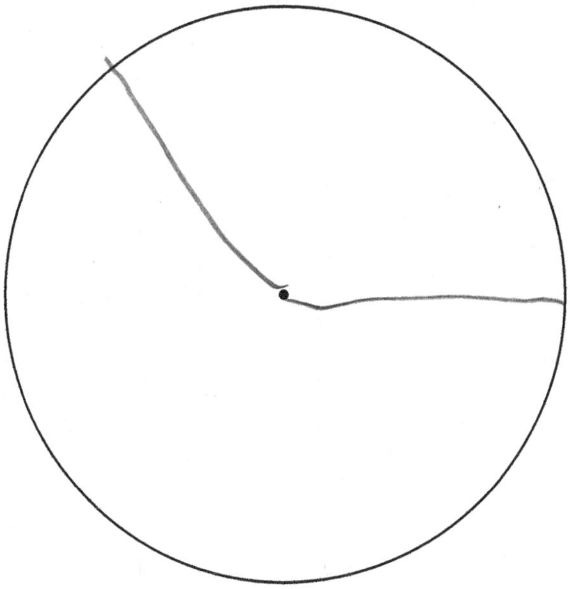

2. straight angle

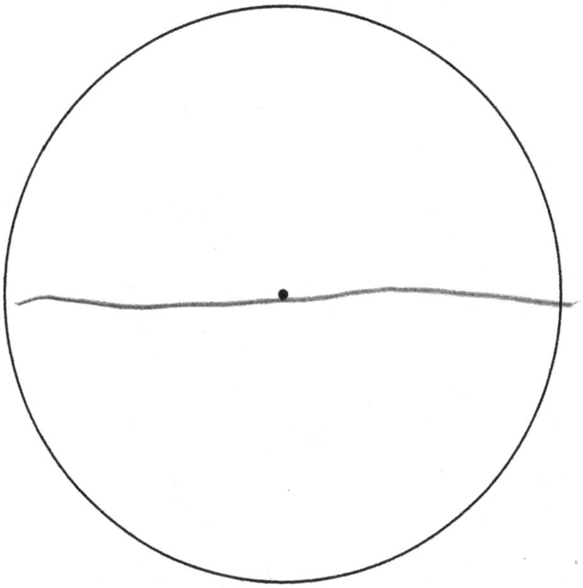

3. acute angle

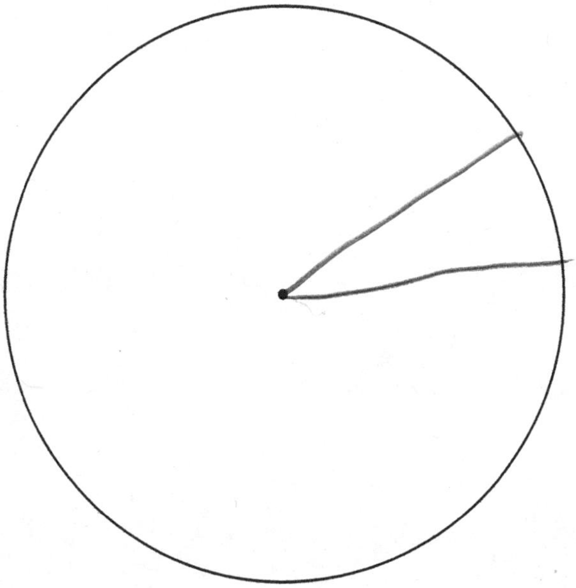

4. three angles with a sum of 360°

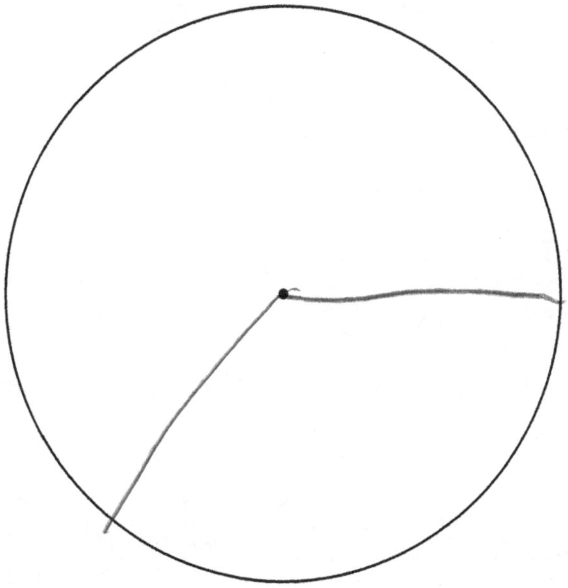

✓ Check Understanding

Write an addition equation that shows the sum of your angle measures in Exercise 4.

____

Draw Angles in a Circle

Use a straightedge and a protractor to draw and shade an angle of each type. Measure and label each angle.

1 obtuse angle

2 straight angle

3 acute angle

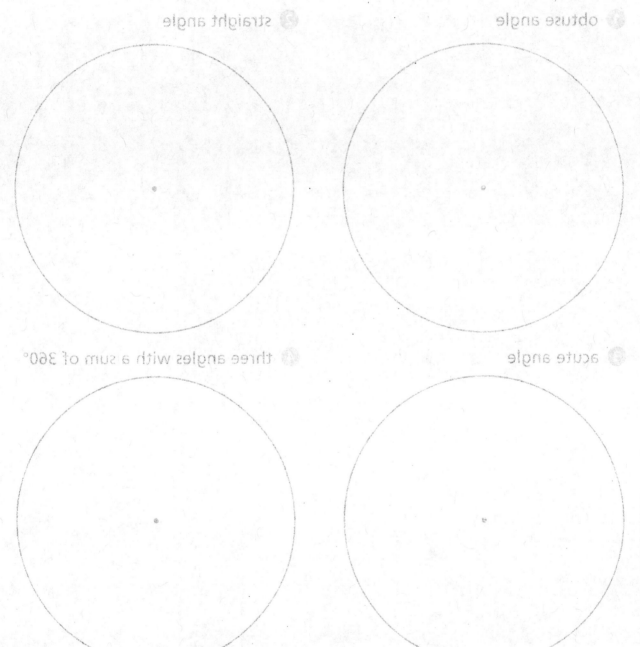

4 three angles with a sum of 360°

Check Understanding

Write an addition equation that shows the sum of your angle measures in Exercise 4.

Name ______________________________

Write the correct answer.

1 Measure angle *ABC*. Tell whether it is an acute, obtuse, or right angle.

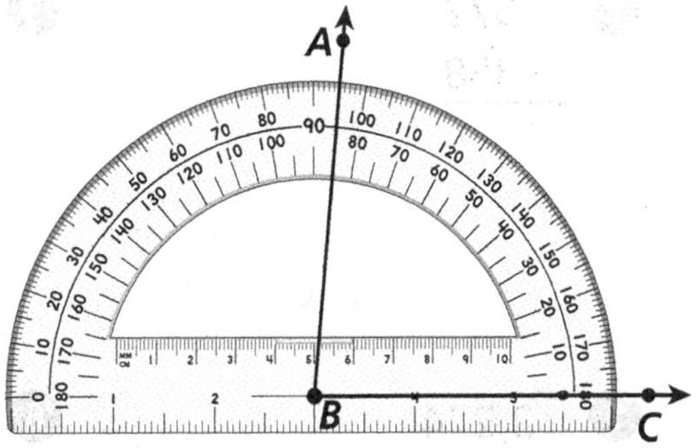
A
B
C

____

2 Liam sketches a 45° angle. Circle the angle Liam sketches.

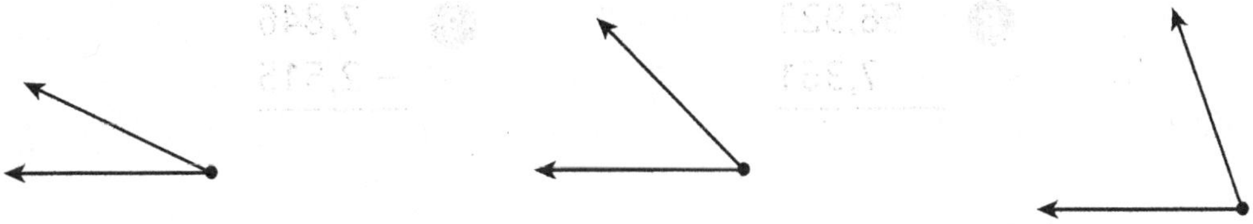

Draw the figure.

3 Ray *EF*

4 Right angle *ABC*

5 Obtuse angle *DEF*

Fluency Check 24

Name ____________________

PATH to FLUENCY

Add or subtract.

1. $\begin{array}{r} 434 \\ +\ 315 \\ \hline \end{array}$

2. $\begin{array}{r} 572 \\ -\ 358 \\ \hline \end{array}$

3. $\begin{array}{r} 374{,}583 \\ +\ 44{,}625 \\ \hline \end{array}$

4. $\begin{array}{r} 506{,}721 \\ -\ 452{,}899 \\ \hline \end{array}$

5. $\begin{array}{r} 3{,}274 \\ +\ 835 \\ \hline \end{array}$

6. $\begin{array}{r} 30{,}430 \\ -\ 18{,}478 \\ \hline \end{array}$

7. $\begin{array}{r} 813 \\ +\ 526 \\ \hline \end{array}$

8. $\begin{array}{r} 56{,}923 \\ -\ 7{,}361 \\ \hline \end{array}$

9. $\begin{array}{r} 7{,}846 \\ -\ 2{,}515 \\ \hline \end{array}$

10. $\begin{array}{r} 676 \\ -\ 421 \\ \hline \end{array}$

11. $\begin{array}{r} 5{,}707 \\ -\ 2{,}644 \\ \hline \end{array}$

12. $\begin{array}{r} 17{,}948 \\ +\ 23{,}324 \\ \hline \end{array}$

13. $\begin{array}{r} 672{,}943 \\ -\ 45{,}867 \\ \hline \end{array}$

14. $\begin{array}{r} 4{,}839 \\ +\ 6{,}127 \\ \hline \end{array}$

15. $\begin{array}{r} 67{,}359 \\ +\ 4{,}418 \\ \hline \end{array}$

Name ______________________

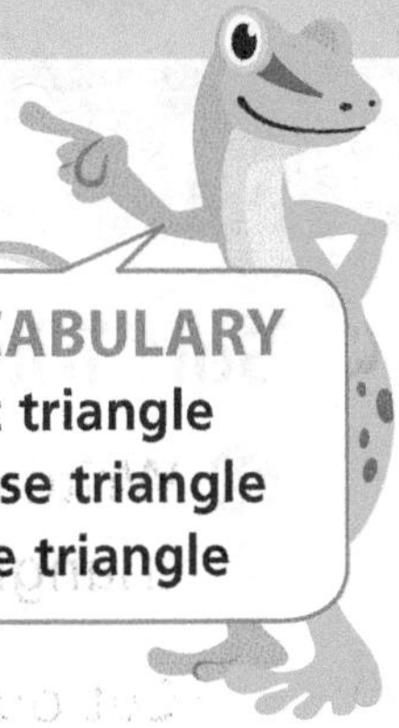

VOCABULARY
right triangle
obtuse triangle
acute triangle

Discuss Angles of a Triangle

The prefix *tri-* means "three," so it is easy to remember that a triangle has 3 angles. Triangles can take their names from the kind of angles they have.

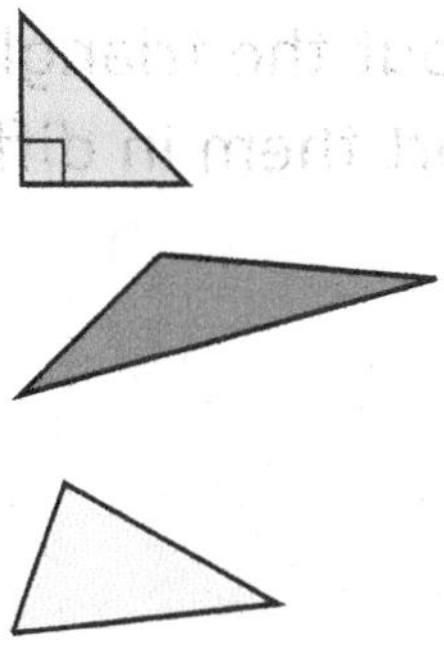

- A **right triangle** has one right angle, which we show by drawing a small square at the right angle.
- An **obtuse triangle** has one obtuse angle.
- An **acute triangle** has three acute angles.

1. You can also use letters to write and talk about triangles. This triangle is $\triangle QRS$. Name its three angles and their type.

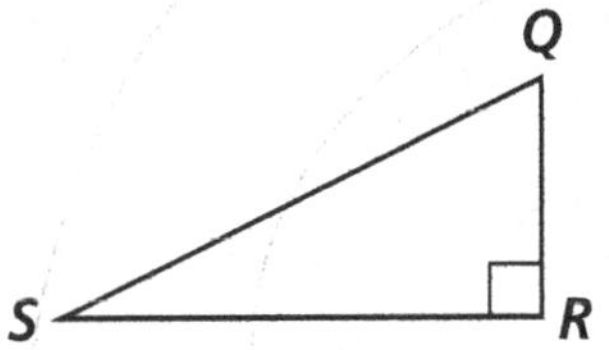
Q
S
R

____

____

____

2. What kind of triangle is $\triangle QRS$? How do you know?

____

____

3. Draw and label a right triangle, an acute triangle, and an obtuse triangle.

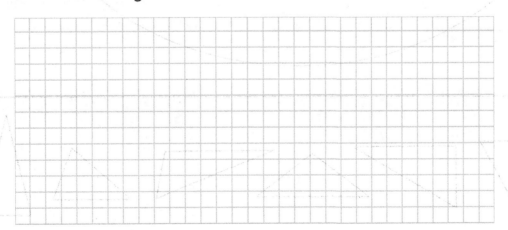

Name ______________________

Sort Triangles in Different Ways

VOCABULARY
Venn diagram

33 Write a capital letter and a lowercase letter inside each triangle below, using the keys at the right.

acute = a
obtuse = o
right = r

Isosceles = I
Scalene = S
Equilateral = E

Cut out the triangles and use the **Venn diagram** below to sort them in different ways.

Triangles

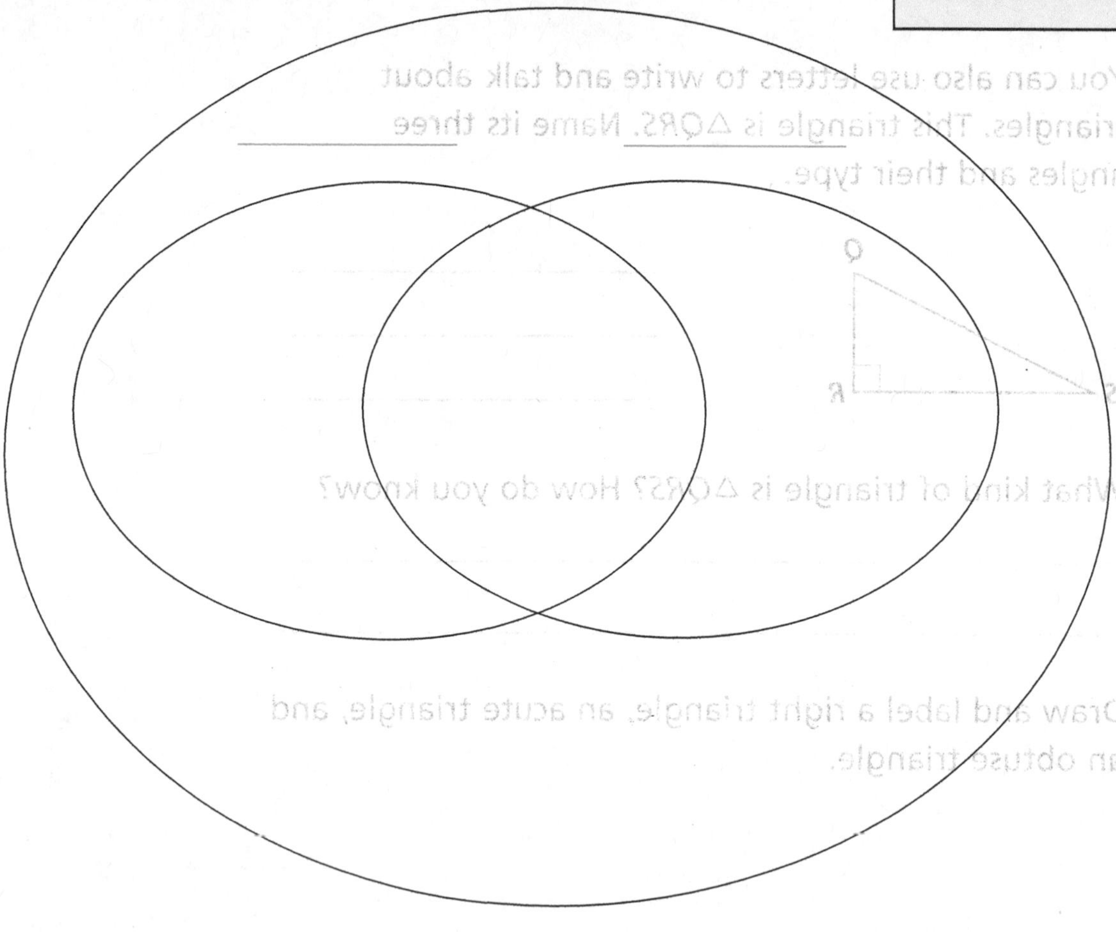

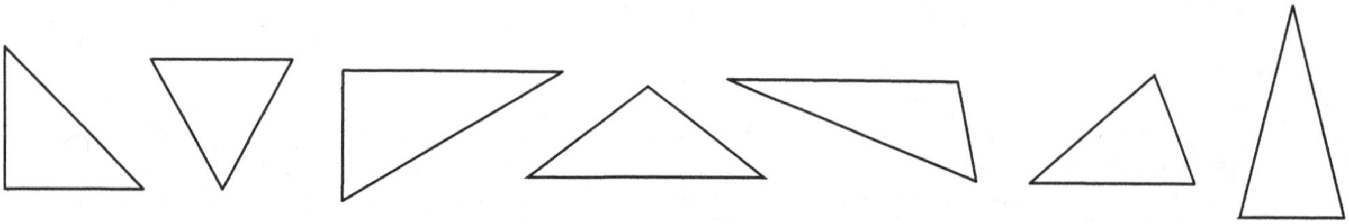

Name ______________________________

What's the Error?

Dear Math Students,

I want to find the measure of $\angle DBE$ in the following diagram.

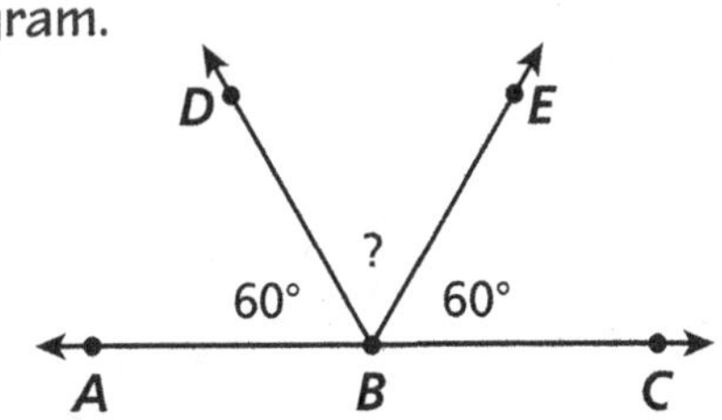
D
E
?
60°
60°
A
B
C

I wrote and solved this equation.

$180° - (60° + 60°) = x$

$180° - 60° + 60° = x$

$120° + 60° = x$

$180° = x$

This answer doesn't make sense. Did I do something wrong?

Your friend,
Puzzled Penguin

19 Write a response to Puzzled Penguin.

____

____

____

____

____

____

____

Check Understanding

Explain how to use an equation to find an unknown angle measure.

Name ______________________________

Write the correct answer.

1. Which three angles can be put together to make a 165° angle?

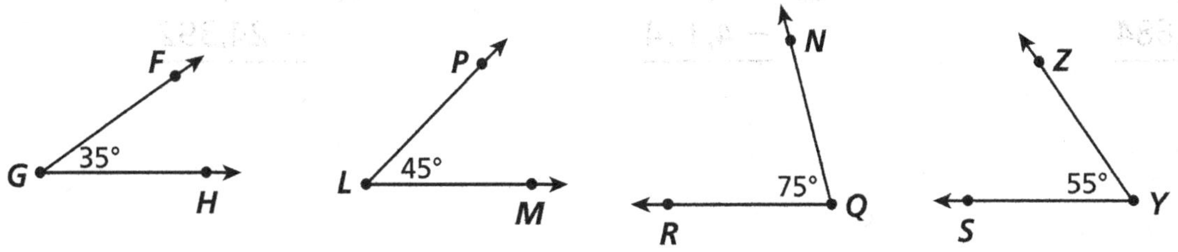
F
G
35°
H
P
L
45°
M
N
75°
R
Q
Z
55°
S
Y

____

2. Jeri measures one of two equal angles in the figure shown. Write an addition equation to find the sum of the angles.

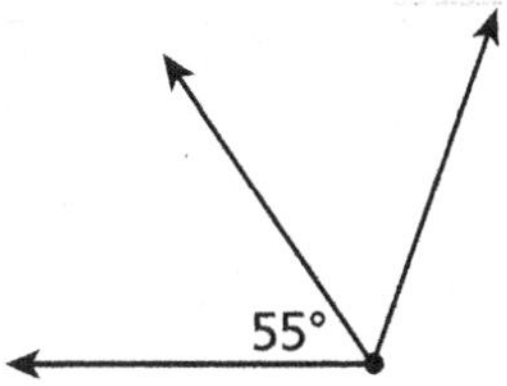
55°

____

3. In the window design shown, the measure of one angle is 60°. Write a subtraction equation to find the unknown angle measure.

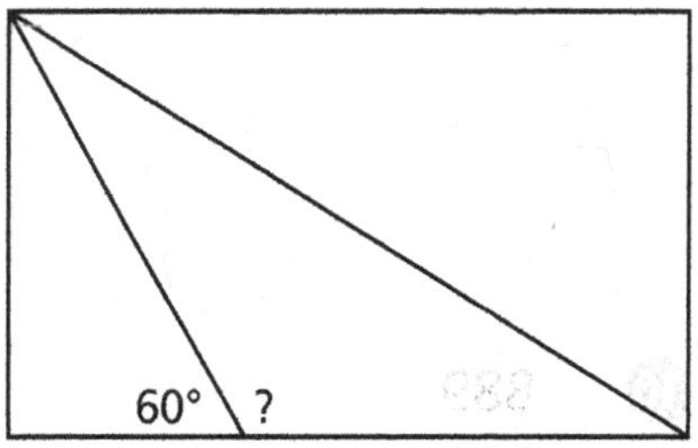
60°
?

____

Name the triangle by its angles.

4. 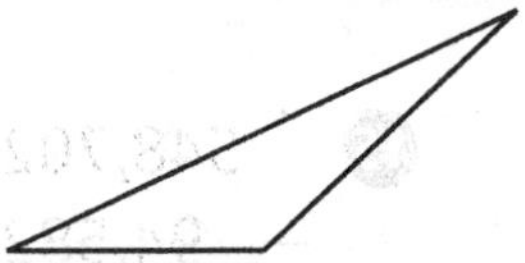

____

5. 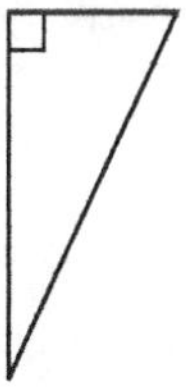

____

Fluency Check 25

Name ____________________

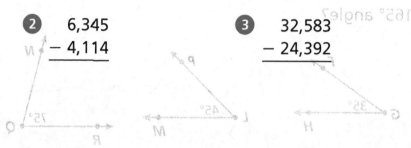

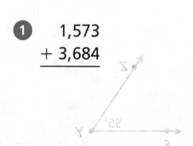

PATH to FLUENCY

Add or subtract.

1. $\begin{array}{r} 1{,}573 \\ +\ 3{,}684 \\ \hline \end{array}$

2. $\begin{array}{r} 6{,}345 \\ -\ 4{,}114 \\ \hline \end{array}$

3. $\begin{array}{r} 32{,}583 \\ -\ 24{,}392 \\ \hline \end{array}$

4. $\begin{array}{r} 428 \\ +\ 361 \\ \hline \end{array}$

5. $\begin{array}{r} 719 \\ -\ 483 \\ \hline \end{array}$

6. $\begin{array}{r} 7{,}832 \\ +\ 556 \\ \hline \end{array}$

7. $\begin{array}{r} 78{,}362 \\ +\ 14{,}839 \\ \hline \end{array}$

8. $\begin{array}{r} 3{,}450 \\ -\ 2{,}137 \\ \hline \end{array}$

9. $\begin{array}{r} 273 \\ +\ 825 \\ \hline \end{array}$

10. $\begin{array}{r} 889 \\ -\ 523 \\ \hline \end{array}$

11. $\begin{array}{r} 387{,}387 \\ +\ 126{,}836 \\ \hline \end{array}$

12. $\begin{array}{r} 20{,}000 \\ -\ 4{,}357 \\ \hline \end{array}$

13. $\begin{array}{r} 708{,}427 \\ -\ 473{,}892 \\ \hline \end{array}$

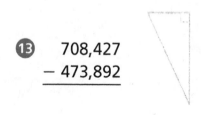

14. $\begin{array}{r} 72{,}497 \\ +\ 3{,}538 \\ \hline \end{array}$

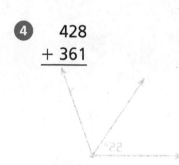

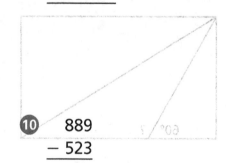

15. $\begin{array}{r} 548{,}702 \\ -\ 94{,}582 \\ \hline \end{array}$

Dear Family:

Your child has been learning about geometry throughout this unit. In this second half of the unit, your child will learn to identify and draw parallel, perpendicular, and intersecting lines as well as lines of symmetry that divide a figure into two halves that match exactly. Your child will be learning how to recognize and describe a group of geometric figures called quadrilaterals, which get their name because they have four (*quad-*) sides (*-lateral*). Six different kinds of quadrilaterals are shown here.

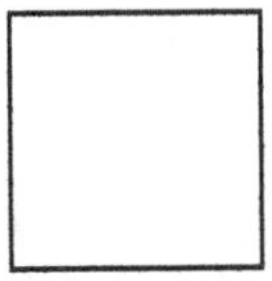

Square
4 equal sides
opposite sides parallel
4 right angles

Rectangle
2 pairs of parallel sides
4 right angles

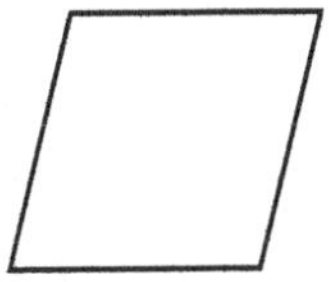

Rhombus
4 equal sides
opposite sides parallel

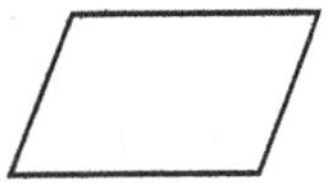

Parallelogram
2 pairs of parallel sides

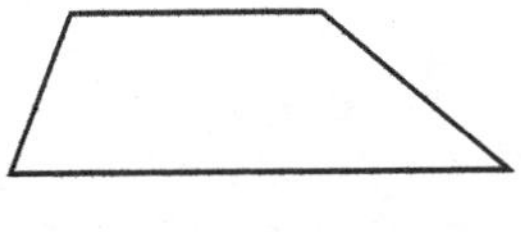

Trapezoid
exactly 1 pair of
opposite sides parallel

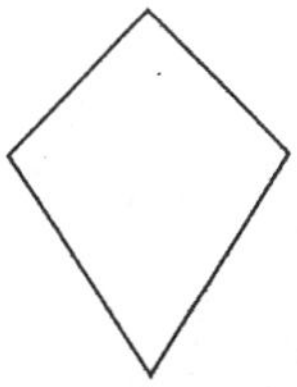

Kite
2 pairs of equal
adjacent sides

The unit concludes with exploring how figures, including quadrilaterals, can be rotated (turned), reflected (flipped), or translated (slid) to prove that they are the same size and shape and are congruent.

If you have any questions or comments, please contact me.

Sincerely,
Your child's teacher

Estimada familia:

Durante esta unidad, su niño ha estado aprendiendo acerca de geometría. En esta parte de la unidad, su niño aprenderá a identificar y dibujar líneas paralelas, perpendiculares y secantes así como líneas de simetría que dividen una figura en dos mitades exactas. Su niño aprenderá cómo reconocer y describir un grupo de figuras geométricas llamadas cuadriláteros, que reciben ese nombre porque tienen cuatro *(quadri-)* lados *(-lateris)*. Aquí se muestran seis tipos de cuadriláteros:

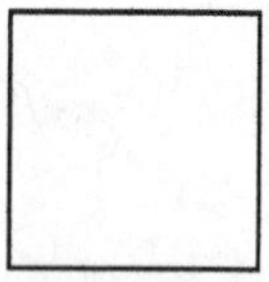

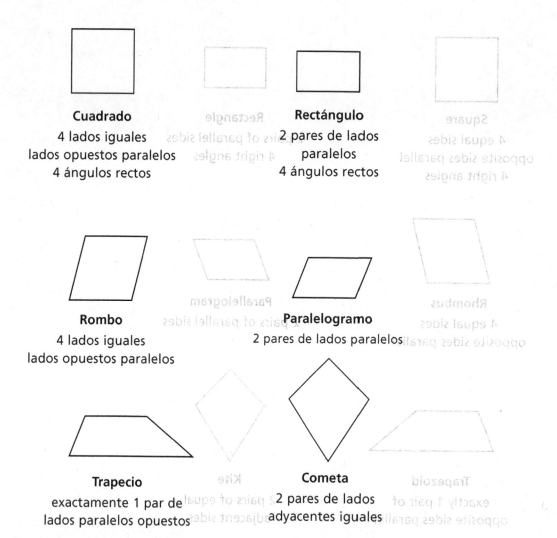

Cuadrado
4 lados iguales
lados opuestos paralelos
4 ángulos rectos

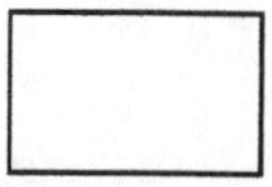

Rectángulo
2 pares de lados paralelos
4 ángulos rectos

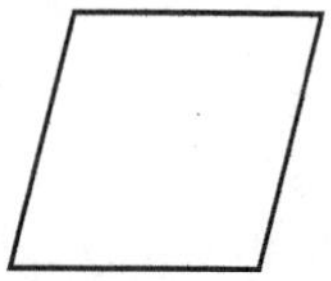

Rombo
4 lados iguales
lados opuestos paralelos

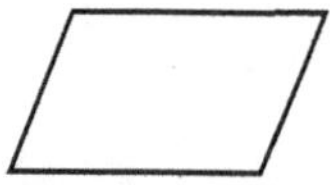

Paralelogramo
2 pares de lados paralelos

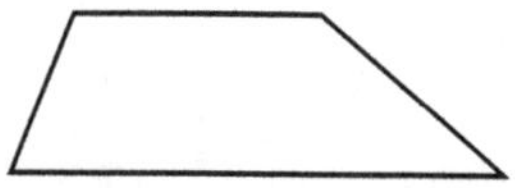

Trapecio
exactamente 1 par de lados paralelos opuestos

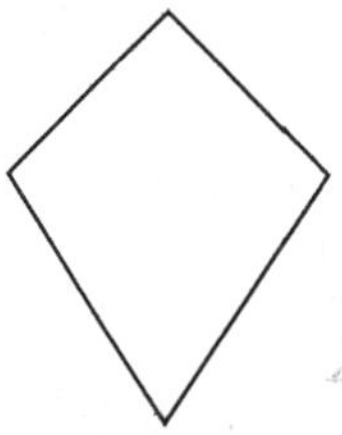

Cometa
2 pares de lados adyacentes iguales

La unidad concluye con la exploración de cómo las figuras, incluyendo los cuadriláteros, pueden girar (rotar), reflejar (voltear) o trasladar (deslizar) para probar que son del mismo tamaño y forma, y son congruentes.

Si tiene alguna pregunta o algún comentario, por favor comuníquese conmigo.

Atentamente,
El maestro de su niño

 Name ____________________

VOCABULARY
parallel lines
intersecting lines

Define Parallel Lines

The lines or line segments in these pairs are **parallel**.

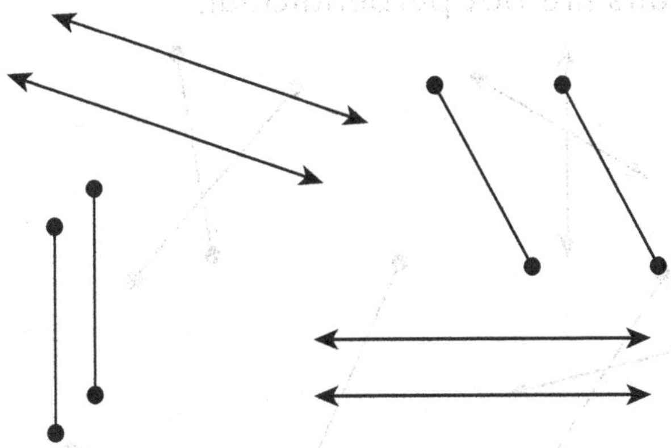

The lines or line segments in these pairs are not parallel.

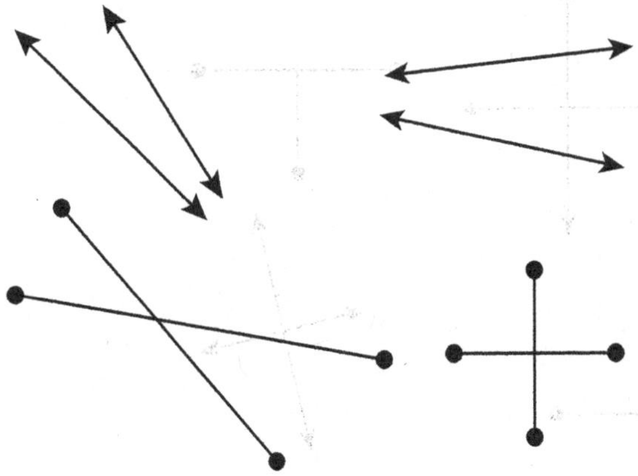

Intersecting lines meet at a point.

1. What do you think it means for two lines to be parallel?
They can go forever without meeting.

2. If two lines are parallel, can they ever be intersecting? NO

Draw Parallel Lines

3. Draw and label a pair of parallel lines.

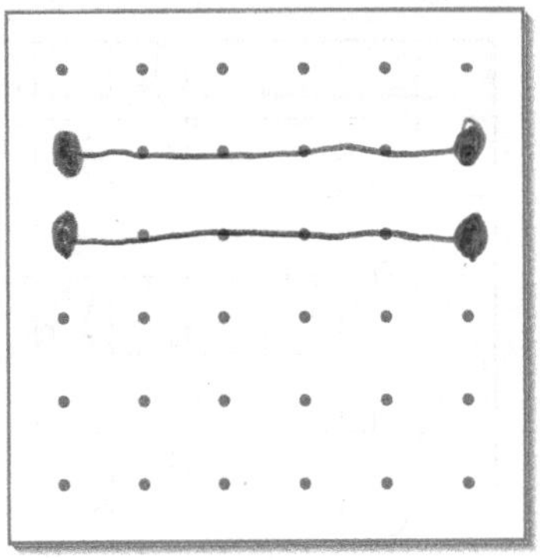

4. Draw and label a figure with one pair of parallel line segments.

Name ______________________________

VOCABULARY
perpendicular lines

Define Perpendicular Lines

The lines or line segments in these pairs are **perpendicular**.

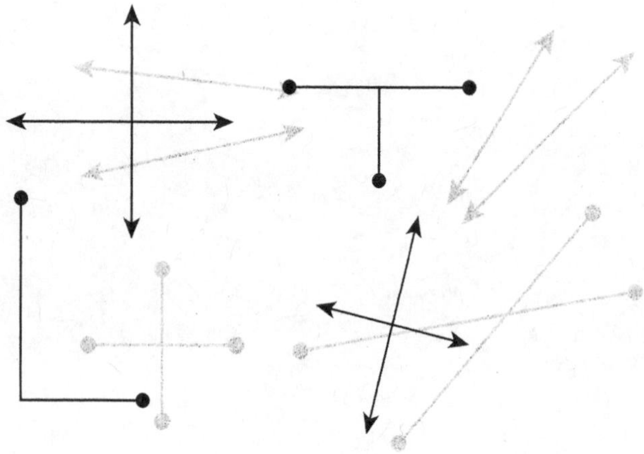

The lines or line segments in these pairs are not perpendicular.

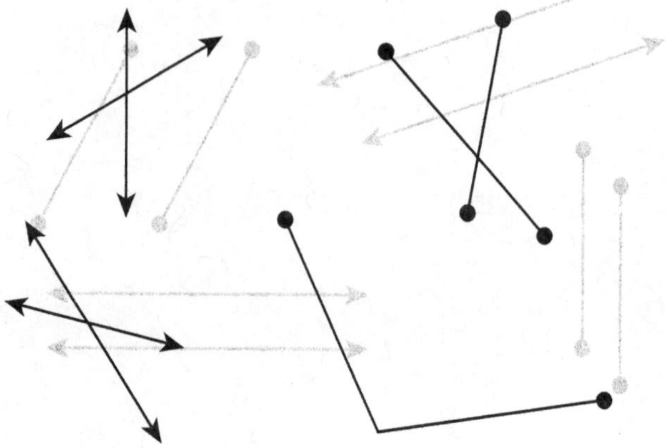

5 What do you think it means for two lines to be perpendicular?

____

____

6 If two lines are perpendicular, will they always be intersecting? __________

7 Are all intersecting lines perpendicular? __________

Draw Perpendicular Lines

8 Draw and label a pair of perpendicular lines.

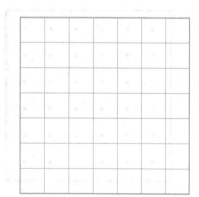

9 Draw and label a figure with one pair of perpendicular line segments.

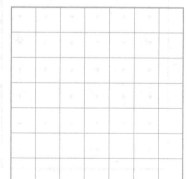

Name

Draw Special Quadrilaterals

5 Draw a quadrilateral that has exactly one pair of opposite sides parallel. What type of quadrilateral is it?

6 Draw a quadrilateral that has two pairs of opposite sides parallel. What type of quadrilateral is it? Is there more than one answer?

7 Draw a quadrilateral that has two pairs of opposite sides parallel, 4 equal sides, and no right angles. What type of quadrilateral is it?

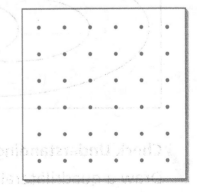

Name ______________________________

Identify Relationships

Why is each statement below true?

8 A rhombus is always a parallelogram, but a parallelogram isn't always a rhombus.

____

____

9 A rectangle is a parallelogram, but a parallelogram is not necessarily a rectangle.

____

____

10 A square is a rectangle, but a rectangle does not have to be a square.

____

____

11 Complete the Venn diagram by placing each word in the best location.

Quadrilateral	Parallelogram	Rhombus
Trapezoid	Rectangle	Square

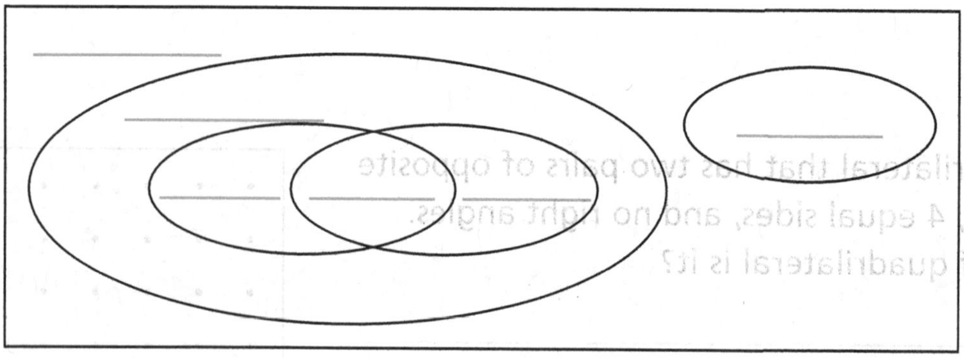

Check Understanding

Draw a quadrilateral that is not a parallelogram.

Name ____________________

Sort and Classify Quadrilaterals

Cut along the dashed lines.

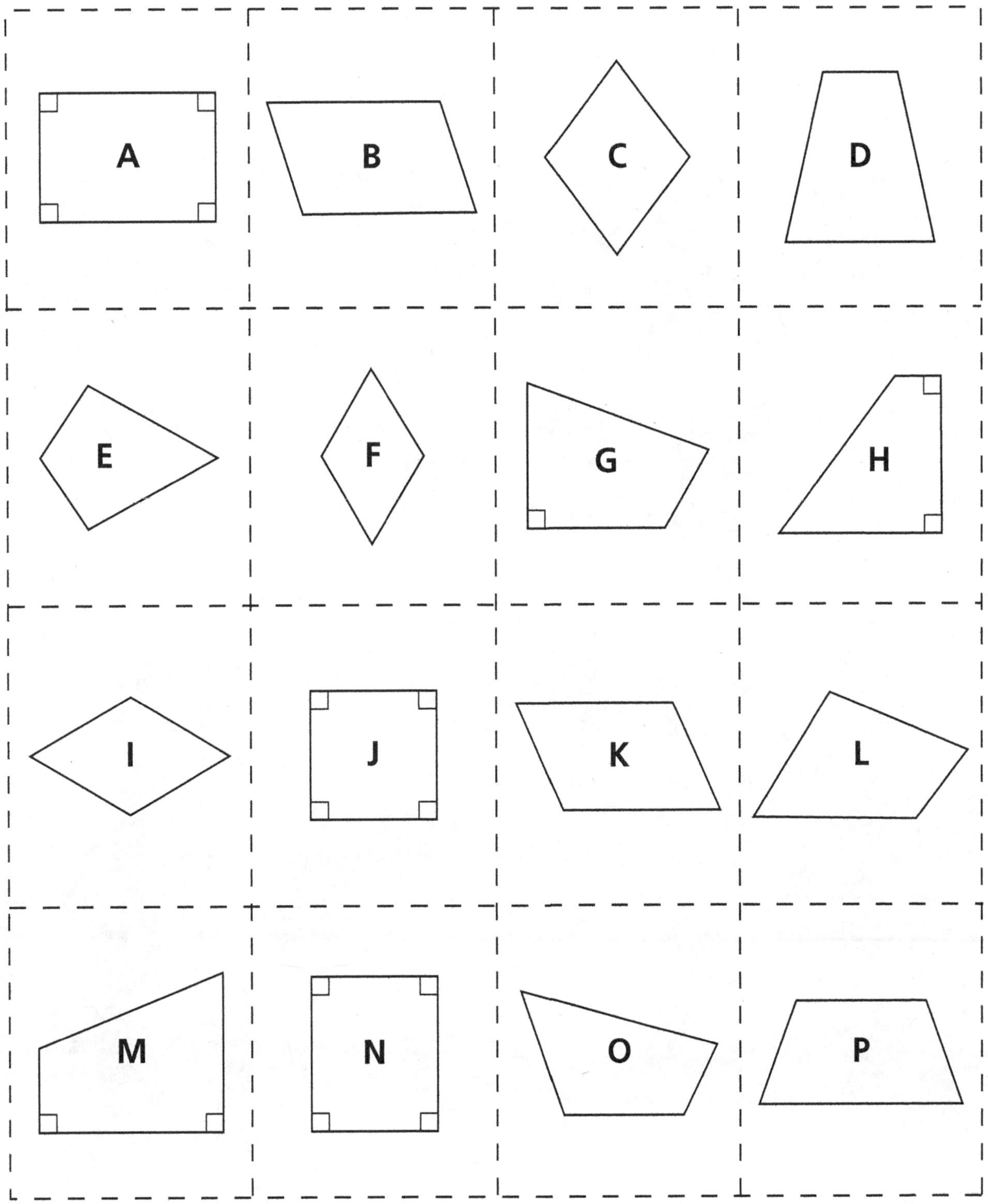
A
B
C
D
E
F
G
H
I
J
K
L
M
N
O
P

Name ______________________

Build Quadrilaterals With Triangles

You can make a quadrilateral by joining the equal sides of two triangles that are the same size and shape.

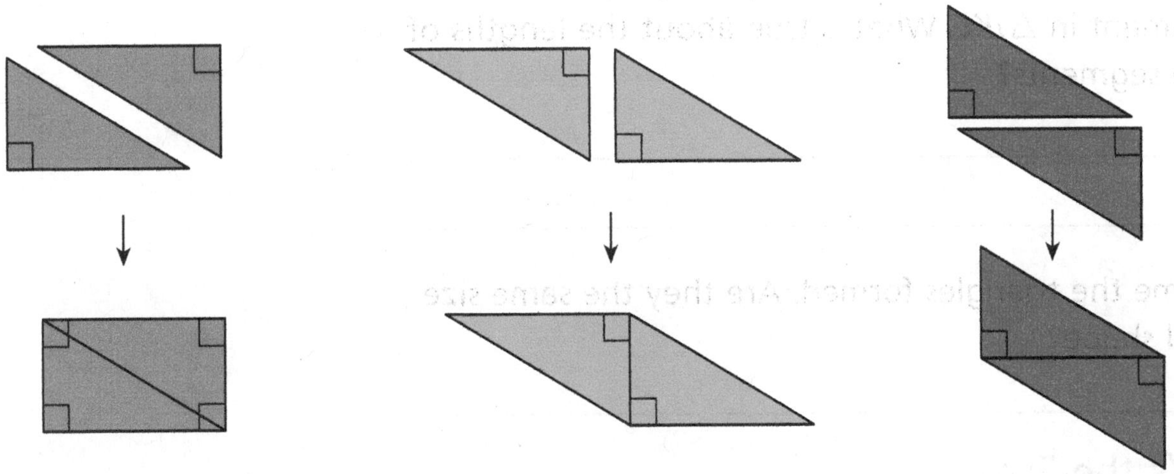

Cut out the triangles below. For each exercise, glue two of the triangles on this paper so that the stated sides are joined. Then write the name of the quadrilateral.

7. $\overline{AB}$ is joined to $\overline{AB}$

8. $\overline{AC}$ is joined to $\overline{AC}$

9. $\overline{BC}$ is joined to $\overline{BC}$

______________________ ______________________ ______________________

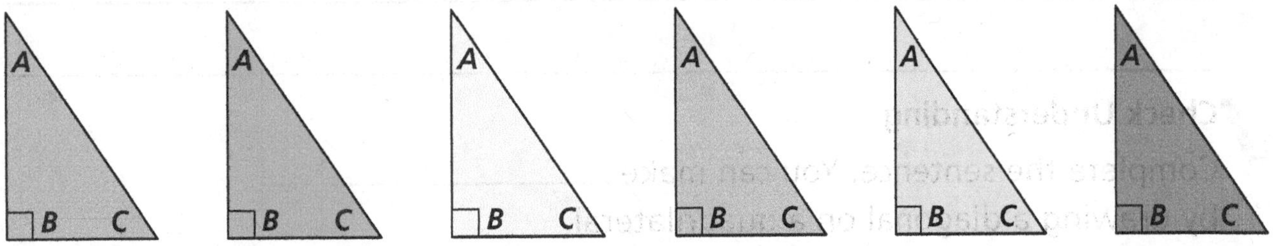
A
B
C
A
B
C
A
B
C
A
B
C
A
B
C
A
B
C

Name ______________________________

Draw Perpendicular Lines in Triangles (continued)

Use your isosceles triangle *JKL* to answer the questions.

22. Name the segments formed by the perpendicular segment in $\triangle JKL$. What is true about the lengths of the segments?

____

____

23. Name the triangles formed. Are they the same size and shape?

____

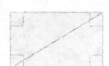

What's the Error?

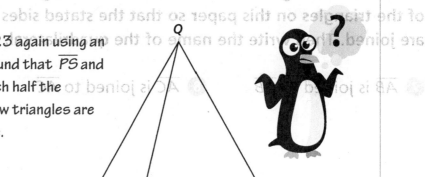

Dear Math Students,

I tried to do Exercises 20–23 again using an equilateral triangle *PQR*. I found that $\overline{PS}$ and $\overline{RS}$ that I formed are not each half the length of side $\overline{PR}$ and the new triangles are not the same size and shape.

Did I do something wrong?

Your friend,
Puzzled Penguin

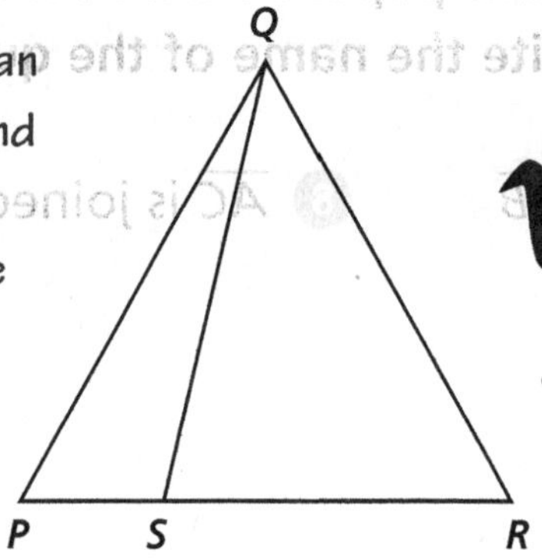
Q
P
S
R

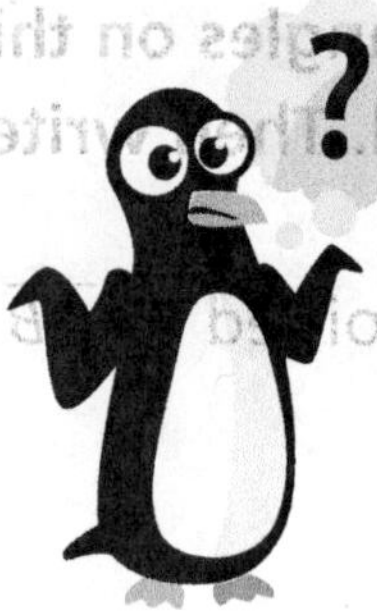
?

24. Write a response to Puzzled Penguin.

____

____

____

____

Check Understanding

Complete the sentence. You can make ______________ by drawing a diagonal on a quadrilateral.

Name ______________________

Tell whether the lines are *parallel* or *perpendicular*.

1 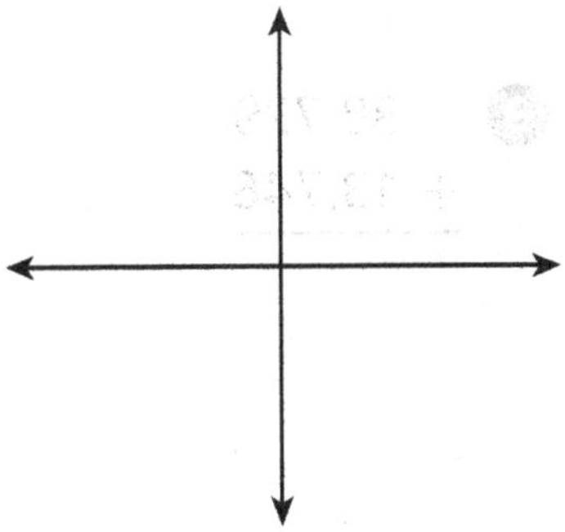

2 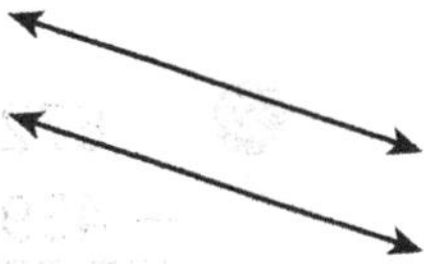

______________________ ______________________

3 Deena draws four line segments to make a figure. The figure has two pairs of parallel sides and no right angles. What figure does Deena draw?

____

4 Gerard made a plaque. It has four sides with two pairs of equal adjacent sides. What shape is the plaque?

____

List all the names for the quadrilateral. Then write the type of triangles you can make with the diagonals.

5 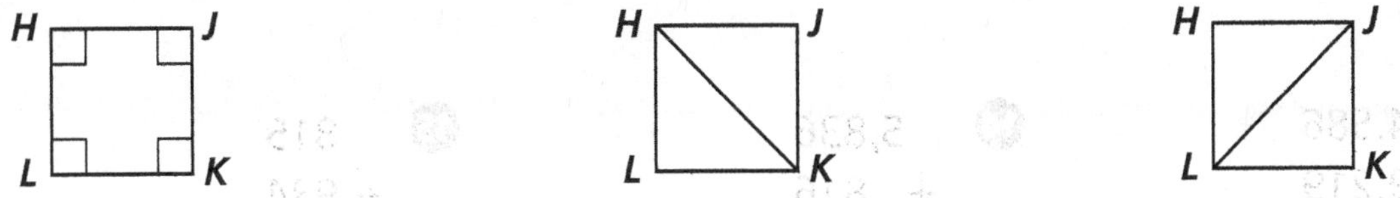
H
J
L
K
H
J
L
K
H
J
L
K

____

____

Name ____________________

PATH to FLUENCY

Add or subtract.

1. $1{,}846 + 4{,}539$

2. $672 - 459$

3. $38{,}729 + 13{,}746$

4. $8{,}695 - 4{,}265$

5. $475{,}932 - 58{,}484$

6. $70{,}007 - 43{,}862$

7. $348{,}421 + 74{,}325$

8. $5{,}016 - 3{,}204$

9. $783 - 411$

10. $209 + 360$

11. $62{,}678 - 3{,}822$

12. $94{,}327 + 3{,}882$

13. $704{,}586 - 479{,}219$

14. $5{,}836 + 816$

15. $815 + 934$

Name ____________________

Sort Polygons Cards

Cut along the dashed lines.

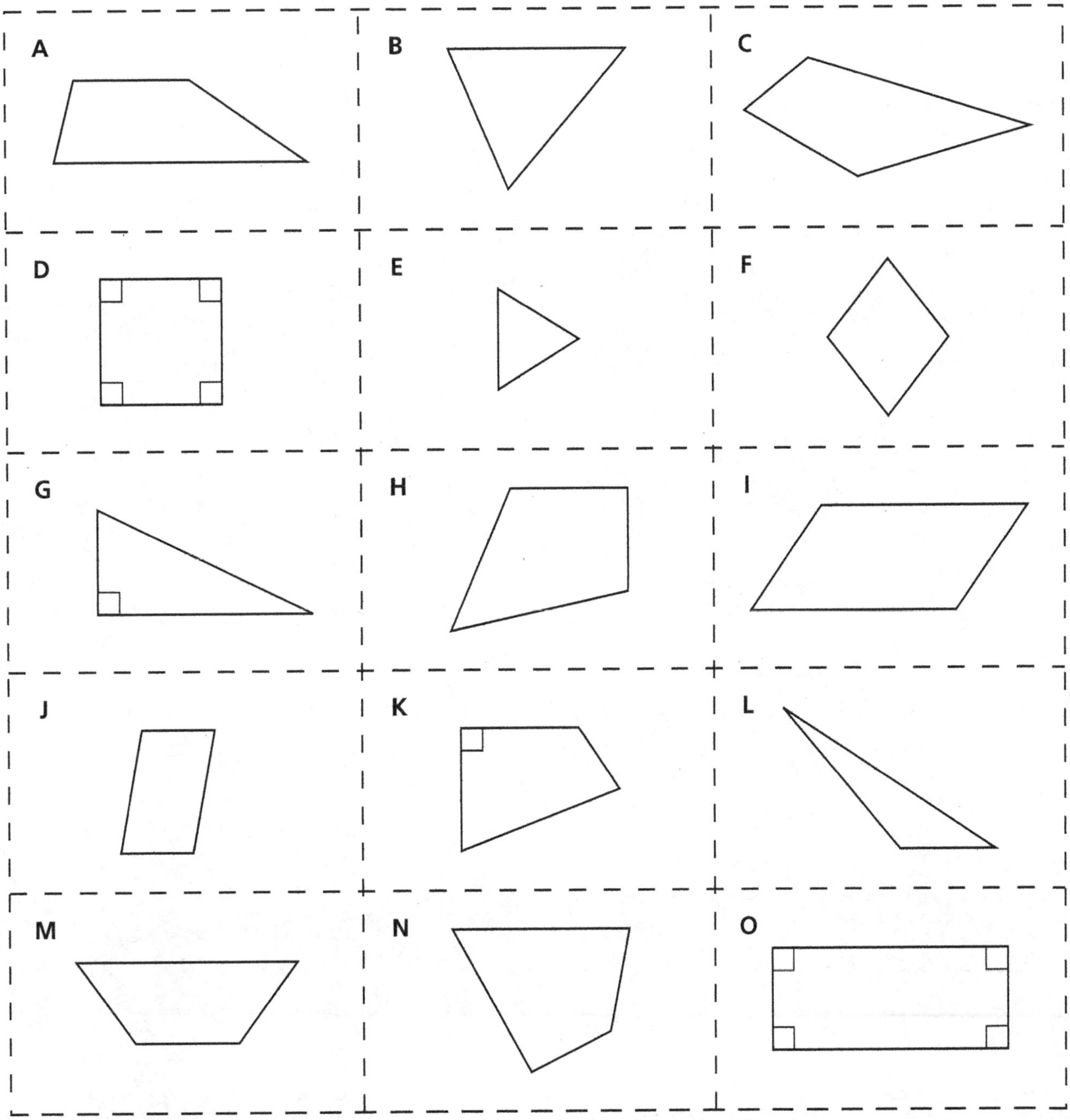
A
B
C
D
E
F
G
H
I
J
K
L
M
N
O

Name ____________________

Draw Lines of Symmetry

A line of symmetry divides a figure or design into two matching parts.

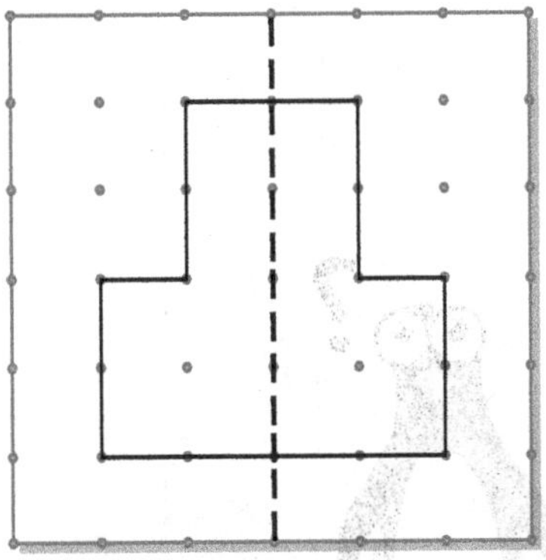

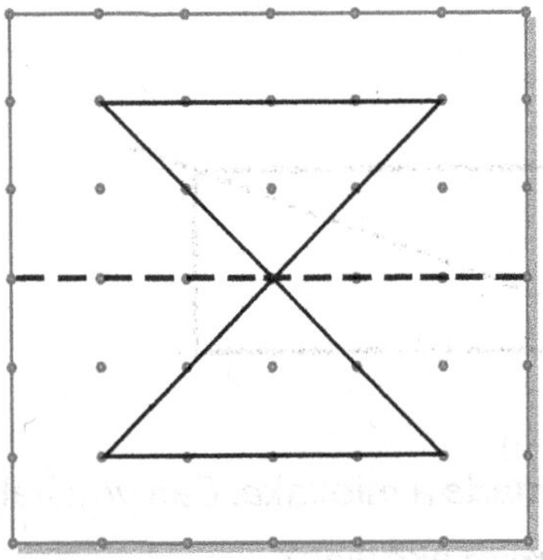

Draw the line of symmetry in the figure or design.

7 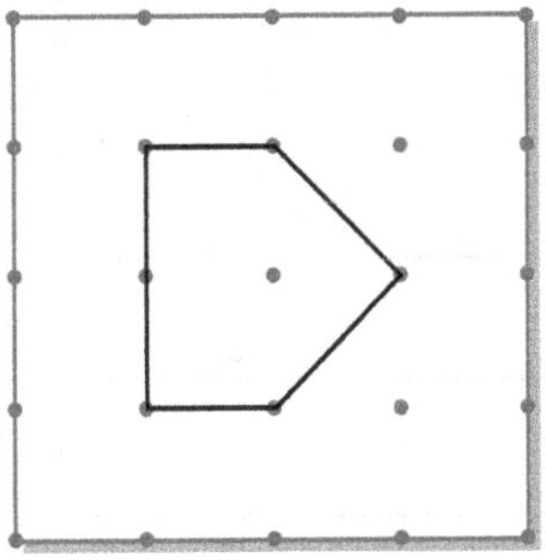

8 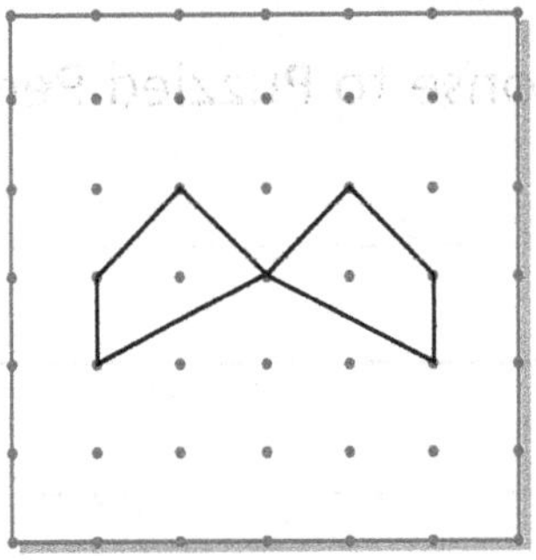

9 Which figures in Exercises 1–6 have more than one line of symmetry?

____

10 Choose one of the figures from your answer to Exercise 9. Draw the figure and draw all of its lines of symmetry.

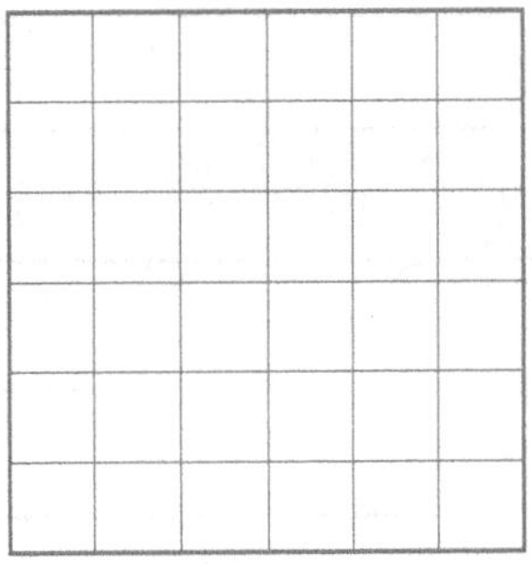

Name

What's the Error?

Dear Math Students,

I drew the diagonal of this rectangle as a line of symmetry.

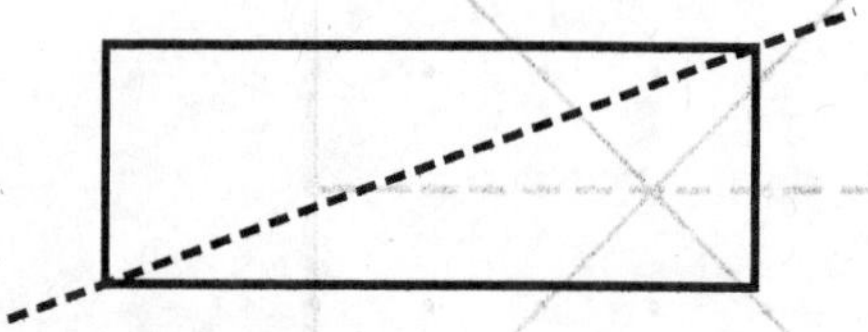

My friend told me I made a mistake. Can you help me figure out what my mistake was?

Your friend,
Puzzled Penguin

11 Write a response to Puzzled Penguin.

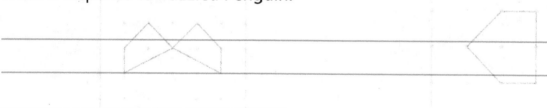

Name

Draw the Other Half

Draw the other half of each figure to make a whole figure or design with line symmetry.

12 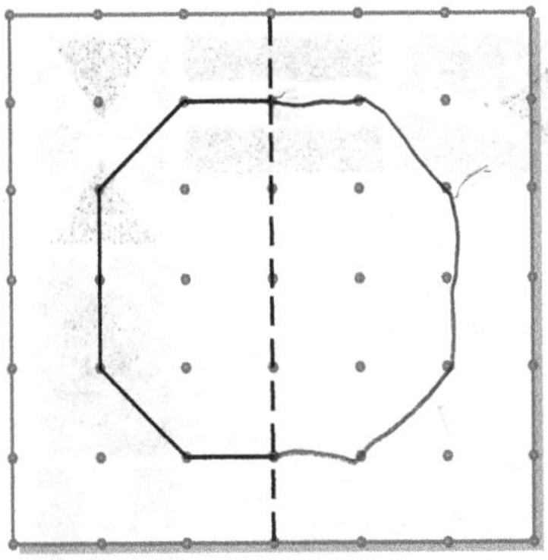

13 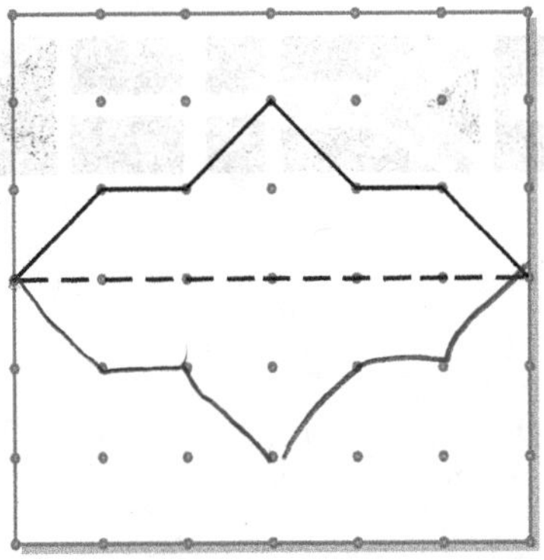

14 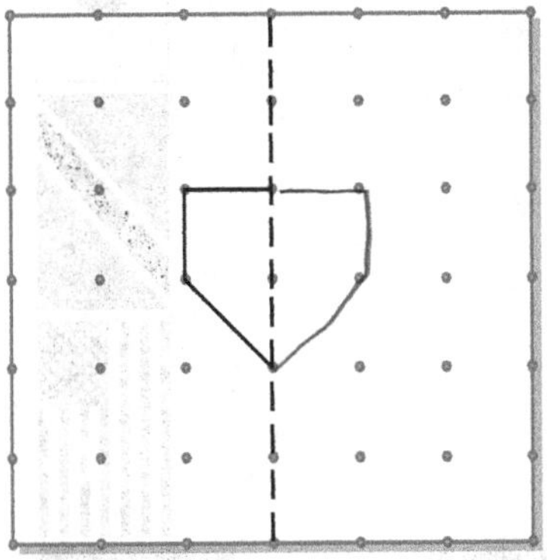

15 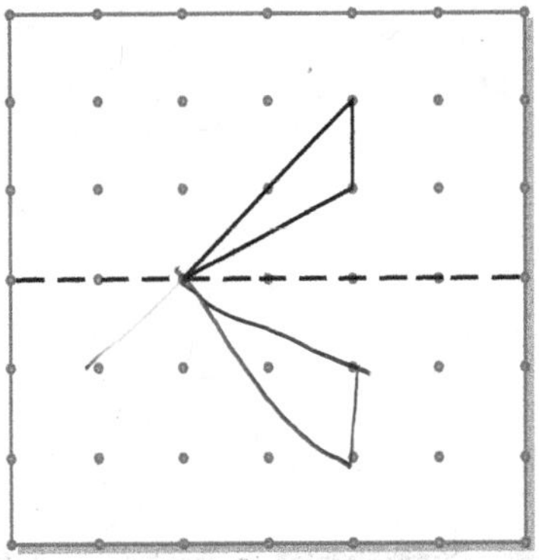

16 Copy one of your answers to Exercises 12–15 onto another piece of paper. Cut out the design and then fold it along the line of symmetry. Check that the two halves of the design match exactly.

Check Understanding

Which of your completed figures in Exercises 12–15 have more than one line of symmetry? ________________

Name

Designer Flags

Design your own flag in the space below. Your flag design should include each of the following: one triangle, one pair of parallel lines, and one 30° angle.

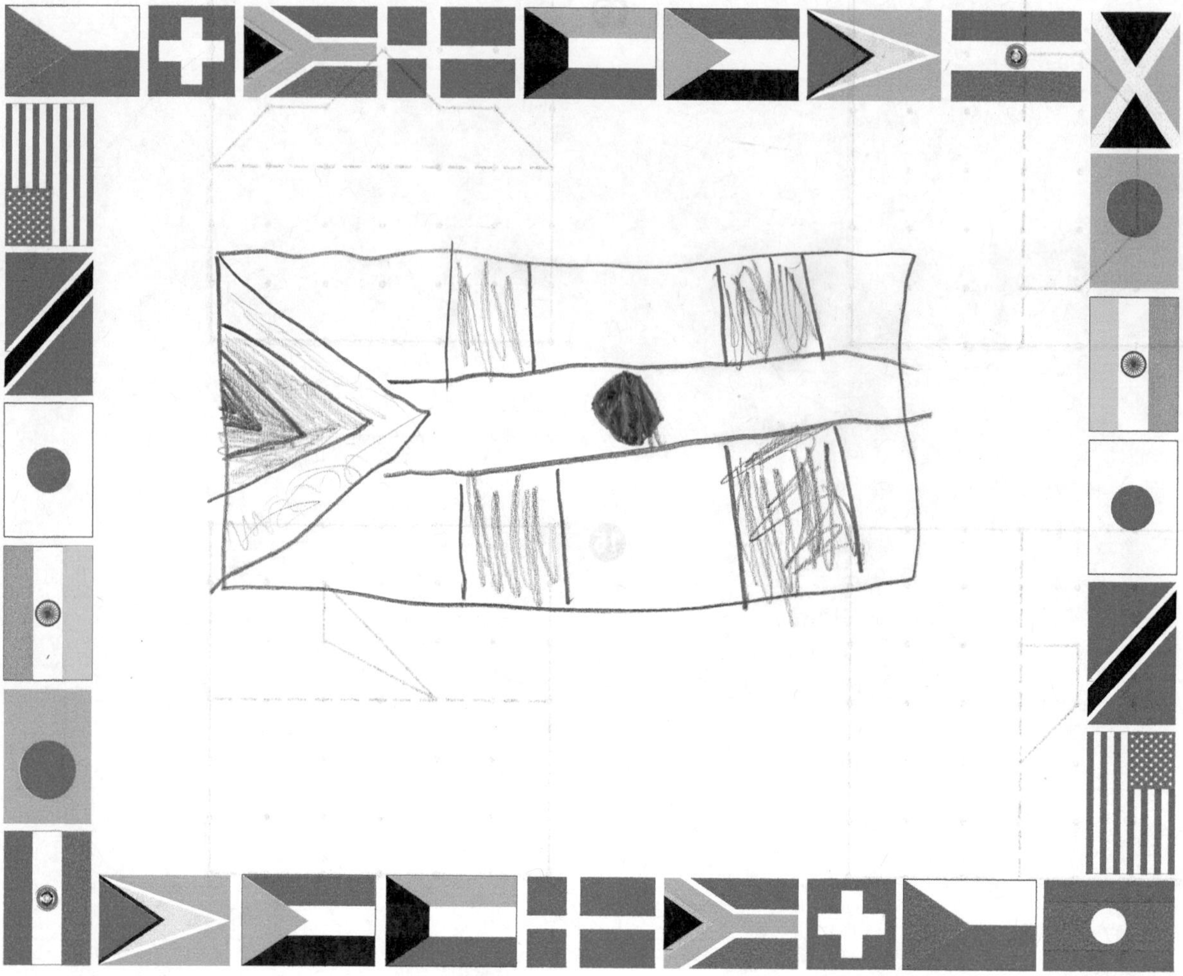

5 What type of triangle did you draw in your flag design? Explain how the sides of the triangle helped you classify the triangle.

6 Compare the flag design you made to the flag design that a classmate made. How are the two designs the same? How are they different? What shapes did you use that your classmate did not use?

Unit 8
Quick Quiz 4

Name ______________________

Look at the figures.

1. Circle the figure with obtuse angles.

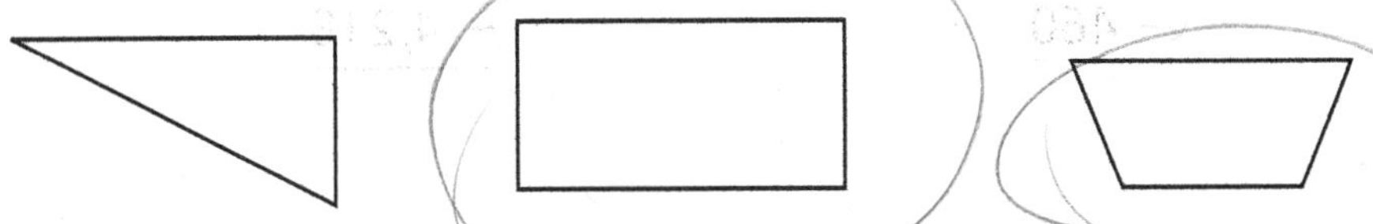

2. Circle the figure that appears to have a right angle.

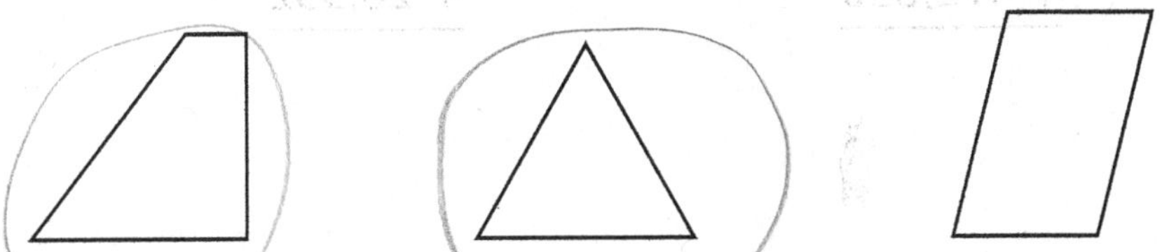

3. Circle the figure that appears to have perpendicular sides.

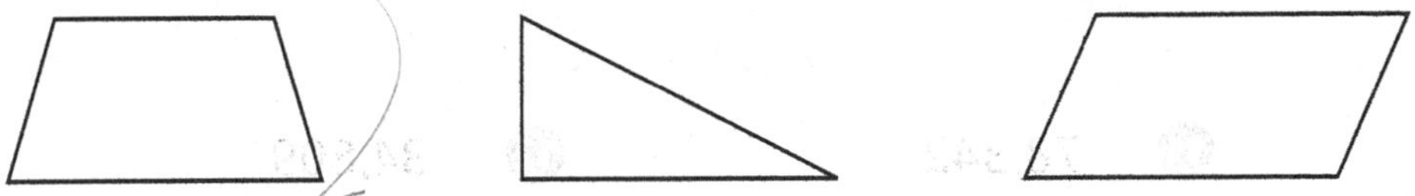

4. Does the figure have line symmetry?

Yes

5. Does the figure have line symmetry?

Yes

Fluency Check 27

Name ______________________

PATH to FLUENCY

Add or subtract.

1. $\begin{array}{r} 352 \\ +\ 337 \\ \hline \end{array}$

2. $\begin{array}{r} 673 \\ -\ 460 \\ \hline \end{array}$

3. $\begin{array}{r} 6,330 \\ -\ 4,218 \\ \hline \end{array}$

4. $\begin{array}{r} 722 \\ -\ 518 \\ \hline \end{array}$

5. $\begin{array}{r} 387,599 \\ +\ 472,850 \\ \hline \end{array}$

6. $\begin{array}{r} 81,275 \\ +\ 28,952 \\ \hline \end{array}$

7. $\begin{array}{r} 5,923 \\ +\ 6,057 \\ \hline \end{array}$

8. $\begin{array}{r} 8,312 \\ +\ 974 \\ \hline \end{array}$

9. $\begin{array}{r} 529 \\ +\ 355 \\ \hline \end{array}$

10. $\begin{array}{r} 40,507 \\ -\ 23,316 \\ \hline \end{array}$

11. $\begin{array}{r} 78,342 \\ -\ 5,761 \\ \hline \end{array}$

12. $\begin{array}{r} 34,809 \\ +\ 7,181 \\ \hline \end{array}$

13. $\begin{array}{r} 6,537 \\ -\ 3,215 \\ \hline \end{array}$

14. $\begin{array}{r} 349,744 \\ -\ 84,589 \\ \hline \end{array}$

15. $\begin{array}{r} 800,000 \\ -\ 526,783 \\ \hline \end{array}$

Name ____________________

VOCABULARY
rotation

Discuss Rotations

A **rotation** is a turn. A number of degrees (°) and a direction (clockwise or counterclockwise) describe a turn.

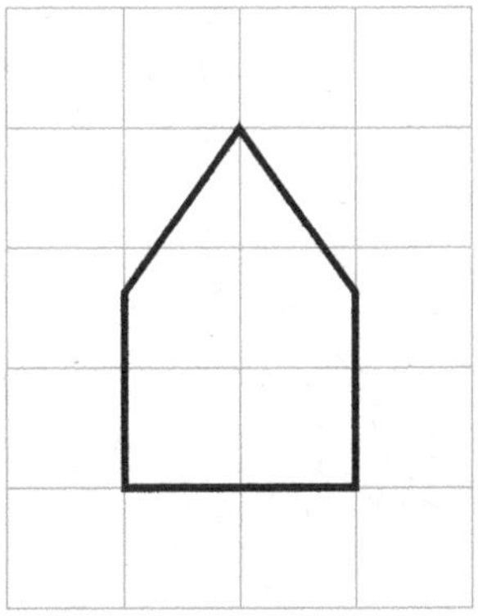

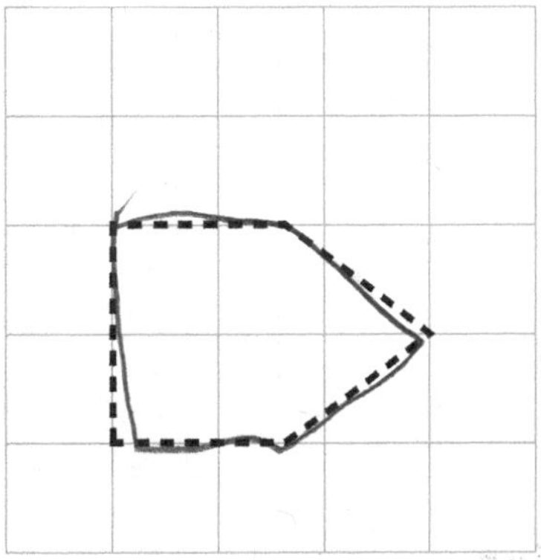

The figure has been rotated 90° clockwise.

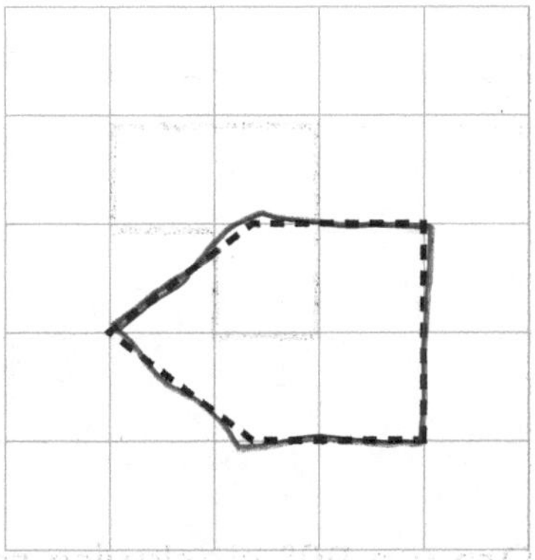

The figure has been rotated 90° counterclockwise.

Draw Rotations

Cut out the figures on page 454A. Use the cutouts to show the rotation.

1. Draw a 90° clockwise rotation.

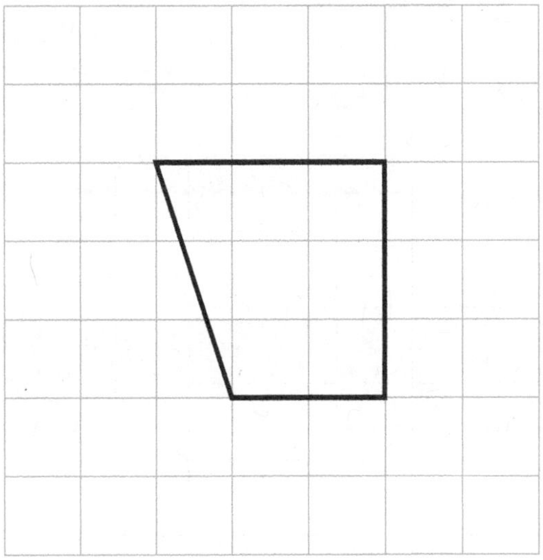

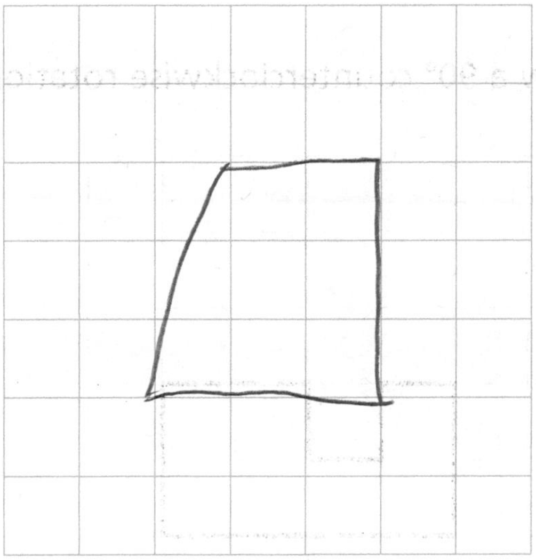

Name ____________________

Draw Rotations (continued)

Use the cutouts to show each rotation.

2 Draw a 90° counterclockwise rotation.

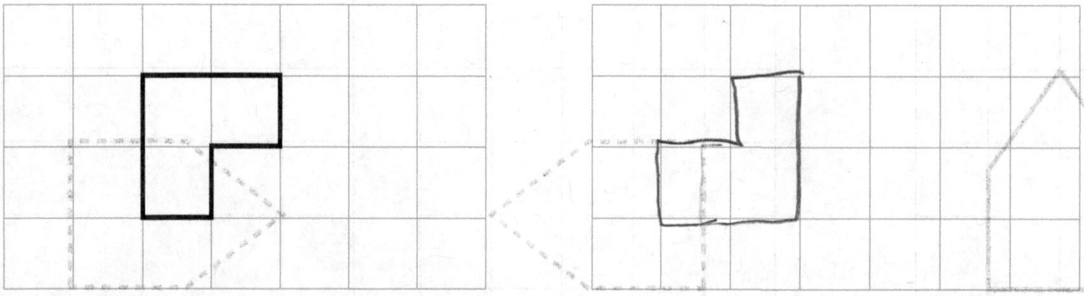

3 Draw a 90° clockwise rotation.

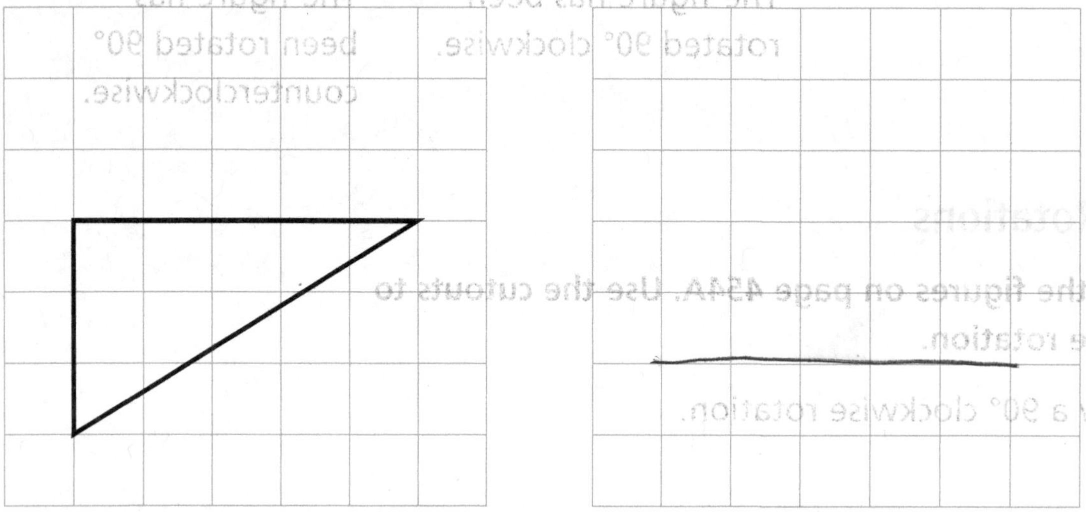

4 Draw a 90° counterclockwise rotation.

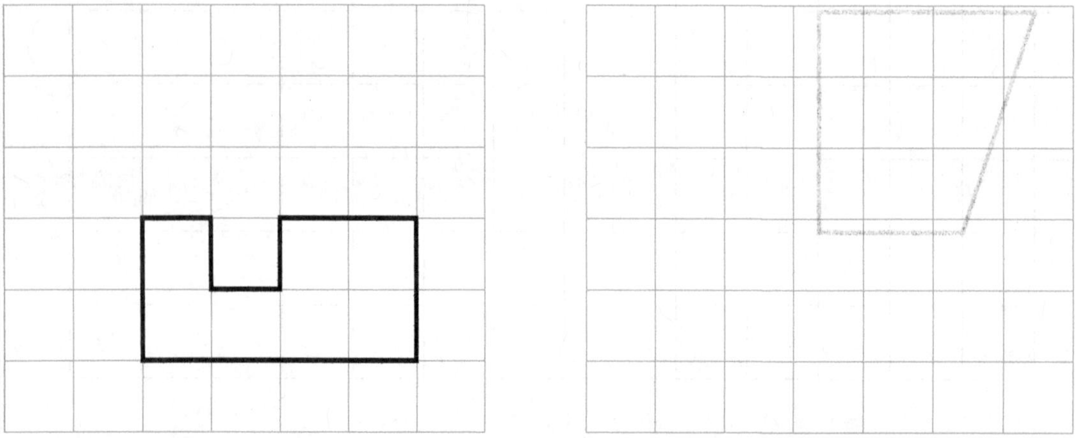

Name ____________________

Discuss Reflections

VOCABULARY
reflection

You can reflect, or flip, a figure across a line. The line is called the line of reflection.

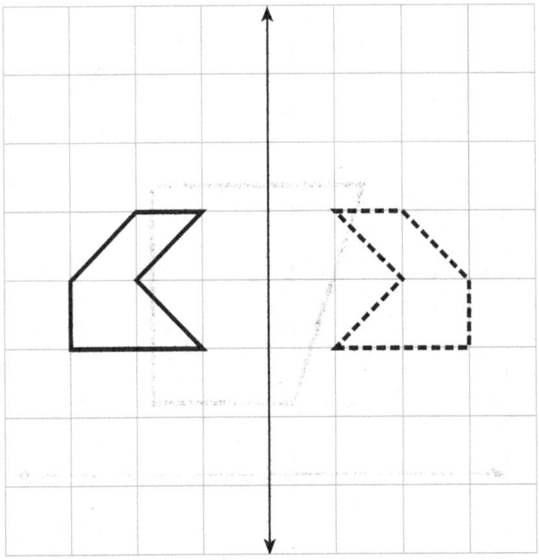

The figure on the left has been reflected over a vertical line.

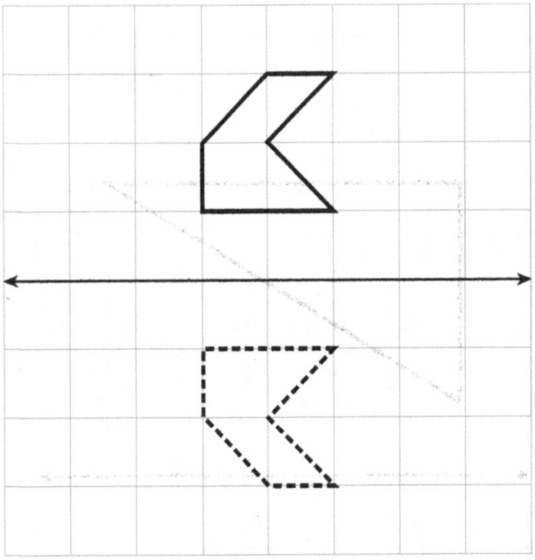

The figure on top has been reflected over a horizontal line.

5. What do you notice about the line in each drawing above?

____

____

Draw Reflections

Use the cutouts from page 454A to show the reflection.

6. Draw a reflection over the line.

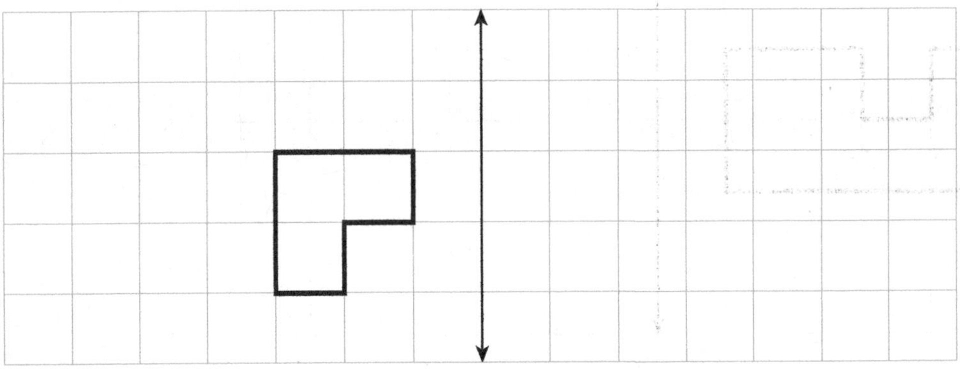

Name ______________________________

Draw Reflections (continued)

Use the cutouts to show each reflection.

7 Draw a reflection over the line.

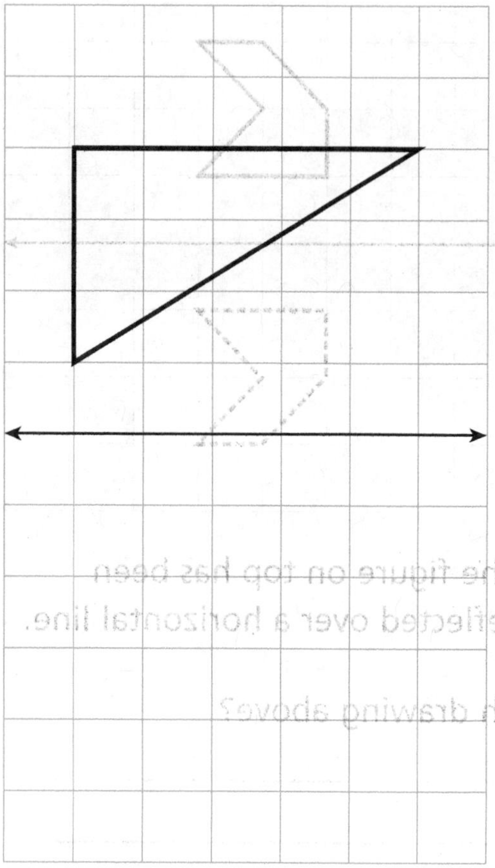

8 Draw a reflection over the line.

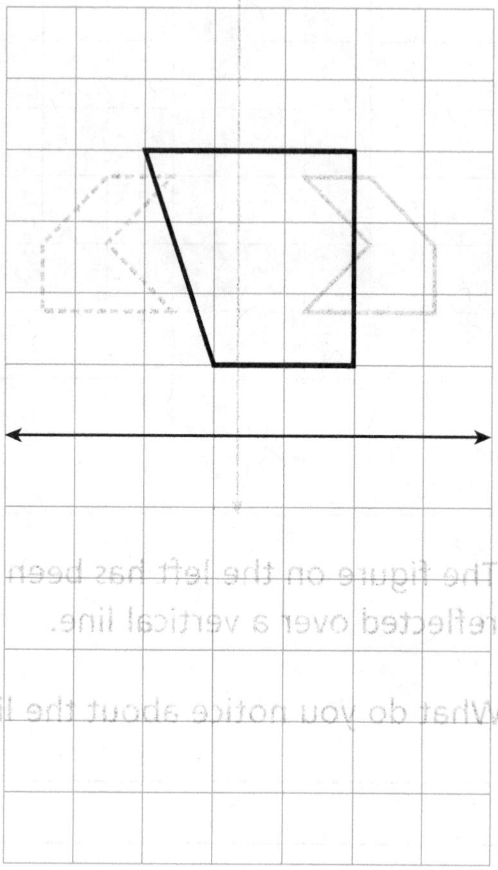

9 Draw a reflection over the line.

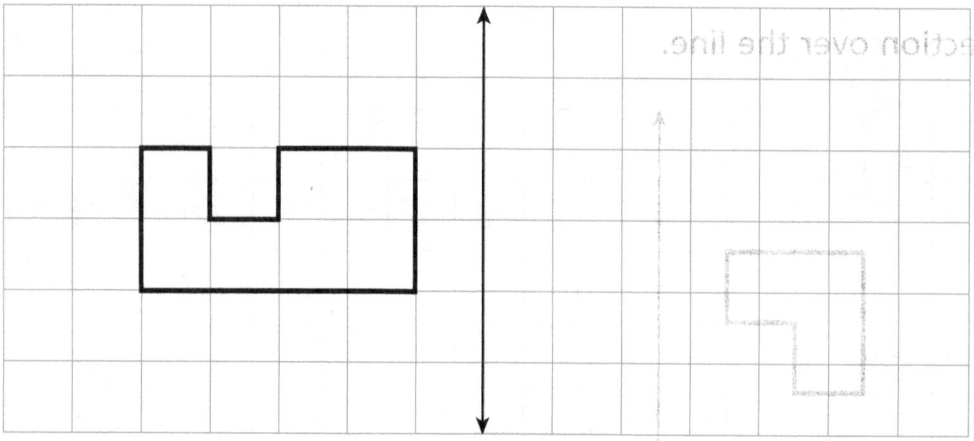

Name

Discuss Translations

VOCABULARY
translation

A **translation** is a slide. When a figure is translated, each of its points move the same distance in the same direction.

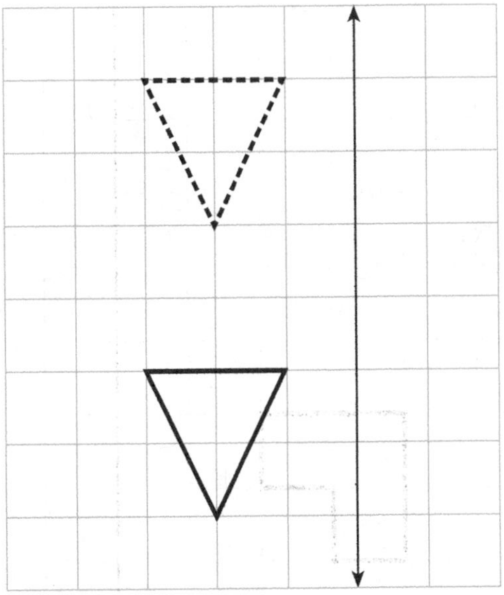

The figure on the bottom has been translated up along the line.

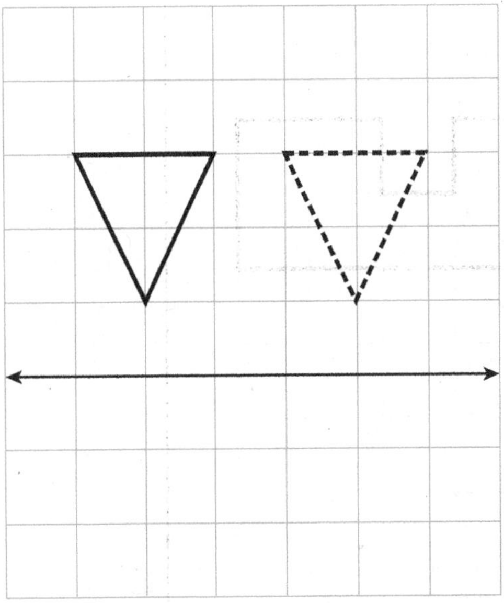

The figure on the left has been translated right along the line.

Draw Translations

Use the cutouts from page 454A to show the translation.

10 Draw a translation along the line.

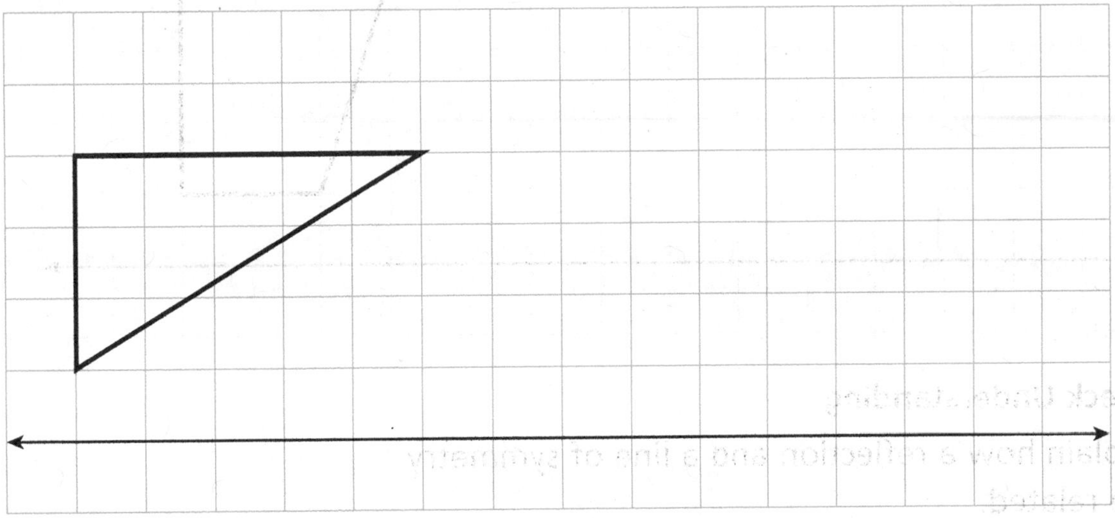

Name ____________________

Draw Translations (continued)

Use the cutouts to show each translation.

11 Draw a translation along the line.

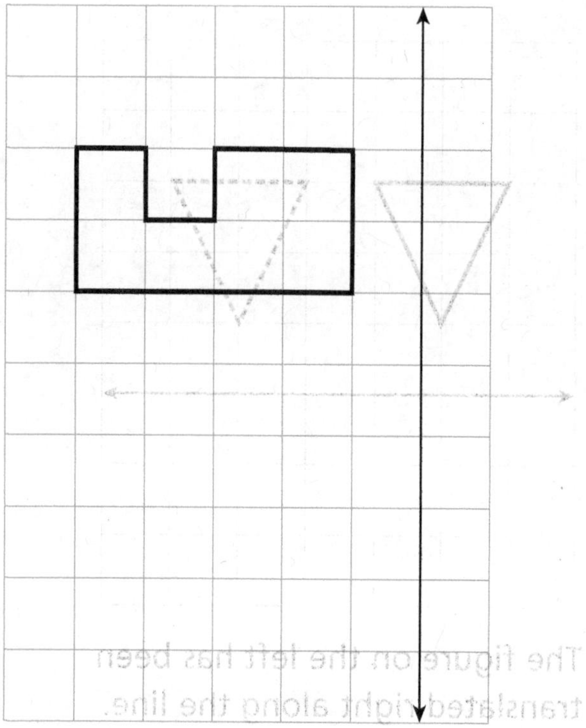

12 Draw a translation along the line.

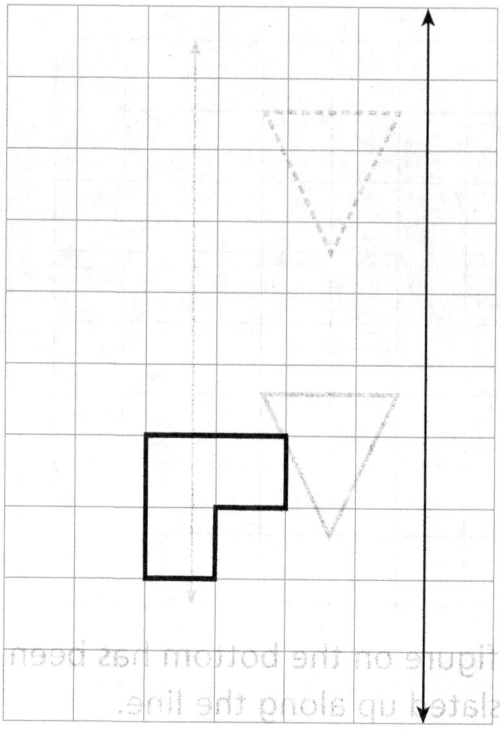

13 Draw a translation along the line.

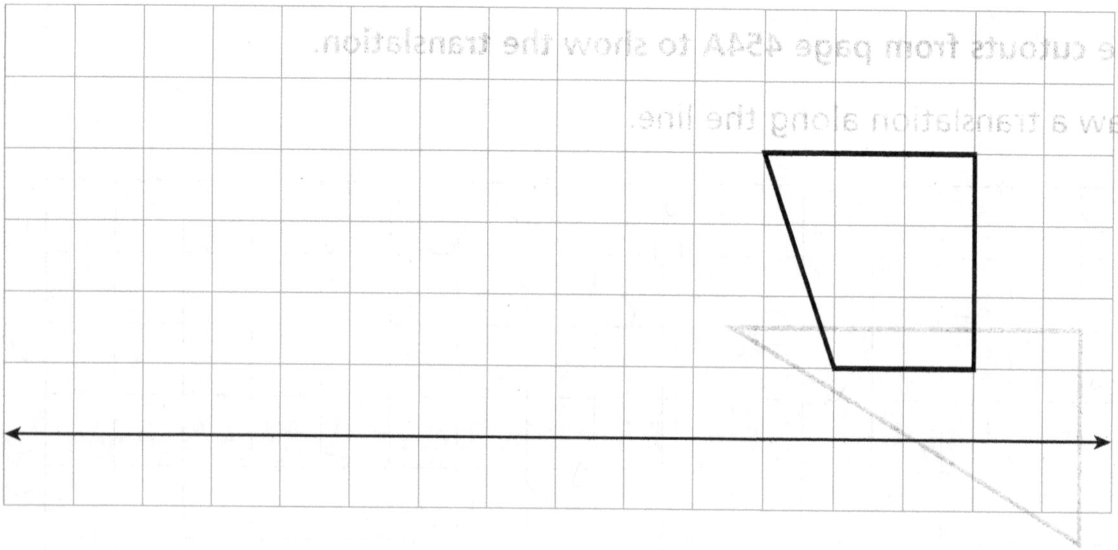

Check Understanding

Explain how a reflection and a line of symmetry are related.

Name

Cutouts

Cut out each figure.

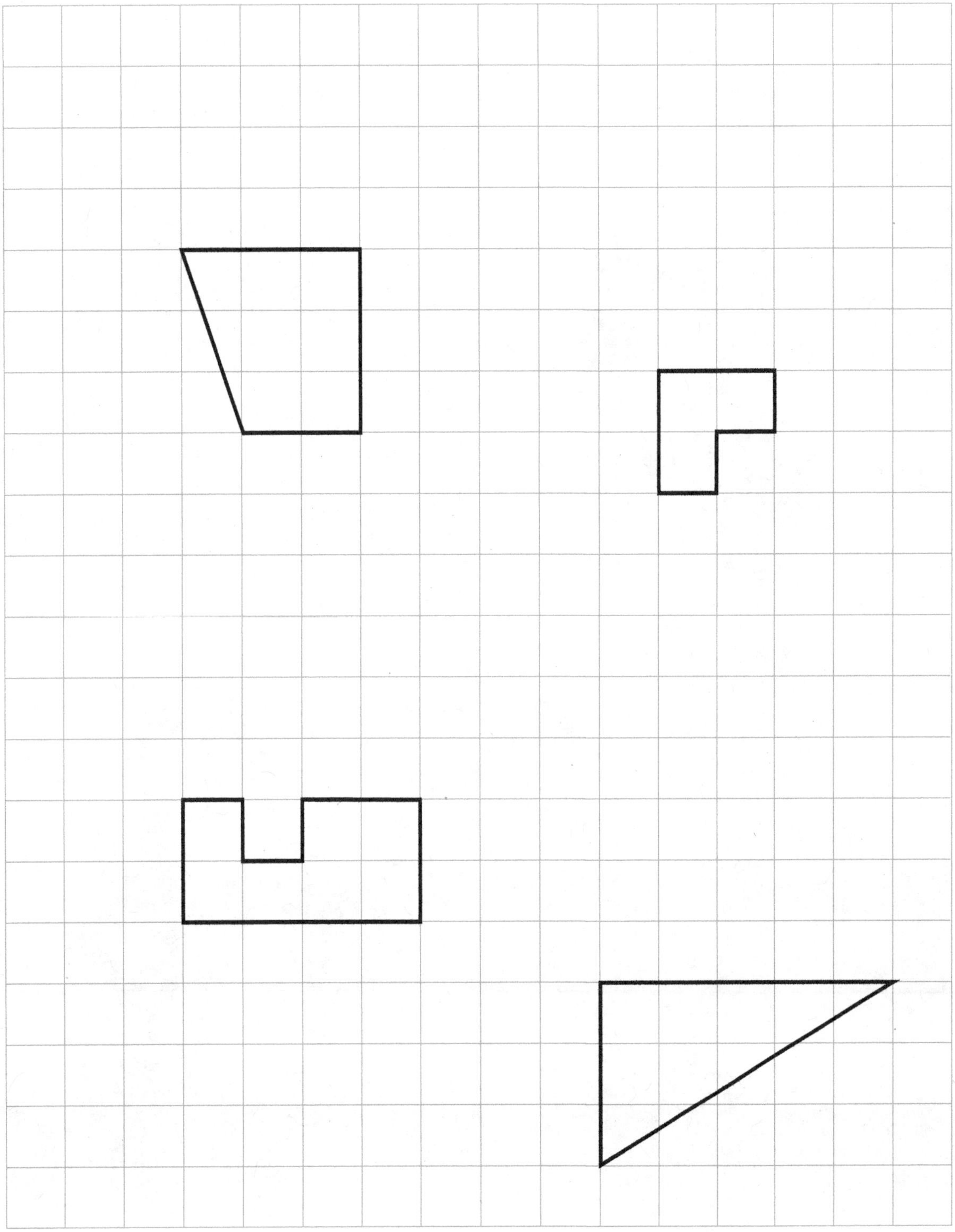

Name ______________________________

VOCABULARY
congruent

Identify Congruent Figures

Congruent figures are the same size and shape.

Figures A and B are congruent. They are the same size and shape.

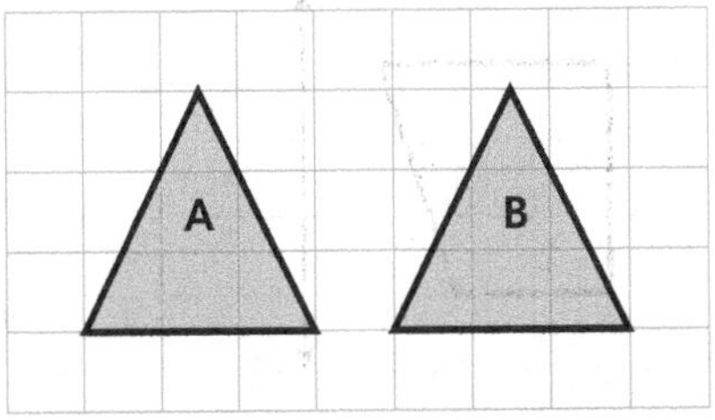
A
B

Figures C and D are congruent. One figure is turned, but they are the same size and shape.

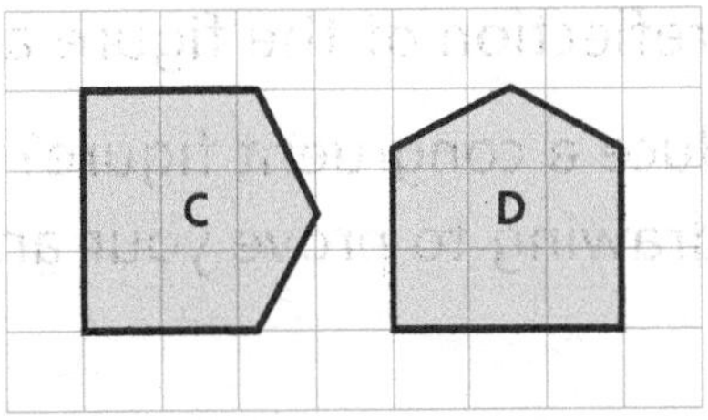
C
D

Figures E and F are not congruent. They are not the same size.

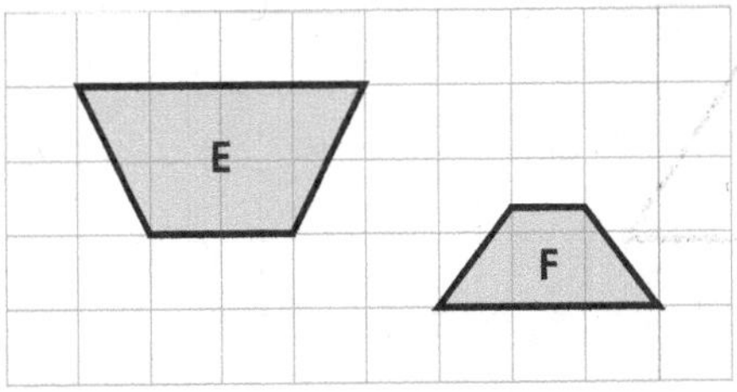
E
F

Figures G and H are not congruent. They are not the same shape.

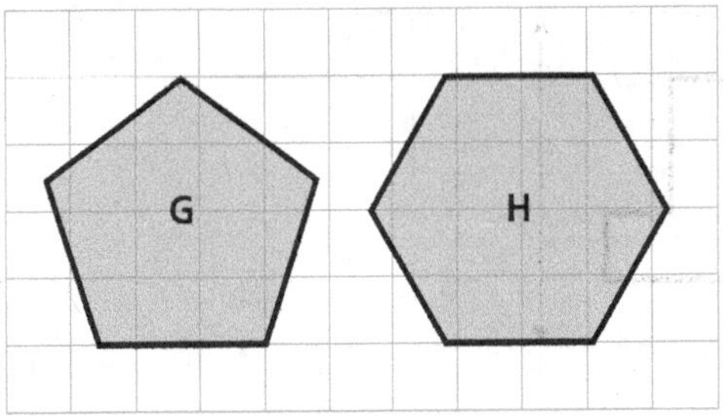
G
H

In each row, loop all of the figures that look congruent.

1

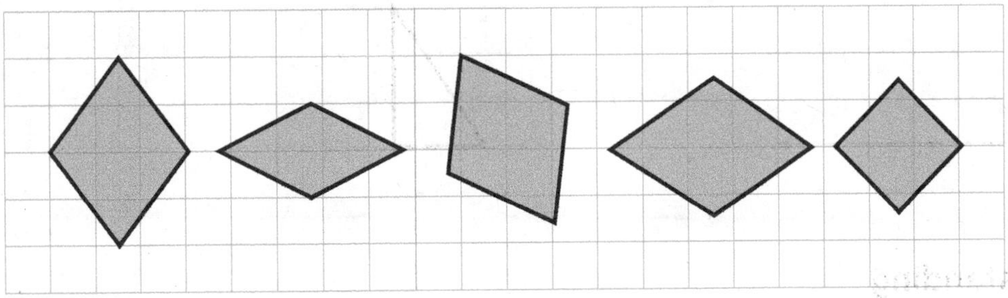

2

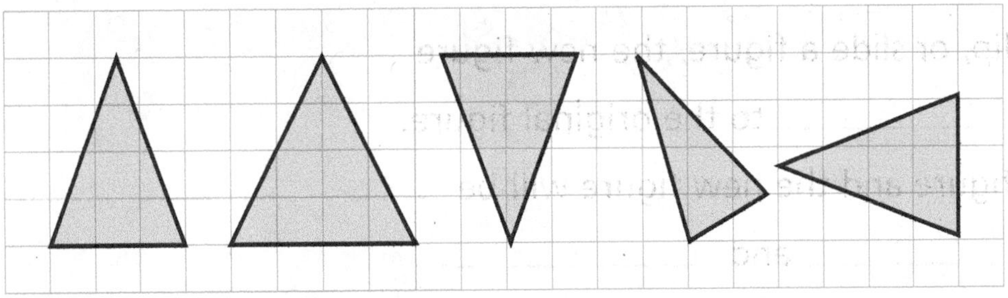

Name ______________________

Transformations and Congruence

VOCABULARY
transformation

You have explored three **transformations,** or changes in the position of a figure.

Will a rotation, reflection, or translation of a figure always produce a figure that is congruent to the original figure?

3 Will the reflection of the figure across the line produce a congruent figure? ________
Make a drawing to prove your answer.

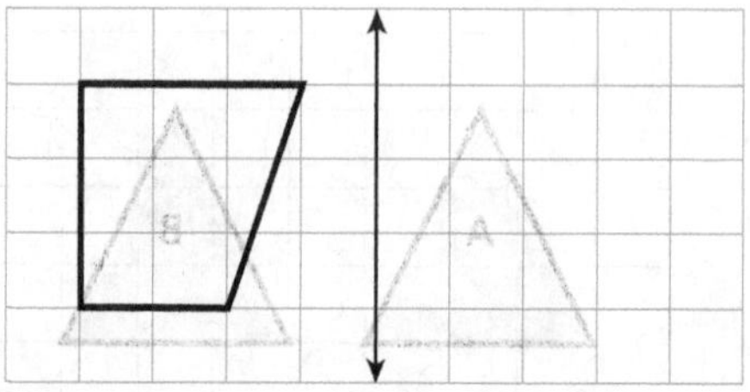

Draw a congruent figure using the transformation given.

4 reflection

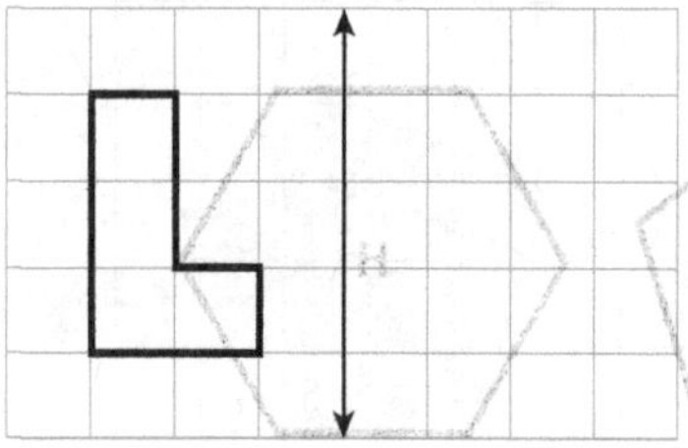

5 90° clockwise rotation

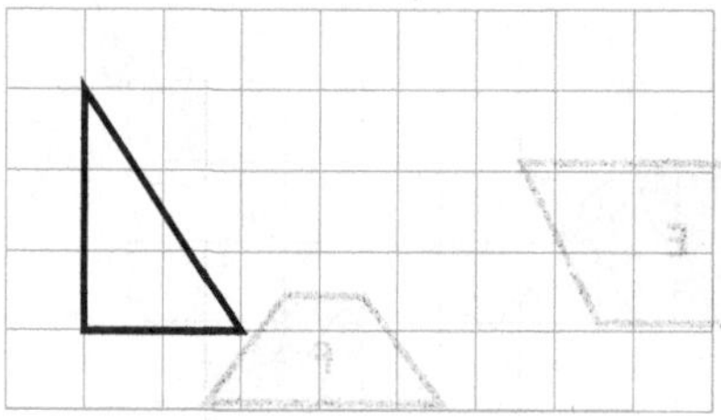

6 translation

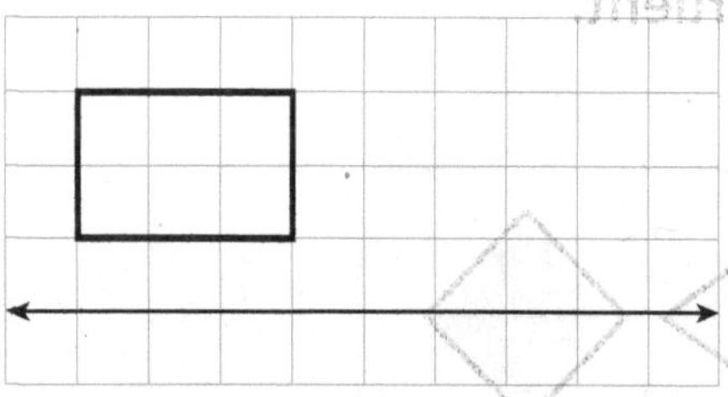

7 90° counterclockwise rotation

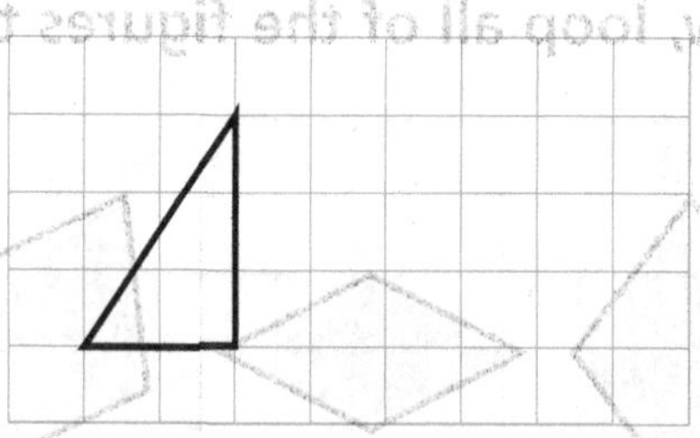

Check Understanding

Complete.

If you turn, flip, or slide a figure, the new figure will be ____________ to the original figure.

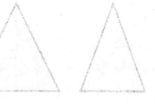

The original figure and the new figure will be the same ____________ and ____________.

Name ____________________

Look at the figures.

1 Draw a reflection over the line.

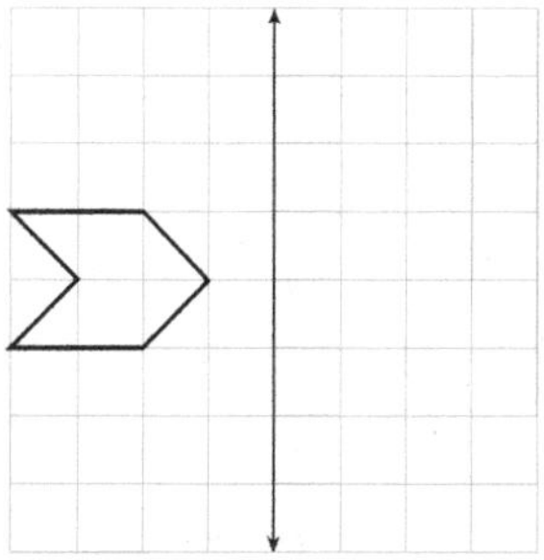

2 Draw a translation along the line.

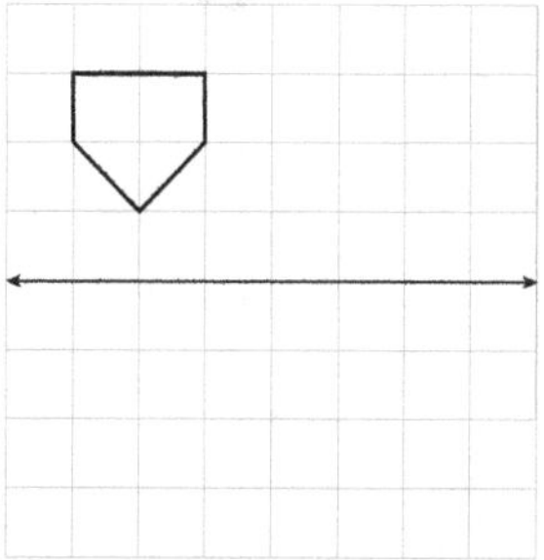

3 Draw a 90° clockwise rotation.

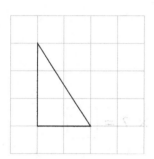

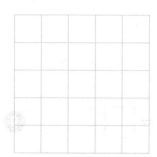

4 Circle the figures that look congruent.

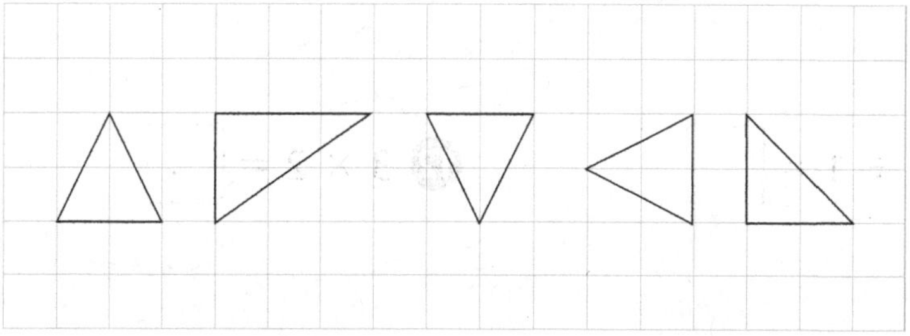

5 Draw a congruent figure using reflection.

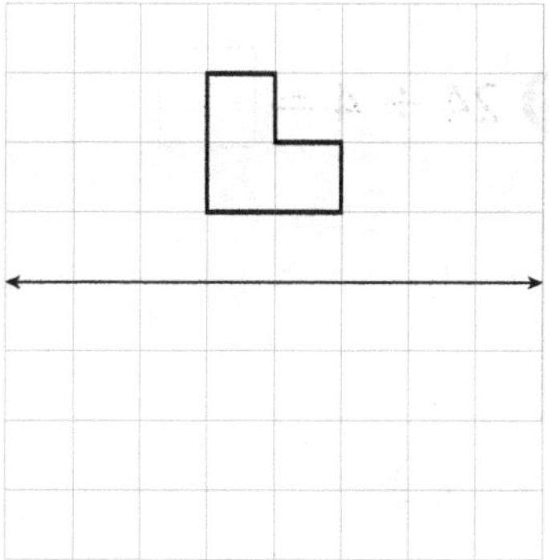

Fluency Check 28

Name ______________________

PATH to FLUENCY

Multiply or divide.

1. $7 \times 0 = \square$
2. $12 \div 2 = \square$
3. $8 \times 3 = \square$
4. $16 \div 4 = \square$
5. $3 \times 7 = \square$
6. $42 \div 6 = \square$
7. $6 \times 8 = \square$
8. $81 \div 9 = \square$
9. $8 \times 7 = \square$
10. $4 \times 1 = \square$
11. $2 \div 1 = \square$
12. $3 \times 2 = \square$
13. $9 \div 3 = \square$
14. $5 \times 6 = \square$
15. $24 \div 4 = \square$

Name ______________________

1. Draw and label line segment *FG*.

2. Use a protractor to measure the angle.

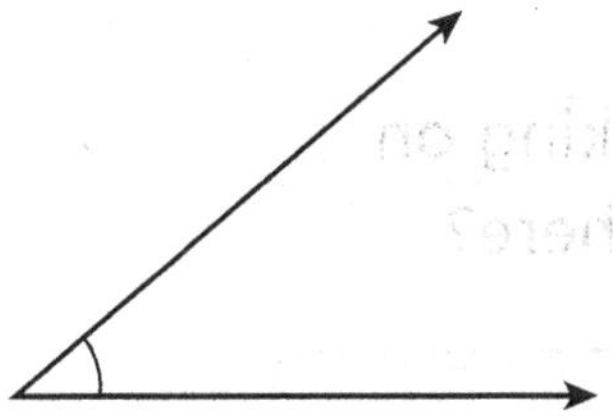

The angle measures ________.

3. Choose the figure that has at least one pair of parallel lines. Mark all that apply.

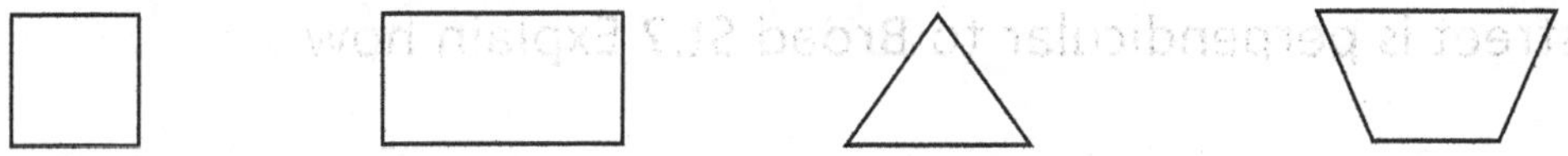

Ⓐ Ⓑ Ⓒ Ⓓ

4. Use the figures. For 4a–4d, select True or False for the statement.

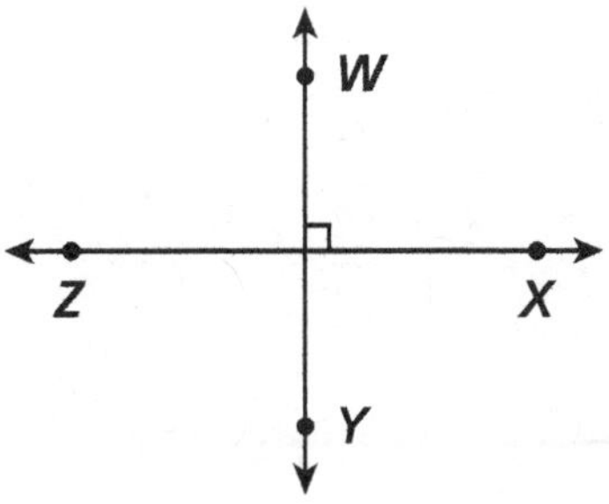
W
Z
X
Y

S
U
R
T

4a. $\overleftrightarrow{SU}$ and $\overleftrightarrow{RT}$ are intersecting lines. ○ True ○ False

4b. $\overleftrightarrow{SU}$ and $\overleftrightarrow{RT}$ are parallel. ○ True ○ False

4c. $\overleftrightarrow{ZX}$ and $\overleftrightarrow{WY}$ are perpendicular. ○ True ○ False

4d. A line drawn through points *R* and *U* is perpendicular to $\overleftrightarrow{RT}$. ○ True ○ False

Name ______________________________

5 The map below shows a section of Fatima's town.

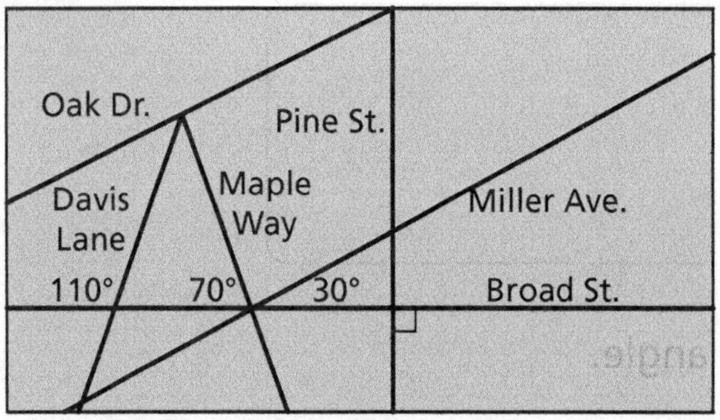
Oak Dr.
Pine St.
Davis Lane
Maple Way
Miller Ave.
110°
70°
30°
Broad St.

Part A Fatima is walking on Oak Drive and Gabe is walking on Miller Ave. Could Fatima and Gabe ever meet? If so, where?

NO!

Part B Which street is perpendicular to Broad St.? Explain how you know.

6 Choose the words that make a true statement.

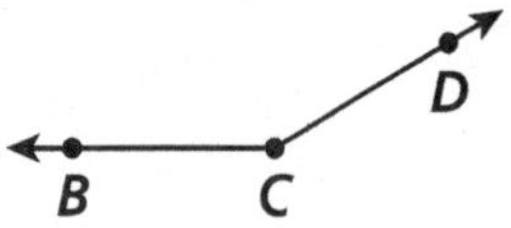
D
B
C

Angle *BCD* is [a right / an acute / an obtuse] angle.

7 Draw all the lines of symmetry for the figure.

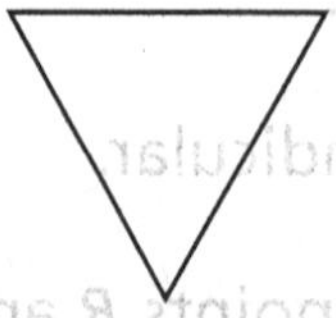

Name ______________________________

8 A gear in a watch turns clockwise, in one-degree sections, a total of 300 times.

The gear has turned a total of ☐ degrees.

9 Lucy is designing a block for a quilt. She measured one of the angles. Use the numbers and symbols on the tiles to write and solve an equation to find the unknown angle measure.

? 110°

40° | 70° | 110° | 180° | + | −

Equation: ☐ ☐ ☐ = ?

Solution: ? = ☐

10 Luke is drawing a figure that has exactly 2 acute angles. For 10a–10d, choose Yes or No to tell if the figure could be the figure Luke is drawing.

10a. 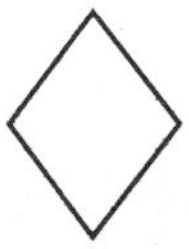 ○ Yes ○ No

10b. 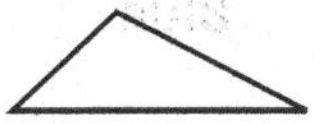 ○ Yes ○ No

10c.  ○ Yes ○ No

10d. 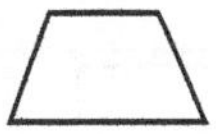 ○ Yes ○ No

11 Triangle *QRS* can be classified

as [an acute / a right / an obtuse] triangle.

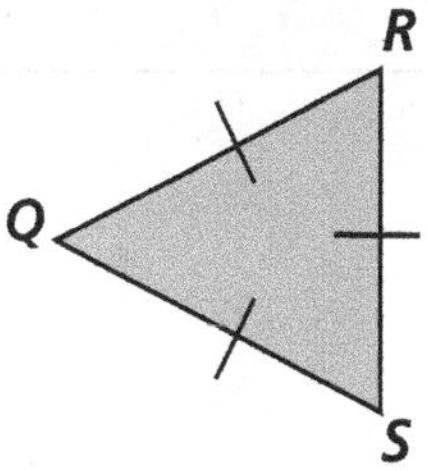
R
Q
S

Name ______________________

12 Draw a congruent figure using translation.

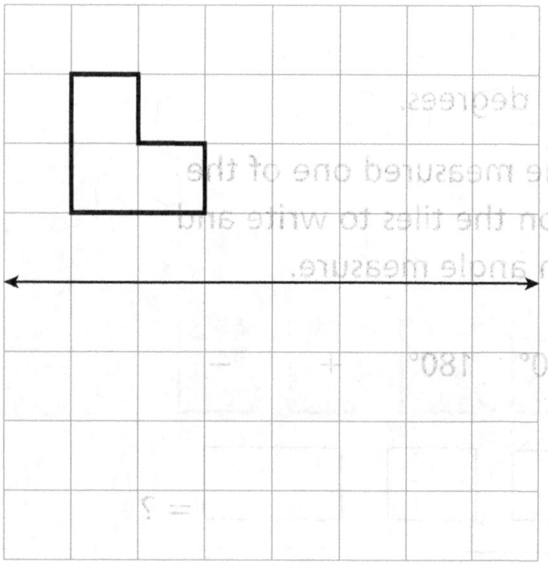

13 A sign has two pairs of parallel sides and two pairs of equal sides. Name one type of quadrilateral that the sign could be.

[ ]

14 The circle represents all of the students in a class. Each section represents the students in the class who chose a certain color as their favorite. The angle measures for some sections are given.

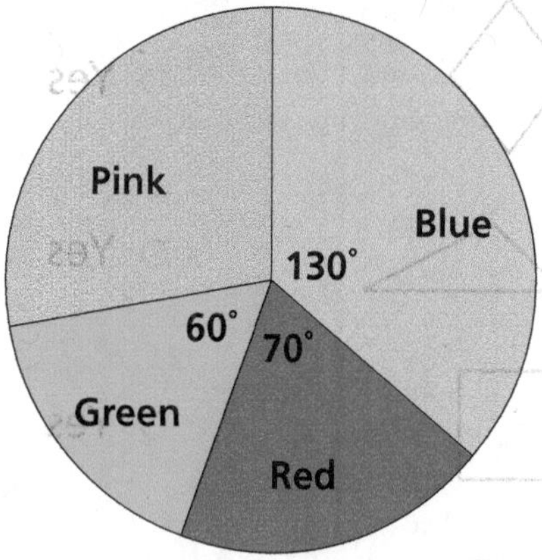
Pink
Blue
130°
60°
70°
Green
Red

Part A

What is the sum of the angle measures for Blue, Red, and Green?

[ ]

Part B

Explain how to find the angle measure for Pink. Then find the measure.

[ ]

Name ____________________

15 Draw one diagonal in the figure to form two obtuse triangles.

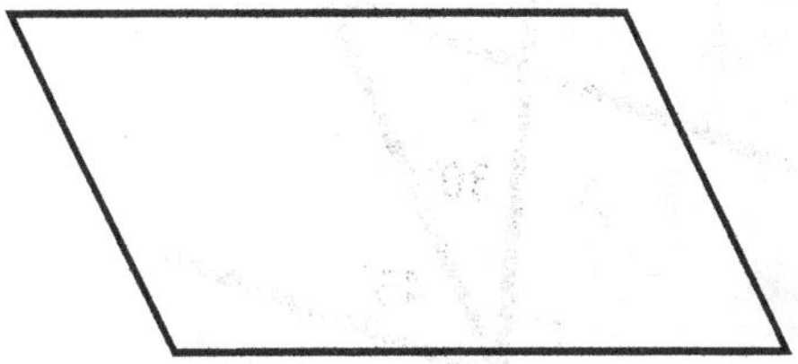

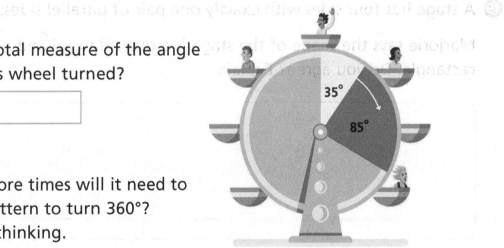

16 Does the figure have a line of symmetry? Explain.

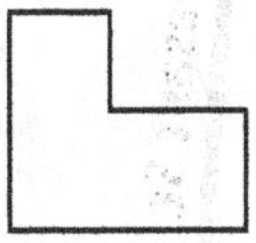

17 A Ferris wheel turns 35° before it pauses. It turns another 85° before stopping again.

Part A

What is the total measure of the angle that the Ferris wheel turned?

120

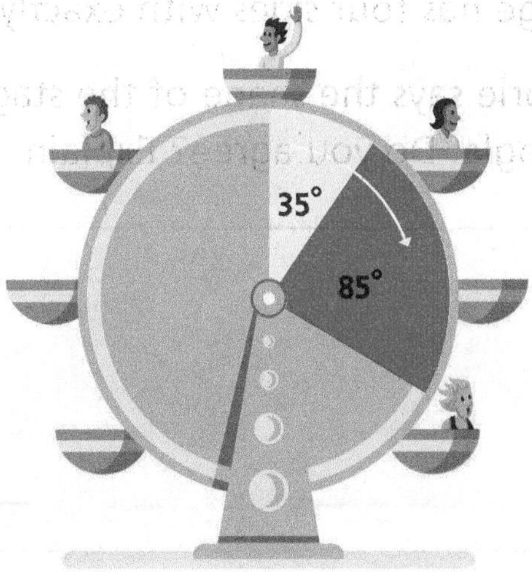
35°
85°

Part B

How many more times will it need to repeat the pattern to turn 360°? Explain your thinking.

2 mare

Name ______________________________

18 Cross Street, West Street, and Carmichael Street form a triangle.

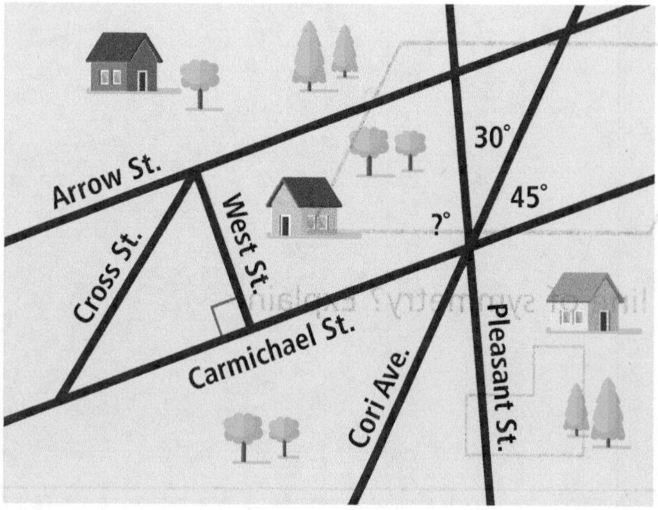
Arrow St.
Cross St.
West St.
Carmichael St.
Cori Ave.
Pleasant St.
30°
45°
?°

How can the triangle be classified? Mark all that apply.

● scalene ○ isosceles ○ equilateral

○ acute ● right ○ obtuse

19 A stage has four sides with exactly one pair of parallel sides.

Marjorie says the shape of the stage is a quadrilateral and a rectangle. Do you agree? Explain.

20 What is the unknown angle measure in this pattern?

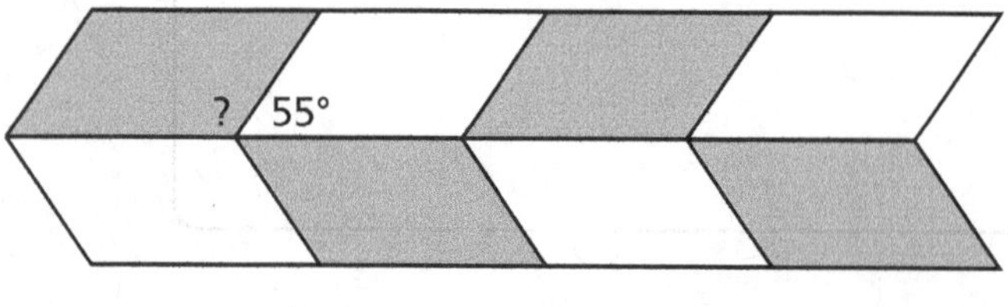
?
55°

Unit 8
Performance Task

Name ______________________

Crack a Secret Code

Meredith developed a secret code using the letters she labeled these polygons. Use what you know about polygons to solve each problem.

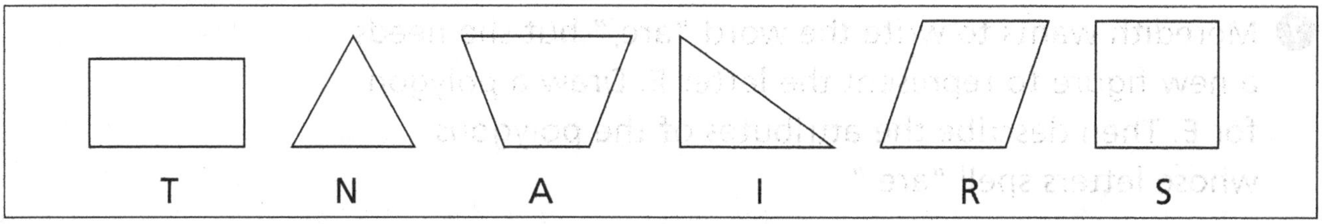
T
N
A
I
R
S

1. Make a word using the letters of all the polygons that are **not** quadrilaterals.

   N I

2. Make a word using the letters of all the polygons that have parallel sides.

3. Make a word using the letters of all the polygons that have perpendicular sides.

4. Make a word using the letters of all the polygons that have acute angles.

5. Meredith wants to use the letters of three polygons to write the word "ran." Write a description for the polygons that she can use.

Name ______________________

6. Meredith thinks she can use all of the polygons to write "strain" using the description "All polygons that have at least two sides with equal side lengths." Is she correct? If not, which figure or figures do not match the description?

7. Meredith wants to write the word "are," but she needs a new figure to represent the letter E. Draw a polygon for E. Then describe the attributes of the polygons whose letters spell "are."

8. Can you write a description for attributes of polygons whose letters spell the word "ant?" Explain why or why not.

9. Explain how polygons *T* and *R* are alike and different.

10. Write your own description for the polygons whose letters spell a word of your choice. Make sure that the attributes you choose for your description are shared with all of the letters in your word and are not shared with any letters not in your word.

Be an Illustrator

Illustrator: Josh Brill

Did you ever try to use shapes to draw animals like the lemur on the cover?

Over the last 10 years Josh has been using geometric shapes to design his animals. His aim is to keep the animal drawings simple and use color to make them appealing.

Add some color to the lemur Josh drew. Then try drawing a cat or dog or some other animal using the shapes below.

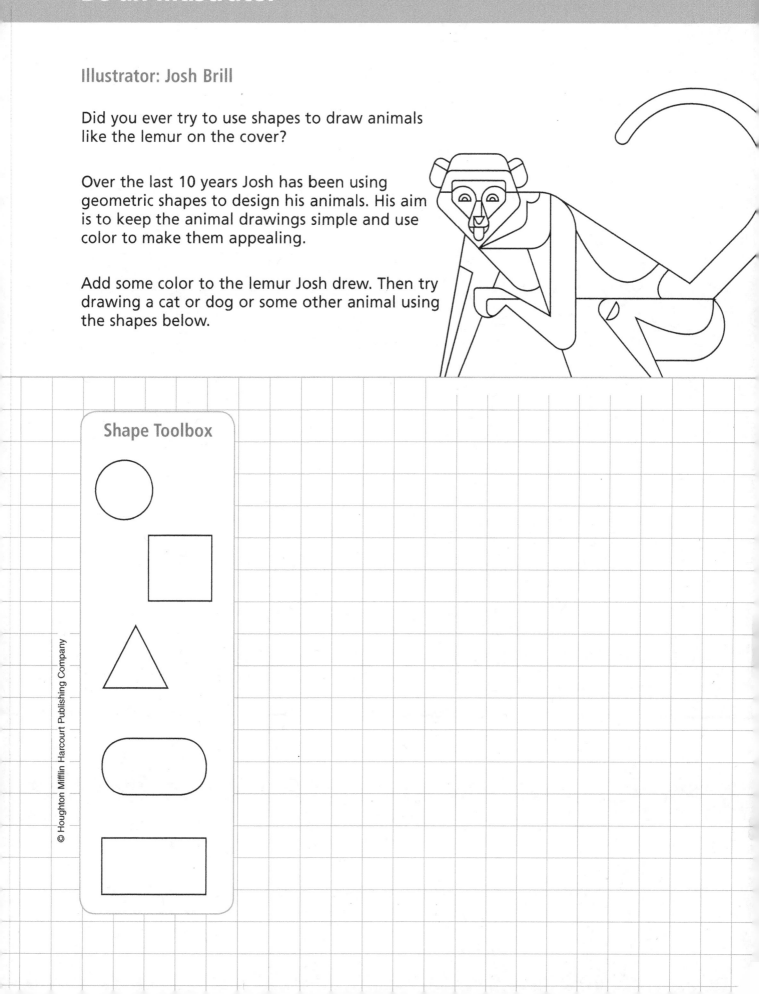

Shape Toolbox

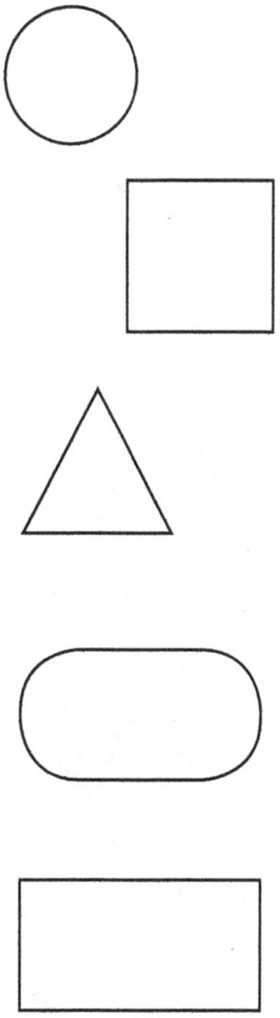